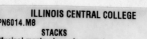

W9-BCG-206

PN 6014 .M8   19138

Musical masterpieces in
    prose /

ISBN 0-87666-585-7
© 1981 Paganiniana Publications, Inc.

Paganiniana Publications, Inc.
211 West Sylvania Avenue
Neptune, N.J. 07753

MUSICAL
MASTERPIECES
IN PROSE

Murray J. Levith

To Tina, Nathaniel, and Will
"If music be the food of love, play on . . . "

CONTENTS

Dr. Murray J. Levith is Associate Professor of English at Skidmore College, Saratoga Springs, New York, where he teaches courses in Shakespeare and Renaissance literature as well as the short story. Professor Levith is also a professional violinist. His interests in literature and music resulted in *Fiddlers in Fiction*, his first collection of masterwork short stories focused on musical subject matter. The continuing popularity of *Fiddlers in Fiction* prompts Dr. Levith's more expansive sequel, *Musical Masterpieces in Prose*. Here again is fiction by the finest practitioners of the art, but this time not limited to stories exclusively about violinists.

ACKNOWLEDGMENTS

"The Fermata," by E.T.A. Hoffmann, from *Tales of Hoffmann*, edited by Christopher Lazare. Published by A.A. Wyn. Reprinted by permission of Harold Ober Associates. Copyright 1946 by Christopher Lazare. All rights reserved.

"The Serenade," by George Bernard Shaw, from *Short Stories, Scraps and Shavings*. Published by Dodd, Mead, 1934. Reprinted by permission of The Society of Authors on behalf of the Bernard Shaw Estate.

"Love Affair With a Double Bass," by Anton Chekhov, from *The Sinner From Toledo and Other Stories*, translated by Arnold Hinchliffe. Published by Associated University Presses and reprinted with their permission.

"Gambrinus," by Alexander Kuprin, is taken from *Gambrinus and Other Stories*, translated by Bernard Guilbert Guerney. Copyright 1925 by the Adelphi Publishing Company. Reprinted with the permission of the Chilton Book Company, Radnor, Pennsylvania.

"The Infant Prodigy," by Thomas Mann. Copyright 1936 and renewed 1964 by Alfred A. Knopf, Inc. Reprinted from *Stories of Three Decades*, by Thomas Mann, translated by H.T. Lowe-Porter, by permission of Alfred A. Knopf, Inc.

"A Mother," from *Dubliners* by James Joyce. Copyright 1967 by the Estate of James Joyce. Reprinted by permission of Viking Penguin, Inc.

"Flute Dream," by Hermann Hesse. Reprinted by permission of Farrar, Straus and Giroux, Inc., "Flute Dream" from *Strange News from Another Star and Other Tales* by Hermann Hesse, translated by Denver Lindley. Translation copyright 1972 by Farrar, Straus and Giroux, Inc. Translated from the German, Marchen, copyright S. Fischer Verlag 1919, Copyright 1955 by Suhkamp Verlag, Berlin.

"Mr. Reginald Peacock's Day," by Katherine Mansfield. Copyright 1920 by Alfred A. Knopf, Inc. and renewed 1948 by J. Middleton Murry. Reprinted from *The Short Stories of Katherine Mansfield*, by Katherine Mansfield, by permission of Alfred A. Knopf, Inc.

"The King's Favor," by Stephen Crane, from *Tales, Sketches, and Reports*, edited by Fredson Bowers and Edwin H. Cady. Reprinted by permission of the University Press of Virginia.

"Olympians," by Kenneth Burke, from *The Complete White Oxen*. Copyright 1968 by Kenneth Burke; reprinted by permission of the University of California Press.

"Guitar," from *Not Without Laughter*, by Langston Hughes. Copyright 1930 by Alfred A. Knopf, Inc. Reprinted by permission of Alfred A. Knopf, Inc.

INTRODUCTION

I have an economist friend who complains that we literary types are "unscientific," that we approach a given story from a different vantage each time (looking now at character, then structure, or imagery, theme, Freud, etc.), that we never move from step A to step B, that there are only variables in our so-called "methodology," that (in short) we don't "get anywhere." Economists should talk!

This collection is in part an answer to my friend, for besides an economist he is a musician. Just as no two composers—Bach, Beethoven, Berg—approach, say, the concerto form in exactly the same way, so too with stories about the single subject of music: it elicits the widest range of writerly responses. For some authors music is a metaphor, a way of talking about, for example, "spirit," non-verbal communication, or art in general. For others it is simply one subject chosen from infinite possibilities. When William Faulkner was asked why he wrote about the South, he replied to the effect that he had to write about "something." Why not the South? Why not music?

For the reader a fine work of literature, as life itself, is jewel-like—many faceted but of a piece. Turn it a fraction and a new surface is caught by the light. Change a perspective (get older, travel, learn a new skill, etc.) and another "reading" of a story suggests itself. No, there can never be a rigid step A to step B to "understanding" a work of fiction. Such methodology is too simplistically linear. What most readers realize is that any literary structure is multi-dimensional: there are countless numbers of points of view.

Here then is a collection of stories, each item of which is as unique as each author. Further, each story will mean different things to different readers, and different things to the same reader at different times. These works reflect multivarious literary creation on a single general subject, and ask for a multiplicity of "methods" of literary analysis to discover their meanings. If all goes well, the reader will want to return to a story again and again, each time bringing something "new" in his or her experience to a reading. Subsequently, the story should, as with all art, send the reader back enriched to life itself.

I have selected what I take to be the best short fiction of the masters—foreign and domestic, men and women—on the subject of music. The individual pieces are wide-ranging in style, specific matter, and historical orientation. I have divided the stories into European and American sections, and arranged them chronologically.

Arleen Targan executed the lovely illustrations for the stories, and I feel especially lucky to have had so talented an artist who is also so sensitive a reader. Warm thanks are also due my student assistants, Maureen Bouley and Maureen Hille, for helping in many ways with this project. Gloria Moore and Alvin Gamage and the staff of the Skidmore College Library were, as usual, helpful beyond the call of duty. Finally, Dr. Eric Weller, Dean of the Faculty of Skidmore College, has always believed in and encouraged my projects. I thank him and Skidmore College for their support.

Murray J. Levith
Skidmore College
Saratoga Springs,
New York

THE FERMATA

E.T.A. Hoffmann
1776-1822

E.T.A. Hoffmann's writing is often thought to exemplify the spirit of German Romanticism. But before Hoffmann's literary career came a number of other careers, most notably a musical one. By the age of thirteen he could play several instruments. He was at various times in his life a composer, conductor, musical director, and critic. Some of his stories, like "The Fermata" (1815), have musical subject matter.

Hummel's amusing and vivacious picture, "Company in an Italian Inn," won immediate renown when it was shown in the autumn of 1814 at the Art Exhibition in Berlin, where it delighted everyone who looked at it. Under an arbor almost hidden in foliage, the painting shows a table well furbished with wine flasks and fruit, and seated facing each other on the opposite sides two Italian ladies, one singing, the other playing a guitar; standing somewhat in the background between them, an abbot acts as music director. With baton raised, he is awaiting the moment when the Signora, with a long trill, shall end the cadence in the midst of which—as her eyes are directed towards Heaven—the artist has just caught her; looking at the picture, one knows that the abbot's hand will then descend sharply, while the guitarist gaily dashes off the dominant chord. The abbot is filled with admiration—indeed, with exquisite delight; yet his attention, at the same time, is tautly concentrated. It is plain that not for the world would he miss the proper downward beat. He hardly dares to breathe. If he could, he would stop every bee's buzzing, the movement of every fly. So much the more, then, is he irritated by the bustling intrusion of the host, who must needs choose just this decisive and supreme moment to come in with the wine! Beyond the arbor, one can see a tree-arched avenue, where a horseman has just pulled up for a refreshing drink, which is at this moment being handed up to him, so that he can enjoy it without dismounting.

"The more I look at this singer," said Edward, "who, it is true, seems a bit old for her gay costume but, none the less, is obviously fired with the true inspiration of her art; the more I am delighted by the grave but truly Roman profile and lovely form of the guitarist, and the more amused I become by the earnest mien of my estimable friend the abbot, the more the whole painting seems to me instinct with the freedom and vitality of actual life. It is plainly a caricature, in the higher sense of that term; but it also suggests a certain charm and joy. I should like to step into that arbor and open one of those little wine bottles that are tempting me on the table. I tell you more—I fancy that I can already catch something of the bouquet of that rare vintage! And I feel—come, now, it would be a sin if this cheerful solicitation were wasted on the cold, insensitive atmosphere that surrounds us here! Let us go and drain a flask of Italian wine in honor of this fine picture, in honor of art, and in honor of merry Italy, where life is exhilarating and pleasure is given its due!"

While Edward was thus running on in lively—if somewhat disconnected—sentences, Theodore stood silent, deeply absorbed in his own sober reflection. "Yes, that is what we will do. Come along," he said at last, starting up as if he were waking from a dream. It was plain, nevertheless, that he had some difficulty in tearing himself away from the picture. And as, almost mechanically, he followed his friend, he had to stop at the door, and turn around for another lingering and longing look at the singer and the guitarist, and the abbot who was directing their performance. . . .

Edward's proposal, however, was very easy to execute! The friends crossed the street diagonally, and very soon they were seated in the little blue room of the Sala Tarone, before a flask of wine which was the very image of those in the painting they had just left.

"It seems to me," said Edward—as Theodore remained thoughtful and silent, even after several glasses of wine—"it seems to me that you are more deeply impressed by that painting than I am; and that your impression is not so agreeable as mine."

Theodore still did not break his silence for a moment. "I assure you that I did not lose anything of the brightness and grace of that animated composition," he said at last. "And yet," he added, slowly, "it is very strange: that picture is a true and accurate representation of a scene out of my own life. The faithful portraits of the individuals concerned are nothing short of startling. And you will agree with me that such swift memories themselves, unexpectedly and extraordinarily brought to life as if by the stroke of a magician's wand, must exert a sudden and remarkable power over the mind. That is how it stands with me at this moment."

"What!" exclaimed Edward, in astonishment. "A scene out of your own life? Do you mean to say that the picture represents an episode which you have actually seen and can actually remember? I saw at once that the two ladies and the priest were eminently successful pieces of portraiture; but I could never for one moment have dreamed that you had met them in the flesh, in the course of your own personal experience! My dear friend, do tell me about it! We are entirely alone here. Nobody else will come into the café at this hour. Tell me what happened, who they are, how it all came about."

"I will gladly do that," Theodore responded. "But I must go a long way back. You must bear with me if I carry you back to my childhood!"

"Never mind that! Go ahead!" rejoined Edward. "As a matter of fact, I don't know as much as I'd like to about your early youth. And if the story lasts a long time, the worst that can happen is that we shall have to empty a bottle more than we'd bargained for. To that, I know, nobody will have any objections: neither ourselves nor Signor Tarone."

Thus encouraged, Theodore embarked upon his recital. "It can surprise nobody," he began, "that in planning my future I threw everything else aside and devoted myself entirely to the noble art of music. For even as a little boy I would rather play the piano than do anything else; and I spent hours and hours strumming upon my uncle's creaking, jarring, tuneless old instrument. The little town where I lived was badly off for music: there was nobody who could teach an aspiring student except one opinionated old organist, who made a religion of tempo and plagued me almost to death with obscure and unmelodious toccatas and fugues. I would not let myself be daunted, however; I held on like grim death. In fact, although the old fellow was crabbed and faultfinding, he was in his own way something of a master: he had only to play a good piece in his own powerful style, to reconcile me to the man and his art.

"It thus happened that I would often be thrown into a curious state of mind. Especially, many pieces by old Johann Sebastian Bach would seem to me almost like harrowing ghost stories, and I would give myself up to that mood of pleasurable awe to which we are so prone in the days of our fantastic youth. But I entered within the gates of a real Eden when, as sometimes happened in winter, the town bandmaster and his colleagues, supported by a few amateurs of moderate ability, would give a concert, and I would be permitted to play the kettledrum in the symphony. It was not until long afterwards that I realized how extravagant—indeed, how ridiculous—these concerts were. My teacher usually played two piano concerti by Wolff or Karl Philipp Emanuel Bach, a member of the town band would be struggling with Stamitz, while the local tax collector worked away at the flute with unbounded energy, and took in such an immense supply of breath that he blew out both the candles on his music stand, and someone always had to relight them for him.

"As for singing, that wasn't given much attention among us. My uncle, who was a friend of the arts and a great patron of music, always disparaged local talent along this line. His mind still dwelt with exuberant delight upon those days, now long gone by, when the four choristers of the town's four churches would join forces in a performance of *Lottchen am Hofe*. Above all, he was wont, in this connection, to extol the mutual tolerance which united the singers in this work of art—for, you understand, not only were the Catholic and the Evangelical bodies separate and hostile, but the Reformed Community was itself split in two sections: those who spoke German and those who spoke French. The French chorister was not daunted by the *Lottchen*, but, my uncle maintained, sang his part, spectacles on nose, in the finest falsetto that ever proceeded from the human throat!

"Now there was among us at this time—I mean in our town—a spinster named Meibel, whose age was about fifty-five years, and whose only means of livelihood was the scanty pension which she received as a former court singer at the Residenz. And my uncle was rightly of the opinion that Miss Meibel might still do something to earn money in the concert hall. She assumed airs of importance when she was approached on this question, and she required a great deal of coaxing; but at last she consented to appear on our stage, and so we came to have *aria di bravura* at our concerts. She was a singular creature, this Miss Meibel. I still retain the lively recollection of her thin little figure, as, dressed in a parti-colored gown, holding her roll of music in her hand, and looking inexpressibly solemn, she was wont to step to the front of the stage and acknowledge the presence of the audience with a slight inclination of the upper part of her body. Her headdress, especially, was remarkable: I remember that it had a bouquet of china flowers fastened in front, and as she sang these would keep up a continual trembling and nodding, distracting to see. At the end of her song, when the audience had greeted her with unstinted applause, she would first hand her music roll, somewhat haughtily, to my uncle, and would then permit him to dip his thumb and finger into a little porcelain snuffbox, fashioned in the shape of a pug dog, out of which she took a pinch herself with obvious pleasure.

"You will better understand my telling you that we did not pay much attention to singing, when I add that this prima donna of our concert stage had a horrible squeaky voice, which she indulged in all sorts of ludicrous flourishes and roulades. And you can imagine the effect of all this—combined with her ridiculous manners and style of dress—upon a sensitive music-loving lad like myself. My uncle lost no opportunity to shower praise upon Miss Meibel's performance. And I, who could not understand this at all, turned naturally to my organist; he looked with contempt upon vocal efforts in general, and he delighted me down to the ground by parodying the absurd old spinster's antics, with a certain hypochondriac malice which I found irresistibly amusing.

"The more emphatically I came to share my master's scorn for singing, the higher he rated my musical abilities. He took a great and zealous interest in instructing me in counterpoint, so that I was soon composing the most ingenious toccatas and fugues. And it happened that on my nineteenth birthday I was entertaining my uncle with one of these adroit specimens of my skill, when the head porter of our town's leading hotel stepped into the room to announce the visit of two foreign ladies who had just arrived.

"Before my uncle could throw off his dressing gown—its material was of a large flower pattern—and don his coat and waistcoat, his callers entered the room. You know what an electrifying effect every unusual event has upon almost any individual brought up in the narrow confines of a small country town; this sudden encounter was, pre-eminently, of a sort to work a complete revolution in my mind. Picture to yourself two tall and slender Italian ladies, dressed in bright-colored costumes which seemed fantastic to me (though as a matter of fact they were of the latest mode), who approached my uncle with the freedom of professional *artistes*, yet with considerable charm of manner, and addressed him in firm and resonant tones. What the deuce, I asked myself, was that strange language they were speaking? Only now and then was there a sound which bore the slightest resemblance to German. And it was plain that my uncle didn't understand a word. Embarrassed, incapable of intelligible human utterance, he stepped back and pointed to the sofa. The two ladies sat down and talked together—and their voices were like music itself. At length they succeeded in making my good uncle understand that they were singers on tour. They wished to give a concert in our town, and so they had come to him, as the proper man with whom to conduct musical negotiations.

"As they were talking together I picked up their Christian names; and soon I was able to distinguish one from the other. In the confusion of their first overwhelming appearance that had been impossible! Now I noticed that Lauretta, apparently the older of the two, looked about her with sparkling eyes, and talked away at my embarrassed old uncle with an effervescent vivacity which had its natural accompaniment in demonstrative gestures. Teresina, taller, more slender, and with a much more serious face, spoke very little;

but what she said was intelligible. Now and then a rather peculiar smile flitted across her face. It almost seemed as if she were amused by my respected uncle, who had withdrawn into his gay silk dressing gown like a snail into its shell, and was desperately preoccupied with the vain effort to push a treacherous yellow string out of sight within its folds: it was the cord of his nightshirt, and it kept falling out from under his dressing gown, apparently yards and yards long.

"At length the ladies rose to take their leave. My uncle promised to make all arrangements for their concert to be given on the third day following. Then the sisters (we knew now that they were sisters) gave him, and me, a most courteous invitation to take chocolate with them in the afternoon. My uncle, in the meantime, had introduced me as a young musician, which naturally pleased me very much.

"That afternoon, then, we went to the hotel restaurant—but I must confess that we made our way up the steps with a solemn and awkward gait. We both felt odd and out-of-place, as if we were going to meet some adventure to which we were not equal. As a result of careful preparation for the occasion, my uncle had at his tongue's end a great many fine things to say about art, which nobody understood—neither he himself nor any of the rest of us. When these impressive pronouncements had been made (and when I, smiling through my pain with the stoical fortitude of a Scaevola, had thrice burned my tongue with the scalding hot chocolate), Lauretta said that she would sing for us. Teresina took up her guitar, tuned it, and struck a few full chords. It was the first time I had ever heard that instrument, and the characteristic mysterious sounds of the trembling strings made a deep and remarkable impression upon me.

"Lauretta began to sing very softly; but soon she held a note to *fortissimo*, and then quickly broke into a crisp and complicated run through an octave and a half. I can still remember the words with which her song began: '*Sento l'amica speme.*' My heart was as if gripped—and even oppressed—by wonder. I had never had an idea of anything of this kind! But as Lauretta's voice continued to soar, in bolder and higher flights, and as the musical notes fell upon me like the sun's sparkling rays, I was roused from any sense of oppression to, indeed, its liveliest opposite. I felt that all the music within my own spirit, which had lain mute and sleeping all my life, had now been awakened and enkindled, so that it could burst forth in strong and splendid flame. Ah, I had never before heard music; in all my nineteen years, I had never known what music was. . . .

"After this, the sisters sang one of those great imposing duets of Abbot Steffani, which confine themselves to notes of low register. My whole soul was stirred by Teresina's alto, sonorous and pure as silver bells. I couldn't for the life of me restrain my emotion; tears started to my eyes. My uncle coughed warningly and cast indignant glances in my direction, but it was no use: I was really quite beside myself. This seemed to please the sisters. They began to inquire into the nature and extent of my musical studies. I was ashamed, now, of my labors and performances in that line; and with the hardihood born of enthusiastic admiration I bluntly declared aloud what I had already said to myself—that I had today heard music for the first time in my life. . . .

" 'The dear, good boy!' lisped Lauretta, so sweetly and bewitchingly that my head was more than ever in a whirl.

"When I reached home, I was seized with a sort of fury. I pounced upon all the clever toccatas and fugues that I had hammered out, and threw them in the fire; and not only my own compositions, but with them a beautiful copy of forty-five variations on a canonical theme which the organist had written and had done me the honor of presenting to me. And as the double counterpoint smoked and crackled in the flames I laughed with spiteful glee. Then I sat down at the piano, and tried first to imitate the tones of the guitar, then to play the sisters' melodies; I climaxed my efforts by attempting to sing them. My uncle put an end to this at last, about midnight, when he came out of his bedroom and called to me, 'My boy, you'd better just stop that screeching and troop off to bed!' Then he put out both candles, and went back to his own room.

"I had no alternative but to obey. But the mysterious power of song came to me in my dreams—at least I thought it did—and I sang 'Sento l'amica speme' in excellent style!

"The next morning my uncle hunted up everybody who could fiddle and blow, and gathered them together for the rehearsal. He was filled with pride over the idea of showing the visiting *artistes* what good musicians our town possessed; but everything seemed, in stubborn perversity, to go wrong. Lauretta set to work on a fine *scena*, but very soon the orchestra was all at sixes and sevens in the recitative: not one of the players had any idea of the accompaniment. Lauretta screamed, raved, wept with impatience and anger. She poured the bitterest reproaches upon the organist, who was presiding at the piano; silent and obdurate, he got up and marched out of the hall. The orchestra leader (our town bandmaster), whom she had just been railing at as an 'assino tedesco,' tucked his violin under his arm, slammed his hat down on his head with an air of defiance, and likewise made for the door. The members of his company, respectively sticking their bows under the strings of their violins and unscrewing the mouthpieces of their brass instruments, followed him.

"Only the dilettanti were left in the hall; and they gazed about them disconsolately, while the local tax collector expressed the feelings of them all as he exclaimed, with an air of overwhelming tragedy, 'Gracious Heaven! How mortifying I find all this!'

"All my natural diffidence vanished. I could not let our great occasion fail this way! I could not let this promise of real music go unfulfilled! I jumped right in front of the orchestra leader: I begged, I pleaded, in my desperation I promised him six new minuets with double trios for the town's annual ball! And so I succeeded in appeasing him. He went back to his place; his companions followed suit; and soon the orchestra was reconstituted, with the single exception of the organist, who was already outside the building and crossing the market place, and could not be moved, by any shouting or beckoning, to turn back.

"Teresina had looked on at this whole scene with smothered laughter. And Lauretta was now as full of merriment and delight as she had been, a few moments before, of anger. She was lavish in her praise of my efforts; and, since we had now no one at the piano, she asked me if I could play that instrument. Before I knew what I was about, I was sitting in the organist's place, with the music before me. Never in my life had I accompanied a singer, to say nothing of assisting in the direction of an orchestra! But the sisters were kindness itself. Teresina sat down beside me at the piano, and gave me every beat. Lauretta encouraged me with repeated 'Bravos!' The orchestra proved to be co-operative. And things continued to improve. At the second rehearsal everything went off satisfactorily. And when the townspeople crowded the hall for the great concert, the effect of the sisters' singing was something not to be described.

"The Prince's return to the Residenz was soon to be celebrated with a number of festive demonstrations in the capital, and the sisters had been summoned to sing in the theatre and at concerts then. But until the time came for these command performances they decided to remain in our little town, and so it happened that they gave us several more concerts. The admiration of the public reached the point of frenzy. But old Miss Meibel took a pinch of snuff out of her porcelain pug, and gave it as her opinion that 'such impudent caterwauling was not singing; singing,' she added, 'should be low and melodious.' And my old friend the organist never showed himself once, either among the musicians or in the audience.

"But, to tell the truth, I did not miss him! I was the happiest fellow in the world. I spent all of every day with the sisters, copying out the vocal scores of what they were to sing at the capital. Lauretta was my ideal. I endured with patience her unpredictable—not to say outrageous—caprices, her outbursts of passionate violence, the torments she inflicted upon me as her pianist. What did all that matter? She alone had unsealed for me the springs of true music. . . . I began to study Italian, and I tried my hand at a few canzonets. And in what heavenly rapture was I plunged when Lauretta sang one of my compositions, or even praised it! Often it seemed to me that it was not I who had thought out and set to music what she was singing, but that the creative impulse itself only shone forth for the first time as she sang.

"With Teresina, on the other hand, I somehow could not get on familiar terms. She seldom sang. And she did not seem to take much account of all I was doing. Sometimes I even imagined that she was laughing at me behind my back.

"It was indeed different with Lauretta; and when the time came for them to leave the town, I realized for the first time how dear she was to me, and how unendurable it would be to be separated from her. Often, when she was in a mood of tender playfulness, she had touched my cheek, or stroked my head, in a fashion that was none the less caressing because it was also completely artless. And at such times only the realization of her ordinary coolness towards me would restrain my ardent impulse to clasp her in my arms. But now, as I was about to lose her forever, my passion was heightened by despair.

"I possessed a tolerably good tenor voice, which, however, I had never tried to cultivate. Under the spur of my association with the sisters I began to practice assiduously; and frequently Lauretta and I would sing some tender Italian duet (you know them—there are so many!) together. Now it happened that as the hour of departure was drawing near we were singing one of these pieces: 'Senza di te ben mio, vivere non poss' io!' (Without thee, my own, I cannot live!) And—can you blame me that I could not resist it? In desperation I threw myself at Lauretta's feet. And she gently pulled me up again.

" 'But, my friend,' she said, in tones that moved me through and through, 'need we part?'

"And as I stood there, thunderstruck with amazement, she quietly proposed that I should accompany Teresina and herself to the capital. If I intended to devote myself wholly to music, she continued, I must certainly leave this wretched little town sometime or other. What time could be better than now?

"My friend, can you picture to yourself a man struggling in the dark depths of boundless despair, a man who has given up all hope of happiness and fulfillment in this life, and who now—in the very moment when he awaits the blow that is to crush him forever—suddenly finds himself transported to some gloriously bright rose arbor, where unseen but loving spirits whisper to him, 'You are still alive, and we cherish you—you are still alive!'? I repeat—can you imagine this, my good friend? If so, you will know how I felt at this moment. To go along with Lauretta and Teresina to the capital! The dream came to life as an ineradicable resolution. . . .

"But I won't bore you now with the recital of all the details of my procedure: how I set to work to convince my uncle that I ought by all means to go, and now, to the capital—which, as a matter of fact, was not very far away. At length he gave his consent. And, furthermore, he announced his intention of going with me. I did not dare to state my purpose of traveling in company with the two sisters. Again, I was distracted. But at just the right moment my uncle caught a violent cold; he had to stay at home, and I was free!

"I left the town by the stagecoach, but I went only as far as the first stopping place. There I awaited my divinity. My purse, happily, was well-lined. I had thus been able to make all proper preparations for my journey. And I had been seized with the romantic notion of accompanying the ladies in the character of a protecting paladin, and as such a knight should—on horseback. I procured a horse, which its owner assured me was quiet and docile—though I must admit it was not romantically handsome—and I rode back at the appointed time to meet the two fair singers. I soon saw their little carriage coming towards me. It had two seats: Lauretta and Teresina occupied the principal one, while on the other, with her back to the horses, sat their maid, the fat and brown-cheeked little Neapolitan Gianna. In addition, the carriage was packed with boxes, satchels, and baskets, of all shapes and sizes, such as always accompany ladies on their travels. And there were also two pug dogs, which Gianna was holding in her lap, and which began to bark when I gaily saluted the company.

"All had gone very well, and we were completing the last section of the journey, when my steed all at once conceived the idea that it was high time to be returning homeward. Being aware that stern measures were not always blessed with a high degree of success, in such cases, I felt advised to have recourse to milder means of persuasion; but the obstinate brute remained insensible to all my well-meant exhortations. I wanted to go forward. He wanted to go backward. And all the advantage that my efforts gave me was that, instead of taking to his heels for home, he ran around in circles. Teresina leaned out of the carriage and had a hearty laugh. Lauretta held her hands before her face and screamed as if my life were in danger.

"Together, these responses served to give me the courage of despair. I drove the spurs into the brute's ribs. But the result was not what I had hoped for. I was abruptly hurled from his back, and found myself sprawling on the ground. The horse, now, stood perfectly still; and, stretching out his long neck, he regarded me with what I could only take to be a look of derision. I, alas, was unable to rise to my feet: the driver of the carriage had to come and help me. Lauretta, meanwhile, had jumped out, and was weeping and lamenting. Teresina did nothing but laugh. As for me, I had sprained my ankle in my fall: it was impossible for me to mount the horse and ride again. What was I to do? Well, my erstwhile steed was tied to the carriage, while I, perforce, got into it. . . .

"So now, my friend, you can image us all—two rather robust young women, a fat servant girl, two pug dogs, a dozen boxes, satchels, and baskets, and myself as well, all packed into a small vehicle. Imagine Lauretta's complaints over her lack of comfort, crowded in as she was; the maid's witless Neapolitan chattering, the yapping of the dogs, Teresina's sulky silence, and the inexpressible pain I had now begun to feel in my foot, and you will have some idea of my enviable situation!

"Before long, Teresina declared that she could not stand it any longer. The driver stopped the carriage. In a trice she was out on the road, had untied my horse, and was up in the saddle, prancing and curvetting around us. I must indeed admit that she cut a fine figure. The dignity and carriage which marked her ordinary bearing were still more pronounced when she was on horseback. In a few moments she asked for her guitar, and, dropping the reins on her arm, she began to sing proud Spanish ballads with a full-toned accompaniment. Her thin silk dress fluttered in the wind, and light played in sparkling sheen upon its folds, while the white feathers of her hat waved and quivered as if in accompaniment to the air she sang. Altogether, she made such a romantic picture that I could not take my eyes off her, even though Lauretta was scolding her for making herself look like a fantastic simpleton, and was predicting that she would suffer for her senseless daring.

"But no accident occurred. Either the horse had lost his stubbornness, or else he preferred the fair singer to the would-be-paladin. Be that as it may, Teresina did not dismount from the horse and re-enter the carriage until we were almost at the city gates.

"If you had seen me then at concerts and operas, if you had observed my joyous concentration on music of all sorts, if you had heard me as a diligent accompanist at work at the piano on arias, duets, and I don't know what besides—if you had been a witness of all this, my friend, you would have realized, by the complete change in my behavior, that my being itself had been completely changed. Indeed, there was a new and rich spirit within me. I had conquered, cast off, forgotten, all my rustic shyness; and now I sat at the piano with my score before me like an experienced professional, directing my prima donna's performance. My mind was filled with happy melodies. And it was with a reckless disregard of all those laboriously studied rules of counterpoint that I composed for Lauretta a vast variety of canzonets and arias.

"She sang them all: but only in her own room. Why would she never sing any of my pieces at a concert? I could not understand it. And, while Lauretta continued to inspire me, the eyes of my imagination would suddenly be filled also with the sight of Teresina curvetting on her proud steed, with her lute in her hands, like the figure of Art itself in some romantic disguise. Without consciously thinking of Teresina, without having any aim in view, I wrote several songs of a high and serious nature. And something of the difference between the two sisters permeated my mind, although at the time I scarcely realized it. Lauretta played with her notes like some capricious fairy queen, forever regal and forever blessed: there was nothing upon which she ventured that was not crowned with success. But never did a roulade cross Teresina's lips. Nothing more than a simple interpolated note, at most a *mordent*, sounded from her throat when the sisters sang together. Yet her long-sustained notes gleamed like meteors through the darkness of night, and awakened strange spirits who came and gazed with earnest eyes into the very depths of my heart. I do not know, now as I look back upon it, how I remained in ignorance so long!

"The sisters were granted a benefit concert, and in it I joined with Lauretta in a long *scena* from *Anfossi*. As usual, I presided at the piano. We came to the last *fermata*, and Lauretta was exerting all her skill, demonstrating all her art; she warbled trill after trill, like a nightingale; she executed sustained notes, and then long elaborate roulades—a whole *solfeggio*. In fact, I thought that this time she was almost carrying the thing too far. As I was musing to this effect, I felt a soft breath on my cheek: Teresina stood behind me. And at this moment Lauretta took a good start with the intention of swelling up to a 'harmonic shake,' and so passing back into *a tempo*. The Devil entered into me: I jammed down the keys with both hands; the orchestra followed suit; and it was all over with Lauretta's trill, just at the supreme moment when she was to sweep her audience to the highest pitch of astonishment.

"She turned to me with such a look of fury that I felt almost annihilated, crushed her roll of music in her hand, and threw it at my head; then she rushed, as if smitten by madness, through the orchestra, and into the off-stage waiting room. As soon as we had played through the piece, I followed her.

"She wept and raved. 'Out of my sight, you blackguard!' she screamed, as soon as she saw me. 'You devil, you've completely ruined me! Ruined my reputation, my honor—and my trill. Out of my sight, you devil's brood!'

"She made a rush as if to attack me physically, but I escaped through the door. And while someone else was performing on the stage, Teresina and the music director succeeded in so far pacifying her as to win her consent to coming out again. But she made one condition: I was not to be allowed to touch the piano.

"Then, in the last duet that the sisters sang, Lauretta did contrive to introduce the swelling 'harmonic shake,' and was rewarded with a storm of applause. Whereupon she settled down into the best of humors.

"But I could not get over the outrageous treatment which I had received at her hands in the presence of a large audience; and I made up my mind that I would leave her the next morning, and return to my native town. I was actually engaged in packing my things when Teresina came into my room. Observing what I was about, she exclaimed in astonishment, 'What! Are you going to leave us?' And I gave her to understand that after the affront which Lauretta had put upon me I could not think of remaining any longer in her society.

" 'And so,' responded Teresina, 'you are going to let yourself be driven away by the preposterous conduct of a little fool, who is now heartily sorry for what she has done? I ask you, where else than with us can you better live in your art? And let me tell you, too, that it only depends on yourself and your behavior, to keep her from such pranks as this. You are too pliable, too soft, too gentle. What is more, you rate her powers too highly. It is true that her voice is not bad, and it has a wide range. But those fantastic warblings and flourishes, those extravagant runs, those never-ending shakes—what are they but delusive artifices of style, which people admire in the same way that they admire the foolhardy agility of a tightrope walker? Do you really think that such things as that can make any deep impression, that they can stir the heart? The "harmonic shake" which you spoiled,' she continued with emphasis, 'is a thing I cannot tolerate. When she attempts it, I always feel anxious and pained. And then this scaling up into the region of the third line above the stave—what is that but a violent straining of the natural voice? And the natural voice, after all, dear friend, is the only thing that really moves the heart. . . . I like the middle notes and the low notes; a sound that goes through to the heart, a quiet and easy transition from note to note—those are the things I love above all. No useless ornamentation; a firm, clear, strong note; a definite expression, which reaches and transports the mind and the soul—that's real, true singing, and that's how I sing.

" 'If you can't be reconciled to Lauretta,' she added, a little wistfully, 'then think of Teresina, who indeed likes you so much that you shall, in your own way, be her musical composer. Don't be cross—but all your elegant canzonets and arias cannot match this single piece. . . . And in her lovely, resonant voice she sang a simple devotion canzona which I had written a few days before.

"I had never dreamed that it could sound like that. I felt the power of the music going through and through me. Tears of joy and rapture stood in my eyes. I grasped Teresina's hand, and as I pressed it to my lips I swore, over and over and over again, that I would never leave her.

"Lauretta showed a certain envious attitude towards my intimacy with her sister, but she suppressed any obvious sign of vexation; for the fact was, as I soon realized, that she could not do without me. In spite of her skill in singing, she read badly, and she was uncertain in time and beat. Teresina, on the contrary, sang everything at sight, and her ear for time was perfect in its accuracy. Never did Lauretta give such free rein to her capricious and violent temper as when her accompaniments were being practiced: they were never right; they were nothing but a necessary evil anyway; the piano ought not to be heard at all; it must always be *pianissimo*. So there was nothing to do but give way to her again and again, and alter the time just as the whim happened to strike her at the moment. Now, however, I took a firm stand against her. I combatted her impertinences. I taught her that an accompaniment devoid of energy was nothing short of inconceivable, and that there was a marked difference between supporting the song—carrying it along—and letting it run riot, without time and without form. Teresina faithfully lent her assistance in all this. And now I composed nothing but church pieces, and wrote all the solos for a voice of low register. It is true that Teresina also tyrannized over me not a little, but I submitted to her despotism with a good grace. She had, I assured myself, more knowledge of good German seriousness, and (so at least I thought) deeper appreciation of it, than her sister could possess.

"When we were touring in south Germany, some time after the incident I have just recalled, we met, in a little town, an Italian tenor who was making his way from Milan to Berlin. My fair companions were delighted with their fellow countryman. And he, for his part, attached himself closely to them, and cultivated Teresina's acquaintance, especially, with such eagerness and success that to my great vexation I soon came to feel that my rôle among them was only secondary. At last affairs came to a sudden climax. One day, as I was about to enter the sisters' sitting room with a roll of music under my arm, the voices of my companions and the tenor, engaged in an animated conversation, fell upon my ear. My name was mentioned. I pricked up my ears. Unashamed, I listened. Lauretta was telling the whole tragic story of the concert in which I had cut short her trill by prematurely striking the concluding notes of the bar. 'Assino tedesco!' the tenor exclaimed.

"I felt as if I must rush into the room and throw the flighty hero out of the window; but I restrained myself. I continued to listen, however. And I heard Lauretta go on to say that she had been minded to send me about my business immediately, but had been so moved to compassion by my clamorous entreaties as to tolerate me for some time longer, since I was studying singing under her. This, to my utter amazement, Teresina confirmed.

" 'Yes, he's a good child,' I heard the latter add. 'He's in love with me now, and he sets everything for the alto. He is not without talent, but he must rub off that stiffness and awkwardness which are so characteristic of the Germans. I hope to make a capable composer out of him. Then he shall write me some good things—for as yet there is very little written for the alto voice—and after that I shall let him go his way. He's a terrible bore,' she went on, 'with his billing and cooing and lovesick sighing; and he bothers me much too much with his tedious compositions, which so far have been poor stuff.'

" 'I at least got rid of him,' Lauretta interrupted. 'And you know, Teresina, how the fellow pestered me with his arias and duets.'

"And now she began to sing a duet of my composing, which formerly she had praised very highly. The other sister took up the second voice; and both in tone and in execution they burlesqued me in the most shameful manner. The tenor laughed until the walls rang with the echo of his mirth. My limbs seemed frozen. But at once I came to an irrevocable decision. I quietly slipped away from the door and back to my own room, the windows of which looked out upon a side street. Opposite was the post office. The post-coach for Bamberg had just driven up to take on the mails and passengers. The latter were standing ready waiting in the gateway, but I still had an hour to spare. . . .

"Hastily packing my things, I generously paid the whole of the bill at the hotel, and hurried over to catch the post-chaise. As I crossed the broad street I saw the fair sisters and the Italian standing at the window, and leaning out to hear the sound of the post-horn. I leaned back in the corner of the chaise, and dwelt with a good deal of satisfaction upon the crushing effect of the bitter and scathing letter which I had left behind for Lauretta and Teresina at the hotel."

With evident gratification, Theodore tossed off the rest of the fiery Aleatico which Edward had poured into his glass. The latter, opening a new bottle and skilfully shaking off the drops of oil which floated on top of the wine, remarked, "I should not have dreamed Teresina capable of such artfulness and falsity. I cannot banish from my mind the recollection of the charming picture she made—on your mind and through you on mine—as she sat singing Spanish ballads on horseback, while the steed gracefully pranced and cur-vetted along the road."

"That was her climactic point," Theodore interrupted. "I still remember the strange impression which the scene made upon me. I forgot my pain. She seemed to me like a creature of some higher race. It is indeed true that such moments are turning points in one's life, and that in them images arise which time is powerless to dim. Whenever I have succeeded in any fine *romanza*, it has always been when Teresina's image has stepped forth from the treasure house of memory, in clear bright colors, at the moment of writing it."

"At the same time," said Edward, "let us not forget the artistic, and 'temperamental,' Lauretta. And, casting all rancor to the winds, let us drink to the health of the two sisters."

They did so. And as he raised his glass Theodore exclaimed, "Oh, how the fragrant breezes of Italy rise from this wine and fan my cheeks! My blood courses through my veins with quickened energy. Oh, why was I obliged so soon to leave that glorious land?"

"As yet," interrupted Edward, "as yet, in all that you have told me, there has been no connection, so far as I can see, with the delightful painting we were looking at. And so I believe that you still have something to tell me about these two sisters. Of course I perceive that the two ladies in the picture are none other than Lauretta and Teresina—but come, you must have something more to say."

"You are right," replied Theodore. "They are Lauretta and Teresina; and I still have something more to say, to which my sighs and ejaculations, my longing for the lovely land of Italy, will form a fitting introduction. . . .

"A short time ago," he now plunged again into his narrative, "perhaps two years since, as I was about to leave Rome, I made a little excursion on horseback. Before a village inn, as I went riding along, I saw a charming young girl; and the thought came to me, how pleasant it would be to receive a glass of wine from the hands of that pretty child. I pulled up before the door, in an avenue so thickly planted with shrubs that only patches of sunlight could make their way through the leaves. In the distance I heard sounds of singing, and the tinkling of a guitar. And I pricked up my ears and listened, as I became conscious that the two female voices were affecting me in quite a singular way.

"Strange recollections were stirring dimly in my mind, but they refused to take definite shape. By this time, however, I was so interested that I got down from my horse, and slowly approached the vine-covered arbor from which the music seemed to proceed—eagerly listening, meanwhile, to catch every sound. The second voice had fallen silent. The first sang a canzonet alone. As I drew nearer, the sense of familiarity faded; the initial attraction ceased to beckon me; but I was still interested. The singer was now in the midst of an elaborate and florid *fermata*. Up and down she warbled, and down and up; at length, holding one note for a long time, she stopped. Then all at once a woman's voice broke out in a torrent of abuse, maledictions, vituperations, curses. A man protested. Another man laughed. The second female voice joined in the altercation. The quarrel waxed louder and more violent, with true Italian fury. At last I stood directly in front of the arbor, and an abbot rushed out and almost knocked me down. As he turned his head to look at me, I recognized my good friend Signor Lodovico, my musical newsmonger from Rome."

" 'What in the name of wonder—' I exclaimed. But he interrupted me, screaming.

" 'Oh, sir, sir!' he cried. 'Save me! Protect me from this mad fury, this crocodile, this hyena, this tiger, this devil of a woman! It is true that I did what I did: I was beating time for her to Anfossi's canzonet, and I brought down my baton too soon while she was in the midst of the *fermata*. I cut short her trill. I admit it. But why did I meet her eyes, the devil-goddess! Deuce take all *fermate*, I say!'

"In a most curious state of mind, I hastened into the arbor, taking the priest back with me. And at first glance I recognized the sisters Lauretta and Teresina. The former was still shrieking and raging. Her sister was still earnestly remonstrating with her. The host of the inn, his bare arms crossed over his chest, was looking on and laughing, while a serving-girl was placing fresh flasks of wine on the table. And now my entrance still more strangely complicated the scene.

"For both sisters knew me at once. No sooner had they caught sight of me than they literally threw themselves upon me, apparently in a transport of affection. 'Ah, Signor Teodoro!' they exclaimed, and both embraced me. The quarrel of a moment before was totally forgotten.

" 'Here you have a composer,' said Lauretta to the abbot, 'who is as charming as an Italian, and as strong as a German.' Then both sisters, continually interrupting each other, began to recount the happy days we had spent together, to tell how they had discovered my musical abilities while I was still a youth, to praise my compositions, to recall our hours of practice together; never did they enjoy singing anything, they said, but what I had arranged or composed.

"Teresina at length informed me that a manager had engaged her as his first singer in tragic parts for his next music festival; but now, she said, she would give him to understand that she would sing for him only on condition that the composition of at least one tragic opera was entrusted to me. The tragic was above all others my special field, she averred, and so on, and so on.

"But now Lauretta maintained that it would be a great pity if I did not follow my bent for the light and the graceful—in a word, for *opera buffa*. She had been engaged as prima donna for this type of composition; and it was simply a matter of course—it went without saying—that no one but I should write the piece in which she was to appear. . . .

"You may imagine what my feelings were, as I stood there between the two! In short, you perceive that the company which I had just joined was the one which Hummel painted, and that the painting shows the group at precisely the moment when the priest is about to cut short Lauretta's *fermata*."

"But," Edward broke in, "did they not make any allusion to your departure, or to the scathing letter you left behind?"

"Not with so much as a syllable," Theodore answered. "And you may be very sure that I said nothing about any of that. The fact is, I had long ago banished all animosity from my heart, and had come to look upon my adventure with the two sisters in the light of a merry prank. I did, however, make one oblique reference to the subject, not addressing them, but speaking to the priest. I told him that, several years before, the same mischance had befallen me, in one of Anfossi's arias, as had been his ill luck today; I painted the period of my association with the sisters in tragicomic colors, and, throwing off many a keen side-blow, I gave them an unmistakable understanding of the superiority which the ripe experience of the intervening years had given me, both in life and in art.

" 'And a good thing it was,' I concluded, 'that I cut that *fermata* short. For it was evidently meant to last through eternity. And I am firmly of the opinion that if I had left the singer alone I should be sitting at the piano now.'

" 'But, Signor,' said the priest, 'what director is there who would dare to lay down rules for the prima donna? Your offense was much more heinous than mine, for you were in the concert hall, and I was here in a leafy arbor. Besides, I was director in imagination only; what I did was of no importance whatever. And if the sweet fiery glance of those heavenly eyes had not fascinated me, moreover, I should not have made an ass of myself.'

"The abbot's last words had a calming effect; for although Lauretta's 'heavenly eyes' had begun to flash with anger as he was speaking, she was quite appeased by the time he had finished with his pretty compliment.

"We spent the evening together. It was fourteen years since I had left my fair friends, and many changes had taken place in that time. Lauretta, though she looked somewhat older, had by no means lost her charm. Teresina had worn somewhat better, and her figure was as graceful as before. Both were dressed in rather gay colors, and their manners were exactly as I remembered them—that is, they were, let us say, fourteen years younger than the ladies themselves. At my request, Teresina sang some of the serious songs which had once so deeply affected me, but I fancied that they did not sound quite the same as when I had first heard them. And Lauretta's singing, also, seemed to me to be quite different from my recollection of it, even though her voice had not appreciably lost anything in power or range.

"The sisters' behavior to me, their feigned ecstasies, their crude praise—even though this last took the form of gracious patronage—had done much to put me in a bad humor; and now my mood deteriorated still further in the obtrusivenss of this comparison between the romantic images in my mind and the not overly pleasing reality. I was restored to a more amiable temper at last by the drolleries of the priest—who in the most saccharine phrases imaginable was playing the *amoroso* to both sisters at once—as well as by numerous glasses of the good wine. And we ended by spending a very pleasant evening in perfect concord and companionable gaiety. The sisters were most pressing in urging me to accompany them to their home, so that we might at once discuss the parts which I was to write for them and begin to make our plans without delay. But, needless to say, I did not accept their invitation. And I left Rome without making any effort to find out where they lived."

"And yet, after all," Edward reflected, "it is to them that you owe the awakening of your musical genius. . . ."

"That I know well!" Theodore replied. "I admit that I owe this to them, and many good melodies besides. And that is just the reason why I did not want to see them again. Every composer, as I said a minute ago, has experienced certain impressions which time does not obliterate. The spirit of music spoke, and the artist heard the creative word which suddenly awoke the answering spirit within himself; and that inner spirit was never to sleep again. Thus it is unquestionably true that when a melody has been called in this way from the depths of the composer's being, it seems to belong to the singer who fanned the artist's first inner spark. It is as if one heard her voice, and merely recorded what she had sung.

"But it is in the human heritage of us weak mortals," Theodore continued, "that we are all too prone to drag what is super-earthly down within the narrow enclosure of this earthly life where we, poor clods, dwell. And so it comes to pass that the singer becomes the lover, or even the wife. The spell is broken. And all that melody of her nature, which was formerly the revelation of glorious things, is now voiced in complaints about broken soup plates or the ink-stains on fresh linen. Happy is the composer who never again, as long as he lives, sets eyes upon the woman who by some mysterious power kindled the flame of music within him! Even though the young artist's heart may be rent by anguish and despair when he must part from his lovely enchantress, nevertheless it is precisely so that she will continue to exist for him as a divinely beautiful strain of music itself: it is so that she will live on and on in his heart and mind, never losing her youth or her loveliness, and forever engendering harmonies in which he forever feels the presence of his love. For what is she, now, but the Highest Ideal which, working its way from within outward, is at last reflected in external form?"

"A strange theory, but not impossible," Edward commented. And the two friends, arm in arm, made their way from the Sala Tarone, and out into the street.

THE SERENADE

George Bernard Shaw
1856-1950

George Bernard Shaw's mother gave singing lessons, and thus the great Irish playwright was exposed to music from an early age. Most of Shaw's own musical education, however, was self-taught, though he did study cornet formally for awhile. But he balked at the time and practice it took to develop an adequately controlled lip for the instrument. Some of his frustration seems to be recalled in his amusing story "The Serenade" (1885).

I celebrated my fortieth birthday by one of the amateur theatrical performances for which my house at Beckenham is famous. The piece, written, as usual, by myself, was a fairy play in three acts; and the plot turned upon the possession of a magic horn by the hero, a young Persian prince. My works are so well known that it is unnecessary to describe the action minutely. I need only remind the reader that an important feature in the second act is the interruption of a festival by the sound of the horn, blown by the Prince in the heart of a loadstone mountain in which he has been entombed by a malignant fairy. I had engaged a cornist from the band of my regiment to blow the horn; and it was arranged that he should place himself, not upon the stage, but downstairs in the hall, so that the required effect of extreme distance should be produced.

The entertainment began pleasantly. Some natural disappointment was felt when it became known that I was not to act; but my guests excused me with perfect good humor when I pleaded my double duty as host and stage manager. The best seat in the auditorium was occupied by the beautiful Linda Fitznightingale. The next chair, which I had intended for myself, had been taken (rather coolly) by Porcharlester of the 12th, a young man of amiable disposition, and of some musical talent, which enables him to make the most of a somewhat effeminate baritone voice which he is weak enough to put forward as a tenor.

As Linda's taste for music approached fanaticism, Porcharlester's single accomplishment gave him, in her eyes, an advantage over men of more solid parts and mature age. I resolved to interrupt their conversation as soon as I was at leisure. It was some time before this occurred; for I make it a rule to see for myself that everything needed at the performances in my house is at hand in its proper place. At last Miss Waterloo, who enacted the heroine, complained that my anxiety made her nervous, and begged me to go to the front and rest myself. I complied willingly and hastened to the side of Linda. As I approached, Porcharlester rose, saying, "I am going to take a peep behind: that is, if non-performers may be admitted."

"Oh, certainly," I said, glad to be rid of him. "But pray do not meddle with anything. The slightest hitch—"

"All right," he said, interrupting me. "I know how fidgety you are. I will keep my hands in my pockets all the time."

"You should not allow him to be disrespectful to you, Colonel Green," said Linda, when he was gone. "And I feel sure he will do no end of mischief behind the scenes."

"Boys will be boys," I replied. "Porcharlester's manner is just the same to General Johnston, who is quite an old man. How are your musical studies progressing?"

"I am full of Schubert just now. Oh, Colonel Green, *do* you know Schubert's serenade?"

"Ah! a charming thing. It is something like this, I think. Diddledi-dum, deediddledi-dum, deedum, deediddledyday."

"Yes, it is a little like that. Does Mr. Porcharlester sing it?"

"He tries to sing it. But he only appears to advantage when he sings trivial music. In nothing that demands serious sentiment, depth of feeling, matured sympathy, as it were—"

"Yes, yes. I know you think Mr. Porcharlester flippant. Do you like the serenade?"

"Hm! well, the fact is—Do *you* like it?"

"I love it. I dream of it. I have lived on it for the last three days."

"I must confess that it has always struck me as being a singularly beautiful piece of music. I hope to have the pleasure of hearing justice done to it by your voice when our little play is over."

"*I* sing it! Oh, I dare not. Ah! here is Mr. Porcharlester. I will make him promise to sing it for us."

"Green," said Porcharlester with ill-bred jocosity: "I dont wish to disturb you groundlessly; but the fellow who is to play the magic horn hasnt turned up."

"Good Heavens!" I exclaimed. "I ordered him for half-past seven sharp. If he fails, the play will be spoilt."

I excused myself briefly to Linda, and hurried to the hall. The horn was there, on the table. Porcharlester had resorted to an infamous trick to get rid of me. I was about to return and demand an explanation, when it occurred to me that, after all, the bandsman might have left his instrument there at the morning rehearsal and had perhaps not come. But a servant whom I called told me that the man had arrived with military punctuality at half-past seven, and had, according to my orders, been shewn into the supper room joining the hall, and left there with a glass of wine and a sandwich. Porcharlester, then, had deceived me. As the servant returned to his duties, leaving me alone and angry in the hall, my attention was curiously arrested by the gleaming brass curves of the instrument on the table. Amid the inanimate objects around me the horn seemed silent and motionless in a way apart, as though, pregnant with dreadful sound, it were consciously biding its time for utterance. I stole to the table, and cautiously touched one of the valves with my forefinger. After a moment I ventured to press it down. It clicked. At a sound in the supper room I started back guiltily. Then the prompter's bell tinkled. It was the signal for the cornist to prepare for his cue. I awaited the appearance of the bandsman with some shame, hoping that he would not discover that I had been childishly meddling with his instrument. But he did not come. My anxiety increased: I hurried into the supper room. There, at the head of the table, sat the soldier, fast asleep. Before him were five decanters empty. I seized his shoulder and shook him violently. He grunted; made a drunken blow at me; and relapsed into insensibility.

Swearing, in my anger, to have him shot for this mutiny, I rushed back to the hall. The bell rang again. This second bell was for the horn to sound. The stage was waiting. In that extremity I saw but one way to save the piece from failure. I snatched up the instrument; put the smaller end into my mouth; and puffed vigorously through it. Waste of breath! not a sound responded. I became faint with my exertions; and the polished brass slipped through my clammy hands. The bell again urgently broke the ruinous silence. Then I grasped the horn like a vice; inflated my lungs; jammed the mouthpiece against my lips and set my teeth until it nearly cut me; and spat fiercely into it. The result was a titanic blast. My ears received a deafening shock; the lamp glasses whirred; the hats of my visitors rained from their pegs; and I pressed my bursting temples between my palms as the soldier reeled out, pale as though the last trumpet had roused him, and confronted the throng of amazed guests who appeared on the stairs.

For the next three months I studied the art of horn-blowing under the direction of an adept. He worried me by his lower middle class manners and his wearisome trick of repeating that the 'orn, as he called it, resembled the human voice more than any other instrument; but he was competent and conscientious; and I was persevering, in spite of some remonstrances from the neighbors. At last I ventured to ask him whether he considered me sufficiently advanced to play a solo in private for a friend.

"Well, Colonel," he said, "I tell you the truth, you havnt a born lip for it: at least, not yet. Then, you see, you blow so tremenjous. If youll believe me, sir, it dont need all the muscle you put into it: it spoils the tone. What was you thinking of playing for your friend?"

"Something that you must teach me. Schubert's serenade."

He stared at me, and shook his head. "It aint written for the hinstrument, sir," he said. "Youll never play it."

"The first time I play it through without a mistake, I will give you five guineas, besides our regular terms."

This overcame his doubts. I found the execution of the serenade, even after diligent practice, uncertain and very difficult. But I succeeded at last.

"If I was you, Colonel," said my instructor, as he pocketed the five guineas, "I'd keep that tune to myself, and play summat simpler for my friends. You can play it well enough here after half an hour's exercise; but when I'm not at your elbow, youll find it wont come so steady."

I made light of this hint, the prudence of which I now fully recognize. But at that time I was bent on a long cherished project of serenading Linda. Her house, near the northern end of Park Lane, was favorably situated for the purpose; and I had already bribed a servant to admit me to the small pleasure ground that lay between the house and the roadway. Late in June, I learned that she intended to repose for an evening from the fatigues of society. This was my opportunity. At nine o'clock I placed my horn in a travelling bag, and drove to the Marble Arch, where I alighted and walked to my destination. I was arrested by the voice of Porcharlester calling, "Hallo, Colonel!" As I did not wish to be questioned, I thought it best to forestall him by asking whither he was bound.

"I am going to see Linda," he replied. "She contrived to let me know last night that she would be alone all this evening. I don't mind telling you these things, Colonel: you are a man of honor, and you know how good she is. I adore her. If I could only be certain that it is myself, and not merely my voice that she likes, I should be the happiest man in England."

"I am quite sure that it cannot be your voice," I said.

"Thank you," he exclaimed, grasping my hand: "it's very kind of you to say so; but I hardly dare flatter myself that you are right. It almost chokes me to look at her. Do you know I have never had the pluck to sing that serenade of Schubert's since she told me it was a favorite of hers?"

"Why? Does she not like your singing of it?"

"I tell you I have never ventured to sing it before her, though she is always at me for it. I am half jealous of that confounded tune. But I would do anything to please her; and I am going to surprise her with it tomorrow at Mrs. Locksly Hall's. I have been taking lessons and working like a dog to be able to sing it in really first-rate style. If you meet her, mind you dont breathe a word of this. It is to be a surprise."

"I have no doubt you will startle her," I said, exulting at the thought that he would be a day too late. I knew that it would take a finer voice than his to bear comparison with the melancholy sweetness, the sombre menace, the self-contained power with which the instrument I carried would respond to a skilful performer. We parted; and I saw him enter the house of Linda. A few minutes later, I was in the garden, looking up at them from my place in the shadow as they sat near the open window. Their conversation did not reach me: I thought he would never go. The night was a little cold; and the ground was damp. Ten o'clock struck—a quarter past—half past—I almost resolved to go home. Had not the tedium been relieved by some pieces which she played on the pianoforte, I could not have held out. At last they rose; and I was now able to distinguish their words.

"Yes," she said, "it is time for you to go." How heartily I agreed with her! "But you might have sung the serenade for me. I have played three times for you."

"I have a frightful cold," he said. "I really cannot. Goodnight."

"What nonsense! You have not the least symptom of a cold. No matter: I will never ask you again. Goodnight, Mr. Porcharlester."

"Do not be savage with me," he said. "You shall hear me sing it sooner than you think, perhaps."

"Ah! you say that very significantly. Sooner than I think! If you are preparing a surprise for me, I will forgive you. I shall see you at Mrs. Locksly Hall's tomorrow, I hope."

He assented, and hurried away, fearful, I suppose, lest he should betray his plan. When he was gone, she came to the window, and looked out at the stars. Gazing at her, I forgot my impatience: my teeth ceased to chatter. I took the horn from my travelling bag. She sighed; closed the window; and drew down a white blind. The sight of her hand alone as she did so would have inspired me to excel all my previous efforts. She seated herself so that I could see the shadow of her figure in profile. My hour was come. Park Lane was nearly still: the traffic in Oxford Street was too distant to be distracting.

I began. At the first note I saw her start and listen. When the completed phrase revealed to her what air I was playing, she laid down her book. The mouthpiece of my instrument was like ice; and my lips were stiff and chilly, so that in spite of my utmost care I was interrupted more than once by those uncouth guggling sounds which the best cornists cannot always avoid. Nevertheless considering that I was cold and very nervous, I succeeded fairly well. Gaining confidence as I went on, I partly atoned for the imperfection of the beginning by playing the concluding bars with commanding sonority, and even achieving a tolerable shake on the penultimate note.

An encouraging cheer from the street as I finished shewed me that a crowd was collected there, and that immediate flight was out of the question. I replaced the horn in my bag, and made ready to go when the mob should disperse. Meanwhile I gazed at the shadow on the blind. She was writing now. Could she, I think, be writing to me? She rose; and the shadow overspread the window so that I could no longer distinguish her movements. I heard a bell ring. A minute later the door of the house opened. I retreated behind an aloe tub; but on recognizing the servant whom I had bribed, I whistled softly to him. He came towards me with a letter in his hand. My heart beat strongly as I saw it.

"All right, sir," he said. "Miss Linda told me to give you this; but you are not to open it, if you please, until you get home."

"Then she knew who I was," I said eagerly.

"I suppose so, sir. When I heard her bell, I took care to answer it myself. Then she says to me, 'Youll find a gentleman somewhere in the pleasure ground. Give him this note; and beg him to go home at once. He is not to read it here.' "

"Is there any crowd outside?"

"All gone sir. Thank you, sir. Goodnight, sir."

I ran all the way to Hamilton Place, where I got into a hansom. Ten minutes afterwards I was in my study, opening the letter with unsteady hands. It was not enclosed in an envelope, but folded in three, with a corner turned down. I opened it and read,

"714, Park Lane, Friday.

"DEAR MR PORCHARLESTER"—

I stopped. Had she then given him credit for my performance? A more immediately important question was whether I had any right to read a letter not addressed to me. Curiosity and love prevailed over this scruple. The letter continued thus:

41

"I am sorry that you have seen nothing in my fancy for Schubert's serenade except matter for ridicule. Perhaps it was an exaggerated fancy; but I would not have expressed it to you had I not believed you capable of understanding it. If it be any satisfaction to you to know that you have cured me of it thoroughly, pray believe that I shall never again hear the serenade without a strange mixture of mirth and pain. I did not know that a human throat could compass such sounds; and I little thought, when you promised that I should hear your voice sooner than I expected, that you contemplated such a performance. I have only one word more: Adieu. I shall not have the pleasure of meeting you at Mrs. Locksly Hall's tomorrow, as my engagements will not permit me to go there. For the same reason I fear I must deny myself the pleasure of receiving you again this season. I am, dear Mr. Porcharlester, yours truly,

LINDA FITZNIGHTINGALE."

I felt that to forward this letter to Porcharlester would only pain him uselessly. I felt also that my instructor was right, and that I have not the lip for the French horn. I have accordingly given it up.

Linda is now my wife. I sometimes ask her why she persists in cutting Porcharlester, who has pledged me his word as an officer and a gentleman that he is unconscious of having given her the slightest ground for offence. She always refuses to tell me.

LOVE AFFAIR WITH
A DOUBLE BASS

Anton Chekhov
1860-1904

Anton Chekhov supported himself and his family during his medical schooling by writing sketches and brief stories, like "Love Affair with a Double Bass" (1886), for popular magazines. Though perhaps best remembered today as a playwright, he was first of all an early master of the short story form and did much to popularize it as an appropriate vehicle for serious writing. Chekhov once said that "medicine was his wife; literature, his mistress."

❧

Smichkov, the musician, was on his way from town to Prince Bibulov's *dacha*, where, to celebrate a betrothal, an evening of music and dancing was to take place. His huge double-bass encased in leather on his back, he walked beside a river where the cool waters flowed along, if not sublimely, then at least with a certain lyricism.

"Why not take a dip?" he thought.

And without much further thinking he stripped and launched his body into the cool stream.

It was a magnificent evening and Smichkov's poetic nature began to be in harmony with his surroundings. But then a most sweet feeling entranced his spirits; for, having swum along a hundred paces, he saw a very lovely girl sitting on the steep bank, fishing. He held his breath, struck quite still, a prey to changing emotions: childhood memories, yearning for the past, a stirring of love.

But, oh God, he thought he was able to love no longer! Since he lost faith in humanity (when his darling wife ran off with Sabarkin, the bassoon player, his friend) his heart was filled with a sense of emptiness and he had become a misanthropist.

"What kind of life is this?" he'd asked himself more than once. "What are we living for? Life is a myth, a day-dream . . . a puppet show. . . ."

But now at the feet of this sleeping beauty (it was easy to see she was asleep) he suddenly felt, despite his will, a thing in his heart akin to love. He stayed a long time before her, feasting his eyes. . . .

"But that's enough . . ." he thought, breathing a deep sigh. "Farewell, lovely vision! It's time now for me to go to His Highness' ball. . . ."

And with yet another glance at the lovely girl he was starting to swim back when an idea flashed across his mind.

"I must leave her a thing to remember me by!" he thought. "I'll hitch something to her line. It will be a surprise from "an unknown stranger."

Smichkov swam quietly to the bank, gathered a bunch of field and water flowers, bound them with a stalk of goose foot and hitched them to the line.

The bunch sank down and with it took the pretty float.

Prudence, the natural order of things and the social position of my hero require that my love story should end just here. But, alas, the fate of an author is relentless. In clear despite of him his story will not end with the bunch of flowers. Against all sober sense and natural law the poor and humble double-bass player had to play a role of great importance in the life of a noble, rich and lovely young lady.

When he reached the bank, Smichkov was horrified: he couldn't see his clothes, someone had stolen them! While he'd been gazing lovingly upon the lovely girl, some unknown villains had made off with everything, except his double-bass and his top hat.

"Curses on you, breed of snakes!" he shouted. "It's not only the loss of clothes that makes my blood boil (for clothes wear out) but the thought that I must go stark naked and offend the laws of decency."

He sat down on his double-bass case and tried to seek a way out of his terrible dilemma.

"I can't walk naked to Prince Bibulov's!" he thought. "There'll be ladies! And what's more the thieves stole my rosin when they made off with my trousers."

He thought and thought in anguish till his temples hurt.

"Ah!" At last he remembered. "Not far from the bank in the bushes there's a footbridge. Till darkness comes I can sit under that bridge and then in the dusk of evening I'll sneak to the nearest peasant's hut."

Having thought the matter over, Smichkov put on his top hat, heaved up his double-bass behind him and trudged towards the bushes. Naked, his instrument on his back, he was like some mythical demigod of the ancient world.

And there, my reader, while my hero sits under the bridge and gives in to grief, we'll leave him for a while and return to the girl who was fishing. What happened to her? When she woke up and could not see her float on the water, she hurriedly tugged at the line. It tautened but neither float nor hook came up. Apparently Smichkov's bunch of flowers had become sodden and heavy in the water.

"Either a big fish is biting," she thought, "or else the hook is caught."

She tugged away at the line for a while and decided that the hook was caught.

"What a pity!" she thought. "In the evening when the fish bite so well! What shall I do?"

And without much thought the eccentric girl threw off her flimsy garments and submerged her lovely body to the marble shoulders in the stream. It wasn't easy to free the hook from the entangling bunch of flowers but work and patience won the day. After some fifteen minutes the lovely girl came radiant and happy out of the water, clutching the hook.

But an evil fate awaited her. The rogues who had stolen Smichkov's clothes, had snatched hers too, leaving only a jar of worms.

"Whatever shall I do now?" She burst into tears. "Can I possibly go about looking like this? No, never! I'd rather die! I'll wait till dusk, then go in the dark to my old nanny Agatha's and send her home for clothes. And in the meantime I'll go and hide under the footbridge."

My heroine, choosing the deepest grass and bending low, ran to the bridge. Creeping under it, she saw a naked man with musician's curls and hairy chest, screamed and lost her senses.

Smichkov was frightened too. At first he took her for a water nymph.

"Is this a mermaid come to lure me?" he wondered and the idea appealed for he had always had a high opinion of his looks. "If she's not a mermaid but a human being, then how do you explain that strange appearance? Why is she here under the bridge? And what's the matter with her?"

While he was considering these questions, the lovely girl came round.

"Don't kill me!" she murmured. "I'm Princess Bibulova. I implore you! You'll get a big reward! Just now I was untangling my hook in the water and some thieves stole away my new dress, my boots and everything!"

"Madam," said Smichkov in a pleading voice, "they stole my clothes as well. What's more they even took away the rosin that was in my trousers."

Double-bass players and trombonists are usually at a loss in crises: but Smichkov was a pleasant exception.

"Madam," he said after a little pause, "I see that my appearance embarrasses you. But you'll agree I can't go off in this state, any more than you can. Here's what I suggest: would you like to lie down in my double-bass case and cover yourself with the lid? That will hide you from me. . . ."

With these words Smichkov heaved his double-bass out of the case. For a moment it seemed a profanation of his sublime art to give up his case but his hesitation was short. The lovely girl lay down inside the case and curled up and Smichkov fastened the straps, feeling delighted that nature had given him such intelligence.

"Now, Madam, you cannot see me," he said. "Lie there and be at ease. When darkness comes, I'll carry you to your father's house. And then I can come back here for my double-bass."

When it was dusk Smichkov hoisted the case with the lovely girl on his shoulder and set off for Bibulov's *dacha*. His plan was this: he would go first to the nearest cottage, get some clothes there and then go on. . . .

"Every cloud's a silver lining . . ." he reflected, stirring up the dust with his bare feet and bending under his load. "For the warm sympathy I've shown his daughter in her plight, Bibulov is sure to reward me handsomely."

"Are you quite comfortable, Madam?" he asked in the tone of a *cavalier galant* requesting her to dance a quadrille. "I beg you, do not stand on ceremony and make yourself quite at home in my case!"

Suddenly it seemed to the gallant Smichkov that before him, shrouded in darkness, two human shapes were moving. Peering more closely, he was sure it wasn't an optical illusion: the shapes were certainly moving and what's more were carrying some sort of bundles. . . .

"Isn't that the thieves?" flashed into his mind. "They're carrying something. It's probably our clothes!"

Smichkov lowered his double-bass beside the path and dashed after the figures.

"Stop!" he shouted. "Stop! Seize them!"

The shapes looked round and seeing they were pursued took to their heels. The Princess heard running footsteps for a time and cries of "Stop!" Then all was still.

Smichkov kept up the chase, and very probably the lovely girl would have lain a long time in a field by the path but for a happy chance. It turned out that two of Smichkov's colleagues, Zhuchkov, the flutist, and Razmahaikin, the clarinetist, were passing at that time along that way to Bibulov's *dacha*. Stumbling upon the case, they stared at each other in surprise and flung up their arms.

"A double-bass!" said Zhuchkov. "But that's our Smichkov's double-bass. But how did it get here?"

"Something has probably happened to Smichkov," Razmahaikin decided. "Either he's drunk or he's been robbed. We'll take it with us."

Zhuchkov hoisted the case on his back and the musicians went on their way.

"What a devil of a weight!" the flutist kept grumbling all the way. "I wouldn't play this lumbering thing for anything in the world! Oh!"

Once they reached Prince Bibulov's *dacha* they put the case in the place reserved for the orchestra and went off to the buffet.

The chandeliers were just being lit. The fiancé Lakeitch, a counsellor at court and an official in the Highways Department, a very pleasant, handsome fellow, was standing in the middle of the ballroom, hands in pockets, chatting about music to Count Shkalikov.

"You know, Count," he said, "I came across a string player in Naples who worked perfect wonders. You don't believe me? On a double-bass, a common or garden double-bass, he produced such devilish trills it made you shiver. He played Strauss waltzes."

"Surely it's impossible . . ." said the Count with doubt in his voice.

"But I assure you. He even performed a Rhapsody of Liszt. I used to share a room with him and once, to pass the time, I learned from him how to play a Liszt Rhapsody on the double-bass."

"A Liszt rhapsody. . . . Hmmmm! You're joking. . . ."

"You don't believe me?" laughed Lakeitch. "Very well, I'll prove it to you. Let's go over to the orchestra."

The fiancé and the count went over to the orchestra, found the double-bass, started hurriedly to undo the straps . . . and oh, horror!

And now, as the reader, giving full rein to imagination, pictures the outcome of this musical controversy, let us return to Smichkov. . . . The poor musician, not having caught the thieves, returned to the spot where he put down his case but did not see his precious burden. Bewildered, he wandered back and forth along the path a few times and, still not finding it, decided he had come to the wrong path. . . .

"It's terrible!" he thought, plucking his hair and going freezing cold. "She'll suffocate in that case. I'm a murderer."

Till midnight he paced up and down the path, searching for his case, but in the end, exhausted, he set off for the footbridge.

"I'll search again at dawn," he decided.

But searching in the dawn brought just the same result and Smichkov decided to wait for nightfall under the bridge.

"I'll find her!" he muttered, taking off his top hat and clutching his hair. "Even if I search a year, I'll find her."

And still today the peasants living in the place relate that in the night time a sort of naked man is to be seen, overgrown with hair and in a top hat. From under the bridge sometimes you can hear the wheezing of a double-bass.

GAMBRINUS

Alexander Kuprin
1870-1938

A legend in his own time for possessing enormous physical strength and a voracious appetite for life, Alexander Kuprin's energy as a writer stems from his close observation of naturalistic detail and his evocative style. "Gambrinus" (1906) is set against a background of real events—pogroms, the first Russian Revolution, the Russo-Japanese War—but Kuprin makes the personal world of his characters the compelling reality. Sashka's music (Art) cannot be repressed no matter how hostile the forces of barbarism become.

1

Such was the name of a certain beer-shop in a bustling seaport town in the south of Russia. Even though it was situated on one of the most populous streets it was hard to find, thanks to its subterranean location. Often a frequenter,—even one well known and well received at the Gambrinus, would contrive to pass by this remarkable establishment, turning back only after having passed two or three neighboring stores.

Sign there was none. People entered the narrow, ever open door directly from the sidewalk. Just as narrow a staircase of twenty stone steps, trodden down and made crooked by many millions of heavy boots, led downward from it. Upon the partition, where the stairs ended, was a bedaubed image, in *alto relievo*, of King Gambrinus,—the splendid guardian spirit of beer brewing,—in all his glory, and approximately twice human height. Probably this sculptured creation was the first work of a beginning amateur, and appeared to be crudely executed in petrified chunks of porous sponge; however, the red jacket, the ermine mantle, the gold crown, and the mug, raised high and with the white froth trickling down, all left no doubt that before the visitor was the great patron of beer brewing himself.

The beer-shop consisted of two vaulted halls, long but exceedingly narrow. The underground moisture always oozed out of the walls in trickling rivulets, and glistened in the light of the gas-jets, which burned day and night, since the beer-shop was entirely lacking in windows. On the vaults, however, one could still make out with sufficient distinctness traces of diverting mural painting. In one picture a large company of German laddies, in green jackets and hats with wood-cock feathers, was holding carouse, their guns slung over their shoulders. All of them, with their faces turned toward the hall, welcomed the public with extended mugs; while two of them, at the same time, were also embracing the waists of two buxom damsels,—servants of the village inn, or, perhaps, daughters of some worthy farmer. Upon another wall was depicted a picnic of the *beau monde*, period of the first half of the eighteenth century: countesses and viscounts in powdered wigs demurely frollicking upon a green meadow with lambs; and, right alongside, under spreading willows, a pond, with swans being gracefully fed by ladies and cavaliers seated in some sort of a gilt nutshell. The next picture represented the interior of a moujik's hut, and a family of happy Little Russians, dancing the thumping *gopak*, with demijohns in their hands. Still farther on a large keg flaunted itself, and upon it, entwined with grapes and leaves of hops, two cupids,—fat unto ugliness, with greasy lips, and shamelessly lubricious eyes,—were clinking shallow goblets. In the second hall, separated from the first by a semi-circular arch, ran a series of pictures from frog life: frogs drinking beer in a green marsh; frogs hunting grasshoppers among thickly-growing reeds; frogs playing in a stringed quartette; frogs engaged in sword play, and so forth. Evidently, the walls had been decorated by a foreign master.

Instead of tables, heavy kegs of oak were placed about the floor, which had sawdust thickly strewn upon it; instead of chairs there were small kegs. To the right of the entrance was raised a small platform, with a piano standing upon it. It was now many years without a break that Sashka the musician,—a Jew, and a meek, droll, tipsy, bald-headed fellow, with the appearance of a moth-eaten ape of indeterminate years,—had played here every evening upon his fiddle for the delectation and diversion of the guests. The years passed by; the waiters with their leather sleeve-protectors changed; the brewers, and the drivers of the beer-trucks, changed; the very proprietors of the beer-shop changed; but Sashka, every evening toward six, was invariably seated upon his platform, fiddle in hand, and a little white dog on his knees; while at one o'clock at night he would walk out of Gambrinus, in the company of the same little dog Bielochka, scarcely able to keep his feet from the beer he had drunk.

However, there was another immutable personage in the Gambrinus,—Madame Ivanova, the dispenser; a full, anaemic old woman, who, from being ceaselessly in the damp, underground place dedicated to beer, bore a resemblance to the pallid, indolent fishes inhabiting the depths of sea-grottoes. She silently directed the help from her bar counter, like the captain of a ship upon his bridge, and smoked all the time, holding the cigarette in the right corner of her mouth, her right eye puckering from the smoke. Only rarely did anyone succeed in hearing her voice, and she responded to all bows by a colourless smile that was always the same.

2

The huge port,—one of the world's largest ports of commerce,—was always thronged to overflowing with ships. Gigantic, dark-rusty armored cruisers entered it. Yellow, thick-funnelled steamers of the Volunteer Fleet, that daily swallowed long trains of merchandise or thousands of convicts, loaded here on their way to the Far East. Spring and autumn, hundreds of flags from all the ends of the terrestrial globe waved here; and from morn to night came the sounds of commands and curses in all possible tongues. From the ships to the countless warehouses, and back again over the shaky gangways, scurried the stevedores: Russian hoboes, ragged, nearly naked, with drunken, puffy faces; swarthy Turks in dirty turbans, and in baggy trousers, wide to the knee but wound tightly about the leg; stocky, muscular Persians, with hair and nails tinged a fiery carrot color by henna. Often two- and three-masted Italian schooners, splendid from afar, would come into the port, with their sails in orderly tiers,—clean, white, and resilient, like the breasts of young women; coming into ken from beyond the lighthouse these graceful ships seemed,—especially on radiant spring mornings,—wonderful white visions, sailing, not upon the water, but in the air, above the horizon. Here, for months at a time, in the dirty-green water of the port, in the midst of flotsam, egg-shells, water-melon rinds, and flocks of white sea gulls, swayed the high-pooped Anatolian barks and the *feluccas* of Trebizond, with their strange coloring, carving, and bizarre ornaments. Occasionally, even certain queer, narrow crafts, under black, tarred sails, with a dirty rag instead of a flag, would sail into the port; having turned the jetty-head,—and well nigh scraping it with the bulwark,—such a ship, careening all to one side and without abating its speed, would fly into any harbor it chose, heaving to, amid polyglot billingsgate, curses and threats, at the first mole that it came to, whereupon its hands,—little men of bronze, entirely naked,—letting out a guttural cackling and with a speed that passed all understanding, would stow away the torn sails, and instantly the dirty, mysterious ship would become bereft of life. And just as mysteriously, some dark night, without showing its lights, it would silently vanish out of the port. The whole bay swarmed of nights with the light shells of the smugglers. Fishermen from far and near brought their fish into the city: in the spring, the small *Kamsa*, that, in its millions, filled their barks to the gunwales; in the summer, the misshapen flounder; in the autumn, mackerel, fat sea-bass, and oysters; and in the winter, ten- and twenty-*poud* white sturgeon, caught, frequently at a great risk to life, many miles out from shore.

All these people,—sailors of different nationalities, fishermen, stokers, rollicking cabin-boys, thieving water-rats, machinists, laborers, boatmen, stevedores, divers,—all of them were young, healthy, and saturated with the pungent odor of the sea and of fish; they knew the arduousness of toil, loved the allure and horror of daily risk, and, above all things, valued strength, the audacity and tang of virile words, and the cleverness that comes of courage; but ashore they gave themselves up with a savage enjoyment to broad debauchery, drinking, and brawls. Of evenings, the lights of the great city, running upward to the heights, would lure them on, like eyes of magic radiance; always holding out promises of some new, joyous thing, never yet experienced,—and always deceiving.

The town was joined to the port by narrow, steep, many-angled streets,—decent folk shunned walking through them at night. At every step one came upon lodging houses, with dirty, closely-barred windows, with the gloomy light of a solitary lamp within. Still oftener met with were shops, where one might sell all the clothing on one's back, down to the sailor's jersey next the skin,—and then dress in any seafaring togs one might choose. Here also were many beer-halls, taverns, cook-shops and inns, with eloquent signs in all languages, and not a few brothels, both wide open and clandestine ones, from the thresholds of which, of nights, crudely bedaubed women with their hoarse voices invited the sailors in. There were Greek coffee-houses, where games of dominoes and "sixty-six" went on; and Turkish coffee-houses, with sets for smoking the *narghili*, where a night's lodging cost a five-*kopeck* copper; there were little oriental taverns, in which were sold snails, *petalidis*, crayfish, mussels, great, warty, ink-squirting squids, and other sea abominations. Somewhere in the garrets and basements, behind close shutters, snuggled gambling dens, in which stoss and baccarat would often wind up in a slit belly or a split skull; and right around the corner, in some little cubby-hole alongside, it was possible to dispose of any stolen thing one liked, from a diamond bracelet to a cross of silver, and from a bale of Lyons velvet to a regulation naval uniform.

These steep, narrow streets, black from coal dust, towards night always became viscid and malodorous, as though they were in a nightmare sweat. And they resembled sewers, or filthy intestines, through which this city of many nations cast forth into the sea all its refuse, all its decay, all its abomination and vice, infecting with them strong muscular bodies and simple souls.

The roistering inhabitants of this region seldom ascended to the dandified city, with its perpetual holiday mood, with its plate-glass, its proud monuments, its glow of electricity,—its majestic policemen, asphalt sidewalks, avenues bordered on both sides with white acacias; with all its deliberate display of cleanliness and well-being. But every one of them, before casting to the winds his hard-earned, greasy, torn, bloated rouble notes, was sure to visit the Gambrinus. This was sanctified by ancient custom, even though it necessitated picking one's way, under the cover of darkness, to the very center of the city.

Many, it is true, were altogether ignorant of the high-faluting name of the glorious King of Beer. Some one would simply propose:

"Let's go to Sashka?"

And the others would answer:

"It's a go! Steer that way!"

And then a unanimous "Heave ho!" would follow.

It was little to be wondered at, that among the folk of the port and the sea Sashka enjoyed greater reverence and celebrity than, say, the local archbishop or governor. And, if not his name, then, beyond a doubt, his ape-like face and his fiddle were at times recalled in Sydney and Plymouth, as well as in New York, in Constantinople, and on the Island of Ceylon, to say nothing of the sounds and bays of the Black Sea, where a multitude of admirers of his talent was to be found among the numbers of the doughty fisher folk.

3

Usually, Sashka arrived at the Gambrinus at a time when it was practically deserted, save for a chance visitor or two. A thick and sour smell of yesterday's beer pervaded the rooms at such a time, and the place was rather dark, because gas was economized during the day. On the sultry days of July, when the stone city languished from the heat and was deafened by the din of the streets, the quiet and coolness of the place were grateful to the senses.

Sashka would walk up to the bar, exchange greetings with Madame Ivanova, and drink his first mug of beer. Sometimes she would ask him:

"Won't you play something, Sashka?"

"What would you have me play, Madame Ivanova?" Sashka, who was especially polite to her, would courteously inquire.

"Something of your own . . ."

Seating himself at his usual place to the left of the piano, he would play some strange, long drawn out, saddening pieces. The underground place somehow grew somnolent and still,—with only the dull rumbling of the city floating in from the street, and the occasional cautious clatter of china by waiters in the kitchen, behind the partition. Hebraic sorrow, ancient as earth itself, all interwoven and entwined by the mournful flowers of national melodies, wept upon the strings of Sashka's fiddle. Sashka's face, with tensed chin and forehead sunk low, with eyes that gazed austerely from under the heavy eyebrows, did not at this twilight hour at all resemble that grinning, winking, dancing face of Sashka which was familiar to all the guests of Gambrinus. His little dog Bielochka sat upon his knees. She had long since grown accustomed not to whine in accompaniment to the music, but the passionately melancholic, sobbing and maledictory strains involuntarily irritated her: she would open her mouth wide in convulsive yawns, her little thin pink tongue curling back, and her entire tiny body and diminutive, tender, black-eyed phiz quivering for a moment.

But now, little by little, the public gathered; the accompanist,—who had finished his by-occupation for the day with some tailor or watch maker,—arrived; sausages in hot water and cheese sandwiches were put out on the counter; and, finally, all the remaining gas jets were lit. Sashka, draining his second mug, would issue a command to his partner: *"The May Parade,—ein, zwei, drei!"* and would begin a tempestuous march. From this moment on he barely managed to bow to the new arrivals, of which each one deemed himself an especially intimate friend of Sashka's, and, after his bow, would survey the other guests proudly. At the same time, Sashka was puckering up now one eye, now the other; the long creases upon his bald, back-sloping skull gathered themselves upward; he moved his lips comically, and smiled in all directions.

Toward ten or eleven Gambrinus, which could hold up to two hundred people and more in its rooms, was packed to overflowing. Many,—almost half,—came with women who wore kerchiefs upon their heads; none took offence at the crowding, a foot stepped upon, a hat crumpled, or somebody else's beer poured over one's trousers; if any grew offended, it was only on account of being in one's cups, to "show off." The dampness of the basement, dully glistening, streamed still more copiously from the walls with their covering of oil colors, while the exhalations of the crowds dripped down from the ceiling, like a fine, heavy, warm rain. Drinking was taken seriously in the Gambrinus. Among the manners of this establishment it was deemed especially clever, while sitting in twos and threes, to cover the table with bottles in such a manner that one's *vis à vis* could not be seen behind a green forest of glass.

At the height of the evening the guests became flushed, hoarse, and all damp. The tobacco smoke made the eyes smart. It was necessary to shout and to lean over the table to hear one another in the general hubbub. And only the indefatigable fiddle of Sashka, sitting on his elevation, triumphed over the stifling atmosphere, over the heat, over the reek of tobacco, gas, and beer, and over the yelling of the unceremonious public.

But the visitors quickly grew tipsy from the beer, from the proximity of the women, from the warm air. Every one wanted his own loved, familiar songs. Two or three men, dim of eye and uncertain of movements, always hovered near Sashka, plucking him by the sleeve and interfering with his playing.

"Sashh! . . . The one that makes you suffer . . . 'Bli . . ."—the supplicant would hiccough,—"'Blige me!"

"Right away, right away," Sashka kept on repeating, nodding his head rapidly, and, without a sound, with the dexterity of a surgeon, slipping a silver coin into his side pocket. "Right away, right away."

"Sashka, that's a low-down trick now. I've given you the money, and it's now for the twentieth time that I'm asking you for *I Was Sailing By Sea To Odessa*."

"Right away, right away. . . ."

"Sashka,—*Marussiya*!"

"Sashka,—*The Nightingale*!"

"*Setz-Setz*, Sashka,—*Setz-Setz*!"

"Right away, right away. . . ."

"*The Chaban*!" a voice, more like a colt's than a human being's, would yell from the other end of the hall.

And, amidst general laughter, Sashka would crow back at him like a rooster:

"Right-a-way. . . ."

And he played without rest all the songs ordered. Apparently, there was not a single one that he did not know by heart. Silver coins poured into his pockets from all sides, and mugs of beer were sent to him from all the tables. When he would climb off his platform to go to the bar, he would be rent into pieces:

"Sashenka . . . Da'ling . . . One tiny mug . . ."

"Sashka, here's to your health. Come here when you're told, you devil,—durn your heart an' liver!"

"Sashka-a, come here and drink some bee-eer!"

The women, inclined, like all women, towards going into raptures over those who tread the boards, and to playing the coquette, to distinguishing themselves before them, and to slavish prostration, called him with cooing voice, with playful, capricious giggling:

"Sashechka, you just gotta have a drink on me. . . . No, no, no,—I'm asking you. And after that, play the cake-walk."

Sashka grinned, bowing left and right and grimacing; he pressed his hands to his heart, threw kisses in the air, drank beer at all the tables, and, having returned to the piano, where a fresh mug was awaiting him, would begin to play some song or other,—a *Parting*, say. Sometimes, to amuse his auditors, he made his fiddle whine like a puppy, or grunt like a pig, or snore in rending bass sounds, all in time with the tune. And the auditors welcomed these antics with benevolent approval:

"Ho-ho-ho-ho-o-o!"

It grew hotter and hotter; the moisture poured down from the ceiling. Some of the guests were already weeping, smiting their breasts; others, with blood-shot eyes, were quarreling over women and over old scores, and trying to get at each other, held back by their more sober neighbors,—parasites, most frequently. The waiters squeezed through by a miracle between the kegs and casks, small and large, among the legs and the torsos, holding their hands, ringed with beer mugs, high above the heads of the sitters. Madame Ivanova, more anaemic, imperturbable and taciturn than ever, directed the activities of the servants from behind the bar-counter, like the captain of a ship during a storm.

All were overcome with the desire to sing. Sashka, all limp from the beer, his own labors, and that crude joy which his music afforded to others, was ready to play any piece that might be desired. And the hoarse people, with discordant, wooden voices, bawled in unison to the sounds of his fiddle, staring one another in the eyes with ludicrous gravity:

> For why should we be pa-arted,
> Ah, why should we live a-part;
> Ain't it better to be united,
> An' treasure love at heart?

While another group alongside, trying to drown out the first (evidently an unfriendly one) with its yelling, was vociferating, by now entirely out of tune:

Oh, his pants is kinda gay,
An' his chestnut hair is sleek;
You can tell just by his walk
That his boots is built to creak.

The Gambrinus was often visited by "Dongolakis,"—Greeks from Asia Minor, who put into Russian ports to trade their fish. They, too, ordered from Sashka their oriental songs, consisting of a dismal, snuffling, monotonous wail of two or three notes; and with gloomy faces, with flaming eyes, they were ready to sing these songs whole hours through. And Sashka also played Italian popular couplets, and Ukrainian snatches, and Yiddish wedding dances, and much else besides. Once a knot of negro sailors dropped into the Gambrinus, in whom, upon beholding the others, a similar desire arose to sing a bit. Sashka rapidly caught by ear the galloping melody, picked out, on the spot, an accompaniment to it on the piano, and lo! to the great delight and amusement of the *habitués* of Gambrinus, the beer-hall resounded to the strange, capricious, guttural sounds of the African song.

A certain reporter on a local paper, a friend of Sashka's, somehow talked a professor in a school of music into going to the Gambrinus to hear the locally celebrated violinist. But Sashka surmised this, and purposely made his violin mew, bleat, and roar more than ever. The guests at Gambrinus were simply splitting their sides with laughing, but the professor uttered contemptuously:

"Buffoonery!"

And went off, without finishing his mug.

4

Not infrequently the exquisite marquises and the feasting German jagers, the fat cupids and the frogs, were, from their walls, witnesses of such broad revelry as was rarely to be seen anywhere save at the Gambrinus.

A party of thieves out on a spree, for instance, would arrive after a good "job"; each with his beloved, each in a cap at a rakish slant; in patent leather boots, with choice tavern manners, with a disdainful air. Sashka played special songs for them,—the thieves' own: *I'm a Ruined Laddie, Don't You Cry, Marussiya, Spring Is Gone*, and others. Dancing they considered beneath their dignity; but their lady friends, all of them not at all bad to look upon, rather young,—some of them almost girls,—danced the *Chaban*, squealing and clicking their heels. Both the men and the women drank a very great deal,—there was only one bad feature; the thieves always wound up their sprees with ancient monetary misunderstandings, and loved to vanish without paying.

The fishermen used to come after lucky hauls, in big gangs of thirty or so. In late fall there were weeks so lucky that every fishery would catch daily some forty thousand mackerel or sea-bass. During such a time the smallest shareholder would earn more than two hundred roubles. But the fishermen were enriched still more by a successful haul of white sturgeon in winter; but then, this was fraught with great hardships. It was necessary to toil heavily, some thirty or forty *versts* from shore, in the night-time; sometimes in inclement weather, when the water inundated the long-boat, immediately turning to ice upon the clothes and oars, while the weather would keep them out at sea for two or three days at a time, until they were cast up some two hundred *versts* away, somewhere in Anap or Trebizond. Some ten yawls would disappear without a trace every winter, and only in spring did the waves bring in the corpses of the doughty fishermen, now on this strange shore, now on that.

But then, when they returned from the sea, safe and successful, a mad thirst of life would possess them on dry land. Several thousand roubles would be gone through in two or three days, in the coarsest, most deafening and drunken carousing. The fishermen got into a tavern or some other gay establishment; threw out all guests that "didn't belong"; closed the doors and shutters tightly; and for whole days at a stretch drank, gave themselves up to love, bawled out songs, beat up the mirrors, the crockery, and the women, and not infrequently one another, until sleep overcame them where they stood,—on the tables; the floor; across beds; among the spittle, cigarette stumps, broken glass, spilt wine and blood stains. Thus would the fishermen carouse for several days running, sometimes changing to another place, sometimes remaining in the same one all the time. Having squandered everything to the last copper, with heads humming, with marks of battle on their faces, a-tremble from the after-effects of drink, morose, cast down and repentant, they would go down to the shore, to their barks, to take anew to their beloved and accursed, their arduous and alluring calling.

Never did they forget to pay a visit to the Gambrinus. They would break their way in,—huge, hoarse, with their red faces, scorched by the ferocious no'-wester of winter; in weather-proof jackets, in leathern breeches and in bull-hide boots up to their hips, in which their friends, in the midst of some stormy night, went down to the bottom like stones.

Out of respect for Sashka they did not expel other guests, even though they did feel themselves masters of the beer-shop, and did smash the heavy mugs against the floor. Sashka played for them their own fishermen's songs, long drawn out, simple, and awesome, like the surge of the sea, and they all sang in unison, straining to the utmost their strong chests and their hardened throats. Sashka acted upon them like an Orpheus pacifying the waves, and there were occasions when some forty-year-old hetman of a bark, a bearded, virile animal, all weather-beaten, would be wallowing in tears, as he led, in a high voice, the singing of the touching words of a song:

> Ah, I'm a poor, poor little laddie,
> Born for to be a fisherman . . .

And sometimes they danced, stamping in one spot, stony-faced, thundering with their thirty-pound boots, and diffusing over the entire beer-hall the pungent salt odor of fish, with which their clothes and bodies had become saturated through and through. They were very generous toward Sashka, and would detain him long at their tables. Well did he know the manner of their hard, reckless existence. Often, as he played for them, he felt in his soul a certain reverential sadness.

But what he loved especially was to play for English sailors from merchant ships. These would come in a crowd, hand in hand,—all of them, as though they had been picked, chesty, broad-shouldered, young, white-toothed, with a healthy glow, with merry, courageous blue eyes. Strong sinews strained their jackets, while their straight, mighty, graceful necks rose up out of their low-cut collars. Some of them knew Sashka from their previous stays in this port. They would recognize him, and, showing their teeth in a cordial grin, would greet him in Russian:

"*Zdraist, zdraist.*"

Sashka, of his own initiative, without being requested, would play *Rule Britannia* for them. Most probably, the consciousness that he found himself at present in a land oppressed by eternal slavery lent an especially proud solemnity to this hymn of English liberty. And when, standing, with heads bared, they sang the final, magnificent words:

"**Britons never, never shall be slaves!**"
even the most riotous of their neighbors involuntarily doffed their hats.

The stocky boatswain, with an ear-ring in one ear, and with a beard that sprouted from his neck just like a fringe, would walk up to Sashka with two mugs of beer; slapping him amicably on the back, he would ask him to play a jig. At the very first strains of this rollicking maritime dance the Englishmen jumped up and cleared a space, moving the kegs to the walls. Permission to do this was asked from strangers by gestures and cheerful smiles; but if any did not comply quickly, that one was treated without any ceremony,—the seat was just knocked away from under him by a well-aimed kick. This, however, was but rarely resorted to, because every one in the Gambrinus was a connoisseur of dancing, and especially fond of the English jig. Even Sashka himself, without ceasing to play, would stand up on a chair to see better.

The sailors formed a ring, clapping their palms in time to the lively dance, the while two of them stepped out into the center. The dance depicted the life of a sailor afloat. The ship is ready to sail; the weather is splendid; everything is ship-shape. The arms of the sailors are crossed on their breasts, their heads thrown back, their bodies still, although their feet are beating a frenzied tatoo. But now a slight breeze has sprung up,—the vessel begins to roll slightly. To a sailor this is nothing but a frolic,—the figures of the dance, however, are becoming more and more complicated and intricate. By now a fresh wind has begun to blow,—it is no longer such an easy matter to walk the deck,—the dancers are slightly rocking from side to side. And then, here is the real gale, at last,—the sailor is tossed from board to board; matters are becoming serious. "All hands aloft,—reef sails!" From the motions of the dancers it is comprehensible, to the verge of laughter, how they clamber with hand and foot up the shrouds, haul at the sails and make fast the sheets, the while the storm rocks the ship more and more. "Stop,—man overboard!" A boat is lowered. The dancers, with heads bent down, straining their mighty, bared necks, row with quick strokes, their backs now bending, now straightening. The storm, however, passes; the rolling abates little by little; the sky clears up, and now the vessel is again running smoothly with a favorable wind, and once more the dancers, their arms crossed, are executing a merry, rapid jig.

Sashka also had occasion to play the *Lezginka* for Georgians, who followed wine-making in the environs of the city. For him there was no such thing as an unfamiliar dance. Whenever a solo dancer, in a tall shako and a long-skirted Circassian coat, was airily careening among the kegs, tossing now one hand, now the other behind his head, while his friends beat time with their palms and encouraged him with shouts, Sashka also could never hold out, and would cry out, with animation: *"Khas! Khas! Khas! Khas!"* There were also times when he played the Moldavian *Jok*, and the Italian *Tarantella*, and waltzes for German sailors.

There were times when fighting—and serious fighting, at that,—took place in the Gambrinus. Old frequenters loved to tell of a legendary pitched battle between sailors of the Russian navy, sent to the reserves from some cruiser or other, and some English seamen. They fought with fists, *casse-têttes*, beer-mugs, and even threw the little kegs that served for seats at one another. It must be said, not to the credit of the Russian warriors, that they were the first to start the row, and were also the first to resort to knives, and that they crowded the Englishmen out of the beer-hall only after a battle of half an hour, although they exceeded them triply in numbers.

Very frequently Sashka's intervention stopped a quarrel which was only a hair's-breadth from bloodshed. He would walk up, jest, smile, grimace,—and immediately goblets would be extended to him from all sides.

"Sashka, just a lil' mug . . . Sashka, one on me . . ." Some would utter nonsensical conglomerations of nouns. Perhaps these simple, wild natures were influenced by this meek and fun-provoking mirth, gaily beaming from his eyes, hidden under the sloping skull? Perhaps it was reverence, of its own kind, before talent, and something in the nature of gratitude? And perhaps it may also have been the additional circumstance that the majority of the *habitués* of Gambrinus consisted of Sashka's perpetual debtors. In the oppressive periods of being "on the rocks," which in the jargon of the port and the sea meant absolute impecuniousness, people turned to Sashka, freely and without fear of refusal, for small sums, or a trifling credit at the bar.

Of course, the debts were never repaid to him,—not through ill intent, but through forgetfulness; but these very debtors, at the height of a spree, repaid the loan tenfold for Sashka's songs.

The lady of the bar would at times lecture him:

"I really wonder, Sashka, how you can have no regard for your money?"

He would parry, argumentatively:

"But then, my dear Madame Ivanova. . . . Am I going to take it into the grave with me, or something? There's enough for Bielochka and me. Bielinka, my doggie, come here."

5

The Gambrinus had song hits of its own, that appeared and had their season.

During Britain's war with the Boers, *The Boer March* flourished. (It seems that the famous fight of the Russian and English sailors is to be referred to this period.) Twenty times of an evening, at the least, would Sashka be compelled to play this heroic piece, and, without fail, all waved their caps and hurrahed at its conclusion, while all those who were indifferent were eyed askance, which was not at all a favorable omen at the Gambrinus.

Then the Franco-Russian celebrations came up. The mayor, with a wry face, granted permission to play the *Marseillaise*. This, also, was called for daily; yet not with as great a frequency as the Boer march,—the hurrahs were thinner and the cap waving was entirely absent. This occurred because, on the one hand, there was no ground for the play of heart-felt emotions; while on the other hand the frequenters of Gambrinus did not sufficiently grasp the political importance of the alliance; and, again, it was remarked that the *Marseillaise* was called for, and the hurrahing done, by the very same people every evening.

A cake-walk tune did become all the rage for a moment; and once some light-headed little merchant, who had strayed in by chance, had danced it among the kegs, without taking off his racoon coat, high galoshes, and fox cap. However, this negro dance was soon forgotten.

But now the great war with Japan came along. The frequenters of Gambrinus began to live at an exhilarated pace. Newspapers appeared on the kegs; the evenings were taken up with war arguments. The most peaceful and simple of men turned into politicians and strategists; but every one of them, in his inmost soul, was on tender-hooks,—if not for himself, then for a brother or, still more often, for some close friend; those days brought out clearly that imperceptible and strong tie which cements men who have long shared toil, danger, and the daily proximity of death.

At first no one had any doubts of Russia's victory. Sashka secured somewhere *The Kuropatkin March*, and would play it twenty times of an evening, with a certain degree of success. But somehow, *The Kuropatkin March* was one evening forever crowded out by a song that some Balaclava fishermen,— "Salty Greeks," or *Pindossi*, as they were locally called,—had brought with them.

Oh, why did they take us to be soldiers?
To the Far East why do they send us to fight?
Can they put this fault upon our shoulders—
That we grew an extra inch in height?

From that time on they would have nothing else at the Gambrinus. Whole evenings through one heard nothing but the demand:

"Sasha,—the one that makes you suffer! The Balaclava one! The one about the reserves!"

They sang and wept and drank twice as much as usually,—as, however, all Russia to a man was drinking then. Every evening some one came to bid farewell, putting on a brave front, strutting like a cook, casting his hat against the floor, with threats of worsting all the insignificant Japs single-handed,—and winding up, in tears, with the pathetic song.

One day Sashka arrived at the beer hall earlier than ever before. The bar manager, having filled his first mug, said, as was her wont:

"Sasha, play something of your own."

His lips suddenly twisted tearfully and the mug began to jump in his hand.

"Do you know what, Madame Ivanova?" he said, as though in bewilderment. "Why, they're taking me for a soldier . . . To the front."

Madame Ivanova threw up her hands.

"Why, it can't be, Sasha! Are you joking?"

"No," Sashka shook his head, despondently and submissively; "I'm not joking."

"But aren't you over the age limit, Sasha? How old are you?"

No one had been interested in this question up to now, somehow. Everybody thought that Sashka numbered just as many years as the walls of the beer-shop, the marquises, the Ukrainians, the frogs, and the guardian of the entrance, the daubed King Gambrinus himself.

"Forty-six." Sashka pondered. "And maybe forty-nine. I'm an orphan," he added, despondently.

"Then just you go and explain everything to the right people."

"I already went, Madame Ivanova; I already explained."

"And . . . Well?"

"Well, they told me: 'You mangy sheeny, you sheeny mug, you just talk a bit more—and you'll find yourself in the cooler . . .' And they hit me right here."

In the evening the news was known to all Gambrinus, and out of sympathy Sashka was made dead drunk. He tried to clown, to grimace, to squint; but nothing save sadness and horror peered out of his meek, droll eyes. One husky workingman, a boiler-maker by trade, suddenly volunteered to go to war in Sashka's stead. The evident folly of such a proposition was plain to everybody, but it touched Sashka; he shed a tear, embraced the master boiler-maker, and presented him with his fiddle on the spot. As for Bielochka, he left her to the bar-manageress.

"Madame Ivanova, do you look after the doggie. Maybe I won't return, after all; so you should have something to remember Sashka by. Bielinka, my little dog! . . . Look, how she's licking her chops . . . Ah, my poor little darling . . . And there's something else I'd ask you, Madame Ivanova. There's some money coming to me from the proprietor, so you should take it and send it away . . . I'll write out the addresses for you. I have a cousin in Homel, he's got a family; and also in Zhmerinka lives my nephew's widow. Every month I send them . . . Well, that's the kind of people us Jews are . . . we like our relatives. As for me, I'm an orphan, I'm all alone. So good-bye, Madame Ivanova."

"Good-bye Sashka. Well, now, let's kiss each other good-bye at least. So many years. . . . And—don't you be angry—I shall make the sign of the cross over you for the journey."

Sashka's eyes were deeply pensive, but he could not refrain from clowning to the very last:

"But, now, won't I croak from the Russian cross?"

6

Gambrinus became empty and abandoned, as though it had been orphaned without Sashka and his fiddle. The proprietor did try, as a sort of a lure, to invite a quartette of strolling mandolinists, of whom one was gotten up as an *opera bouffe* Englishman, with red mutton-chop whiskers and a false nose, in checked pantaloons and a collar that came above his ears, and whose performance on the stage consisted of comic couplets and shameless movements of his body. But the quartette had absolutely no success; on the contrary, the mandolinists were given the birds and pelted with remnants of sausages; as for the star comic, he was on one occasion beaten up by some fishermen from Tendrov, for mentioning Sashka disrespectfully.

However, for old memory's sake, Gambrinus was still visited by those of the fine fellows of the sea and the port whom war had not drawn into death and suffering. At first Sashka was recalled every evening:

"Eh, if we only had Sashka here now! The soul feels so cramped without him . . ."

"Yes-s . . . Where are you soaring now, dear, kind friend Sashenka?"

"In Manchu-u-uria's fields, far away . . ."

Some one would begin a new song of the moment; then, growing confused, become silent, while another would utter unexpectedly:

"There are usually three sorts of wounds: through and through; made by thrusts; and those made by hacking. And there are also those made by tearing . . .

Meself, in vict'ry I rejoice;
Youse, in an arm all torn away . . ."

"Here, stop croaking. . . . Madame Ivanova, isn't there any news from Sashka? A letter, or a bit of a postcard?"

Madame Ivanova now read newspapers whole evenings through, holding the sheet extended at an arm's length, her head thrown back and her lips moving. Bielochka lay upon her knees, occasionally snoring peacefully. The bar manageress was very far now from resembling a wide-awake captain, standing at his post; as for her crew, they wandered about the beer-hall, languid and sleepy.

Whenever Sashka's fate was enquired about, she slowly shook her head.

"Don't know anything. . . . There are no letters, and you can't tell anything from the papers."

Then, slowly taking off her spectacles, she would put them, together with the paper, alongside of the warm, comfortable Bielochka and, turning away, would sob quietly.

At times, bending down toward the little dog, she would say in a piteous, touching voice:

"What is it, Bielinka,—what is it, little doggie? Where is our Sashka? Where is our master?"

Bielochka would lift up her delicate little muzzle, winking her humid black eyes, and, in keeping with the tone of the manageress, would begin a low whine:

"A-oo-oo-oo . . . A-oof . . . A-oo-oo . . ."

But . . . time rounds out and washes away all things. The mandolinists were supplanted by balalaika players, the balalaika players by a female choir of Russians and Little Russians; and finally, one

Leshka—a well-known concertina player, by profession a thief, but resolved on account of marriage to seek the paths of righteousness,—became the most strongly intrenched at the Gambrinus. He had long been known in divers taverns, and for that reason was tolerated here as well; but, outside of that, he was tolerated as a matter of necessity,—for things were going very badly with Gambrinus.

Months were going by; a year passed. None recalled Sashka now, save Madame Ivanova, and even she no longer wept at his name. Another year went by. Evidently, even the little white dog must have forgotten about Sashka.

But, in despite of his dubiousness, not only did Sashka not "croak" from the Russian cross, but was not wounded even once, although he had taken part in three great battles, and had once gone on an attack in front of a battalion, as part of the military band to which he had been assigned to play a flute. At Vafangow he had been captured, and at the conclusion of the war brought by a German steamer to the very port where his friends toiled and rioted.

The news of his arrival spread, like an electric current, through all the harbors, jetties, wharves and workshops. . . . In the evening there were so many people in the Gambrinus that the majority had to stand, the mugs with beer being passed from hand to hand over their heads; and although many went away this day without paying, Gambrinus did more business than ever before. The boiler-maker brought Sashka's fiddle, solicitously wrapped in his wife's kerchief,—which latter he traded for drinks on the spot. From somewhere they searched out the accompanist that Sashka had had last. Leshka the concertina player, a man of self-esteem and self-conceit, did try to assert himself. "I'm paid by the day and I've got a contract!" he reiterated stubbornly. But he was simply chucked out of the door, and most probably would have been beaten, had it not been for Sashka's intervention.

Most assuredly, never a one of the fatherland's heroes of the Japanese war period encountered such a hearty and stormy reception as that which was held in honor of Sashka. Strong, gnarled arms caught him up, raised him up in the air, and tossed him up with such force that they almost dashed Sashka to pieces against the ceiling. And they yelled so deafeningly that the gas flames went out, while a policeman had to drop into the Gambrinus several times and implore them that they "be quieter, because, now, it sounds awful out on the street."

On this evening Sashka played through all the songs and dances beloved of the Gambrinus. He also played Japanese snatches, which he had learned by heart in captivity, but these did not please his audience. Madame Ivanova, just like one brought back to life, again kept vigilantly her little captain's bridge, while Bielka sat upon Sashka's knees and whined for joy. At times, when Sashka stopped playing, some simple-hearted fisherman, who had but just now comprehended the miracle of Sashka's return, would suddenly exclaim, with naïve and jubilant amazement:

"Why, fellows, but this is Sashka!"

And the halls of the Gambrinus would be filled with deep neighing, and joyous ribaldry; and again they seized Sashka and tossed him up to the ceiling,—yelling, drinking, clinking glasses, and spilling beer over one another.

Sashka did not seem at all changed, nor had he aged during his absence: time and misfortunes had affected his appearance as little as they had that of the effigy of the sculptured Gambrinus, the guardian and patron of the beer-hall. But Madame Ivanova, with the sensitiveness of a feeling woman, noticed that that expression of horror and sadness which she had seen in Sashka's eyes when he had been bidding her farewell not only had not disappeared from them, but had become even more intense and significant. Sashka clowned, winked, and puckered the creases on his forehead as of yore, but Madame Ivanova sensed that he was playing a part.

7

All things resumed their wonted course, just as though there had never been any such thing as the war, or Sashka's captivity at Nagasaki. A lucky haul of white sturgeon or *loban* would be celebrated as of yore by the fishermen in their seven-league boots; the sweethearts of the thieves danced as of yore; and Sashka played, the same as ever, the sailors' songs brought from all the harbors of the terrestrial globe.

But motley, changing, stormy times were already approaching. One evening the entire city began to hum and grew agitated, as though alarmed by a tocsin, and at an unusual hour the streets became black with people. Little sheets of paper went from hand to hand, together with the magic word Freedom,—that, on this evening, was repeated time without number by the entire unencompassable, trusting land.

There came a time of indescribably radiant, festal, jubilant days, and their refulgence illumined even the subterranean Gambrinus. Students and workingmen came; came young, handsome maidens. Men, with their eyes flaming got up on the kegs which had seen so much in their days, and spoke. Not all their words were comprehended, but from that vehement hope and great love with which they rang the heart throbbed, opening to meet them.

"Sashka, the *Marseillaise*! Fire away! *The Marseillaise*!"

No, this did not at all resemble that *Marseillaise* which the mayor, averse at heart, had permitted to be played the week of the Franco-Russian transports. Endless processions, with flags and singing, went through the streets. Absolute srangers would, upon meeting, smile to each other and shake hands. . . .

But all this rejoicing vanished momentarily, just as though it had been washed away, like the marks of the little feet of children on a sea shore. One day an assistant to the head of police dashed into the Gambrinus,—a fat little man, gasping, with his eyes popping out, and his complexion a very dark red, like an over-ripe tomato.

"What? Who's the proprietor here?" he bellowed hoarsely. "Fetch the proprietor!"

He suddenly laid eyes on Sashka, who was standing with his fiddle.

"You the proprietor? Silence! What? You'll play anthems, will you? No more anthems of any sort!"

"There will be no more anthems of any kind, your excellency," answered Sashka calmly.

The policeman turned livid, brought his index finger up to Sashka's very nose, and shook it ominously to the right and left.

"None what-so-ever!"

"I hear you, your excellency,—none whatsoever."

"I'll show you revolutions, I will!"

The police chief's assistant flew out of the beer-hall like a bomb, and despondency oppressed everybody after his departure.

And gloom descended upon the entire city as well. Dark, disquieting, loathsome rumors were afloat. People spoke with cautiousness, fearing to betray themselves by a glance, frightened by their own shadow, dreading their own thoughts. The town, for the first time, bethought itself with horror of that cloaka which was in dull turmoil under its feet,—there below, near the sea,—into which cloaka it had been casting its poisonous excreta for so many years. The city put shields about the plate-glass windows of its magnificent stores, guarded its proud monuments with patrols, and, to be ready against any contingency, placed artillery in the yards of its splendid residences. In the meantime, on the outskirts of the city, in noisome cubby-holes and draughty garrets, prayed and wept in horror the chosen people of God,—long since forsaken by the wrathful God of the Bible, but up to the present believing that the measure of its heavy tribulations is not fulfilled.

Down below, near the sea, in the streets that resemble dark, viscid intestines, secret work was going on. The doors of the taverns, tea-houses, and the cheapest of lodging houses, were open wide the whole night through.

The pogrom began in the morning. The same people who, touched by the general pure joyousness and moved by the radiance of an approaching brotherhood, had once marched through the streets singing, under symbols of the liberty they had won through battle,—the very same people were now marching to do murder; and not because they were commanded to do so, nor because they nurtured an enmity against the Jews, with whom they were often on terms of close friendship, nor even out of love for booty (which was problematical),—but because a foul, cunning fiend, that dwells within every man, was whispering in their ears: "Go. Everything shall be unpunished,—the forbidden curiosity of murder, the lust of rape, power over the life of another."

During the days of the pogroms Sashka, with his comical, ape-like, purely Hebraic physiognomy, went freely about the city. He was never annoyed. His was that incontrovertible courage of the soul, that *fearlessness of fear*, which guards even the weakest of men better than all Browning revolvers. But once when, pressed against the side of a house, he was trying to avoid a crowd that was streaming like a hurricane over the entire width of a street, some mason in red blouse and white apron swung at him a cold chisel, snarling:

"Shee-eeny! Kill the sheeny! Get his blood!"

But some one seized his hand from behind.

"Stop, you devil,—why, it's Sashka! You thick-headed fool, damn your mother's heart and liver . . ."

The stone-mason paused. At this drunken, insane, delirious moment he was ready to kill any one at all,—father, sister, priest; even the God of orthodoxy Himself; but he was also ready, like a child, to obey the command of any firmer will.

He bared his teeth in a grin, like an idiot, spat aside, and wiped his nose with his hand. But suddenly his eyes fell upon the nervous little white dog, that, trembling, was hovering about Sashka. Stoop-

72

ing quickly, he seized it by its hind legs, raised it high, dashed its head against the plates of the side-walk, and started running. Sashka watched him in silence. He ran, bending forward, with hands extended, hatless, open-mouthed, his eyes round and white in insanity.

Some brain from Bielochka's head had spattered upon Sashka's boots. Sashka wiped off the spot with a handkerchief.

8

Then ensued a strange period, like the dreaming of a man in paralysis. In the city not a light showed in a single window; but, on the other hand, the fiery signs of *cafés chantants* and the windows of little taverns flamed brightly. The conquerors were testing their power, not being yet sated fully with their impunity. Certain unbridled people, in Manchurian shakos, with ribbons of St. George in the buttonholes of their jackets, made the rounds of the restaurants and with insistent impudence demanded that the national hymn be played, and saw that every one arose. They also broke into private apartments, rummaging in beds and bureaus, demanding whisky, money, and the anthem, and filling the air with their drunken belching.

One day ten of them came into the Gambrinus and took up two tables. They deported themselves in the most provocative manner, treating the help domineeringly, spitting over the shoulders of their unknown neighbors, putting their feet on the seats of others, splashing their beer out on the floor, under the pretense that it was flat. None would have anything to do with them. Everybody knew that these were detectives, and regarded them with the same secret horror and squeamish curiosity with which the general mass of simple folk regard hangmen. One of them was evidently the ringleader. This was a certain Motka Gundossiy,—red-headed, snuffling, with a nose that had been broken; a man of great physical strength (so it was said), a converted Jew, an erstwhile thief, a bouncer in a brothel next, and then a souteneur and catchpole.

Sashka was playing *The Snow Storm*. Suddenly Gundossiy walked up to him, seized fast his right hand, and, turning around to the audience, cried out:

"The Hymn! The National Hymn! In honor of our adored monarch, fellows. . . . The Hymn!"

"The Hymn! The Hymn!" came the droning chorus of the scoundrels in shakos.

"The Hymn!" called out a solitary, uncertain voice in the background.

But Sashka pulled away his hand, and calmly said:

"There won't be any hymns."

"What?" roared Gundossiy; "you won't obey! Oh, you stinking sheeny!"

Sashka bent forward, almost up against Gundossiy, and, his face all puckered up, holding his lowered fiddle by the neck, asked:

"And you?"

"What about me?"

"I'm a stinking sheeny. Well, all right. And you?"

"I'm orthodox."

"Orthodox? And for how much?"

All Gambrinus burst into laughter, while Gundossiy, all white from anger, turned around to his comrades:

"Brethren," he was declaring, in a tremulous, plaintive voice, the memorized words of some other, "Brethren, how long will we stand for the sheenies reviling our throne and holy church? . . ."

But Sashka, getting up on his elevation, with a single sound compelled him to face him again, and never could any frequenter of Gambrinus have believed that this funny, clowning Sashka was capable of speaking with such impressiveness and force:

"You!" cried out Sashka, "you, you son of a bitch! Show me your face, you murderer. . . . Look at me! . . . *Nu!*"

Everything happened within a speeding moment. Sashka's fiddle was raised high, flashed quickly through the air, and—crash!—the tall man in the shako swayed from a ringing blow on the temple. The fiddle flew into pieces. Only its neck, raised victoriously above the heads of the crowd, remained in Sashka's hands.

"He-elp, mateys!" Gundossiy began to roar.

But it was too late to help him. A mighty wall surrounded Sashka, screening him. And the same wall bore the men in shakos out into the street.

But an hour later when Sashka, having finished for the day, was coming out of the beer-hall, several men threw themselves upon him. Some one of their number hit Sashka in the eye, blew a whistle, and said to the roundsman who had come on the run:

"Take him to the boulevard station house. It's a political matter. Here's my badge."

Now for the second time, and definitely, Sashka was considered as put away beneath the ground. Some one had witnessed the entire scene that had taken place on the sidewalk near the beer-hall, and had informed the others of it. And the people who convened in the Gambrinus were worldly-wise, knowing full well just what sort of an institution the boulevard station house was, and just what a thing the revenge of detectives.

But now there was far less disquiet about Sashka's fate than there had been the first time, and he was forgotten far more quickly. Two months later in his place was seated a new fiddler (Sashka's pupil, by the way), whom the accompanist had searched out.

And then, three months later, one quiet autumn evening, as the musicians were playing the waltz *Expectancy*, somebody, in affright, exclaimed in a high voice:

"Fellows,—Sashka!"

All turned around and got up from their kegs. Yes, it was he,— the twice resurgent Sashka, but now bearded, emaciated, pale. They all made a rush for him, surrounding him, squeezing and mauling him, thrusting mugs of beer upon him. But suddenly the same voice cried out:

"Fellows,—look at his arm! . . ."

A sudden silence fell upon them all. Sashka's left arm, screwed up and as though crumpled, was pressed to his side at the elbow. Evidently, it could neither bend nor unbend, while the fingers were forever stuck near the chin.

"What's up with you, matey?" finally asked a hirsute boatswain of The Russian Company.

"Eh, nonsense. . . . That's just a sinew, or something, . . ." Sashka answered, with never a care.

"So-o."

Again there was a brief but total silence.

"Then it's all over with the *Chaban* as well?" asked the boatswain commiseratingly.

"*Chaban*?" repeated Sashka, and his eyes began to sparkle. "Hey there!" he commanded the accompanist, with his usual assurance: "*The Chaban! Ein, zwei, drei!* . . ."

The pianist began the quick tempo of the rollicking dance, looking over his shoulder with mistrust. But Sashka, with his whole hand, took out of his pocket some sort of a small, elongated black instrument, about as large as the palm of the hand and with a stem; he put this stem in his mouth, and, bending his entire body as much to the left as his maimed, motionless arm permitted, suddenly began piping on the ocarina the deafeningly-mirthful *Chaban*.

"Ho-ho-ho!" the spectators went into peals of joyous laughter.

"The devil!" exclaimed the boatswain, and, altogether unexpectedly, even to himself, executed a skillful step and started doing the rapid figures of the dance. Caught up by his impulse all the guests, women as well as men, began dancing. Even the waiters, trying not to lose their dignity, smilingly shuffled in one spot. Even Madame Ivanova, forgetting the duties of a captain on watch, was nodding her head in time to the fiery dance, and snapping her fingers softly. And, perhaps, even old porous Gambrinus himself, gnawed through and through by time, may have been moving his eyebrows, gazing gayly out on the street; and in the hands of the maimed, contorted Sashka, the sorry, naïve penny whistle seemed to be chanting, in a tongue as yet—alas!—comprehensible neither to the friends of Gambrinus, nor even to Sashka himself:

"Nothing matters! Man may be crippled—but art will endure all things, and will all things conquer!"

THE INFANT PRODIGY

Thomas Mann
1875-1941

Thomas Mann felt that music was an especially German art, and that it had peculiarly sinister powers. Such attitudes found their fullest expression in his masterful novel *Dr. Faustus* (1947). But even in his early short story "The Infant Prodigy" (written in 1903, published in 1914), the reader can observe the disturbing quality of music on Bibi, Mann's non-German *Wunderkind*, exploited by a materialistic society.

77

❦

The infant prodigy entered. The hall became quiet.

It became quiet and then the audience began to clap, because somewhere at the side a leader of mobs, a born organizer, clapped first. The audience had heard nothing yet, but they applauded; for a mighty publicity organization had heralded the prodigy and people were already hypnotized, whether they knew it or not.

The prodigy came from behind a splendid screen embroidered with Empire garlands and great conventionalized flowers, and climbed nimbly up the steps to the platform, diving into the applause as into a bath; a little chilly and shivering, but yet as though into a friendly element. He advanced to the edge of the platform and smiled as though he were about to be photographed; he made a shy, charming gesture of greeting, like a little girl.

He was dressed entirely in white silk, which the audience found enchanting. The little white jacket was fancifully cut, with a sash underneath it, and even his shoes were made of white silk. But against the white socks his bare little legs stood out quite brown; for he was a Greek boy.

He was called Bibi Saccellaphylaccas. And such indeed was his name. No one knew what Bibi was the pet name for, nobody but the impresario, and he regarded it as a trade secret. Bibi had smooth black hair reaching to his shoulders; it was parted on the side and fastened back from the narrow domed forehead by a little silk bow. His was the most harmless childish countenance in the world, with an unfinished nose and guileless mouth. The area beneath his pitch-black mouselike eyes was already a little tired and visibly lined. He looked as though he were nine years old but was really eight and given out for seven. It was hard to tell whether to believe this or not. Probably everybody knew better and still believed it, as happens about so many things. The average man thinks that a little falseness goes with beauty. Where should we get any excitement out of our daily life if we were not willing to pretend a bit? And the average man is quite right, in his average brains!

The prodigy kept on bowing until the applause died down, then he went up to the grand piano, and the audience cast a last look at its programmes. First came a *Marche solonnelle*, then a *Rêverie*,

78

and then *Le Hibou et les moineaux*—all by Bibi Saccellaphylaccas. The whole programme was by him, they were all his compositions. He could not score them, of course, but he had them all in his extraordinary little head and they possessed real artistic significance, or so it said, seriously and objectively, in the programme. The programme sounded as though the impresario had wrested these concessions from his critical nature after a hard struggle.

The prodigy sat down upon the revolving stool and felt with his feet for the pedals, which were raised by means of a clever device so that Bibi could reach them. It was Bibi's own piano, he took it everywhere with him. It rested upon wooden trestles and its polish was somewhat marred by the constant transportation—but all that only made things more interesting.

Bibi put his silk-shod feet on the pedals; then he made an artful little face, looked straight ahead of him, and lifted his right hand. It was a brown, childish little hand; but the wrist was strong and unlike a child's, with well-developed bones.

Bibi made his face for the audience because he was aware that he had to entertain them a little. But he had his own private enjoyment in the thing too, an enjoyment which he could never convey to anybody. It was that prickling delight, that secret shudder of bliss, which ran through him every time he sat at an open piano—it would always be with him. And here was the keyboard again, these seven black and white octaves, among which he had so often lost himself in abysmal and thrilling adventures—and yet it always looked as clean and untouched as a newly washed blackboard. This was the realm of music that lay before him. It lay spread out like an inviting ocean, where he might plunge in and blissfully swim, where he might let himself be borne and carried away, where he might go under in night and storm, yet keep the mastery: control, ordain—he held his right hand poised in the air.

A breathless stillness reigned in the room—the tense moment before the first note came. . . . How would it begin? It began so. And Bibi, with his index finger, fetched the first note out of the piano, a quite unexpectedly powerful first note in the middle register, like a trumpet blast. Others followed, an introduction developed—the audience relaxed.

The concert was held in the palatial hall of a fashionable first-class hotel. The walls were covered with mirrors framed in gilded arabesques, between frescoes of the rosy and fleshly school. Ornamental columns supported a ceiling that displayed a whole universe of electric bulbs, in clusters darting a brilliance far brighter than day and filling the whole space with thin, vibrating golden light. Not a seat was unoccupied, people were standing in the side aisles and at the back. The front seats cost twelve marks; for the impresario believed that anything worth having was worth paying for. And they were occupied by the best society, for it was in the upper classes, of course, that the greatest enthusiasm was felt. There were even some children, with their legs hanging down demurely from their chairs and their shining eyes staring at their gifted little white-clad contemporary.

Down in front on the left side sat the prodigy's mother, an extremely obese woman with a powdered double chin and a feather on her head. Beside her was the impresario, a man of oriental appearance with large gold buttons on his conspicuous cuffs. The princess was in the middle of the front row—a wrinkled, shrivelled little old princess but still a patron of the arts, especially everything full of sensibility. She sat in a deep, velvet-upholstered arm-chair, and a Persian carpet was spread before her feet. She held her hands folded over her grey striped-silk breast, put her head on one side, and presented a picture of elegant composure as she sat looking up at the performing prodigy. Next to her sat her lady-in-waiting, in a green striped-silk gown. Being only a lady-in-waiting she had to sit up very straight in her chair.

Bibi ended in a grand climax. With what power this wee manikin belaboured the keyboard! The audience could scarcely trust its ears. The march theme, an infectious, swinging tune, broke out once more, fully harmonized, bold and showy; with every note Bibi flung himself back from the waist as though he were marching in a triumphal procession. He ended *fortissimo*, bent over, slipped sideways off the stool, and stood with a smile awaiting the applause.

And the applause burst forth, unanimously, enthusiastically; the child made his demure little maidenly curtsy and people in the front seat thought: "Look what slim little hips he has! Clap, clap! Hurrah, bravo, little chap. Saccophylax or whatever your name is! Wait, let me take off my gloves—what a little devil of a chap he is!"

Bibi had to come out three times from behind the screen before they would stop. Some late-comers entered the hall and moved about looking for seats. Then the concert continued. Bibi's *Rêverie* murmured its numbers, consisting almost entirely of arpeggios, above which a bar of melody rose now and then, weak-winged. Then came *Le Hibou et les moineaux*. This piece was brilliantly successful, it made a strong impression; it was an effective childhood fantasy, remarkably well envisaged. The bass represented the owl, sitting morosely rolling his filmy eyes; while in the treble the impudent, half-frightened sparrows chirped. Bibi received an ovation when he finished, he was called out four times. A hotel page with shiny buttons carried up three great laurel wreaths onto the stage and proffered them from one side while Bibi nodded and expressed his thanks. Even the princess shared in the applause, daintily and noiselessly pressing her palms together.

Ah, the knowing little creature understood how to make people clap! He stopped behind the screen, they had to wait for him; lingered a little on the steps of the platform, admired the long streamers on the wreaths—although actually such things bored him stiff by now. He bowed with the utmost charm, he gave the audience plenty of time to rave itself out, because applause is valuable and must not be cut short. "*Le Hibou* is my drawing card," he thought—this expression he had learned from the impresario. "Now I will play the fantasy, it is a lot better than *Le Hibou*, of course, especially the C-sharp passage. But you idiots dote on the *Hibou*, though it is the first and the silliest thing I wrote." He continued to bow and smile.

Next came a *Méditation* and then an *Étude*—the programme was quite comprehensive. The *Méditation* was very like the *Rêverie*—which was nothing against it—and the *Étude* displayed all of Bibi's virtuosity, which naturally fell a little short of his inventiveness. And then the *Fantaisie*. This was his favourite; he varied it a little each time, giving himself free rein and sometimes surprising even himself, on good evenings, by his own inventiveness.

He sat and played, so little, so white and shining, against the great black grand piano, elect and alone, above that confused sea of faces, above the heavy, insensitive mass soul, upon which he was labouring to work with his individual, differentiated soul. His lock of soft black hair with the white silk bow had fallen over his forehead, his trained and bony little wrists pounded away, the muscles stood out visibly on his brown childish cheeks.

Sitting there he sometimes had moments of oblivion and solitude, when the gaze of his strange little mouselike eyes with the big rings beneath them would lose itself and stare through the painted stage into space that was peopled with strange vague life. Then out of the corner of his eye he would give a quick look back into the hall and be once more with his audience.

"Joy and pain, the heights and the depths—that is my *Fantaisie*," he thought lovingly. "Listen, here is the C-sharp passage." He lingered over the approach, wondering if they would notice any-

81

thing. But no, of course not, how should they? And he cast his eyes up prettily at the ceiling so that at least they might have something to look at.

All these people sat there in their regular rows, looking at the prodigy and thinking all sorts of things in their regular brains. An old gentleman with a white beard, a seal ring on his finger and a bulbous swelling on his bald spot, a growth if you like, was thinking to himself: "Really, one ought to be ashamed." He had never got any further than "Ah, thou dearest Augustin" on the piano, and here he sat now, a grey old man, looking on while this little hop-o'-my-thumb performed miracles. Yes, yes, it is a gift of God, we must remember that. God grants His gifts, or He withholds them, and there is no shame in being an ordinary man. Like with the Christ Child.—Before a child one may kneel without feeling ashamed. Strange that thoughts like these should be so satisfying—he would even say so sweet, if it was not too silly for a tough old man like him to use the word. That was how he felt, anyhow.

Art . . . the business man with the parrot-nose was thinking. "Yes, it adds something cheerful to life, a little good white silk and a little tumty-ti-ti-tum. Really he does not play so badly. Fully fifty seats, twelve marks apiece, that makes six hundred marks—and everything else besides. Take off the rent of the hall, the lighting and the programmes, you must have fully a thousand marks profit. That is worth while."

That was Chopin he was just playing, thought the piano-teacher, a lady with a pointed nose; she was of an age when the understanding sharpens as the hopes decay. "But not very original—I will say that afterwards, it sounds well. And his hand position is entirely amateur. One must be able to lay a coin on the back of the hand—I would use a ruler on him."

Then there was a young girl, at that self-conscious and chlorotic time of life when the most ineffable ideas come into the mind. She was thinking to herself: "What is it he is playing? It is expressive of passion, yet he is a child. If he kissed me it would be as though my little brother kissed me—no kiss at all. Is there such a thing as passion all by itself, without any earthly object, a sort of child's-play of passion? What nonsense! If I were to say such things aloud they would just be at me with some more cod-liver oil. Such is life."

An officer was leaning against a column. He looked on at Bibi's success and thought: "Yes, you are something and I am something, each in his own way." So he clapped his heels together and paid to the prodigy the respect which he felt to be due.

Then there was a critic, an elderly man in a shiny black coat and turned-up trousers splashed with mud. He sat in his free seat and thought: "Look at him, this young beggar of a Bibi. As an individual he has still to develop, but as a type he is already quite complete, the artist *par excellence*. He has in himself all the artist's exaltation and his utter worthlessness, his charlatanry and his sacred fire, his burning contempt and his secret raptures. Of course I can't write all that, it is too good. Of course, I should have been an artist myself if I had not seen through the whole business so clearly."

Then the prodigy stopped playing and a perfect storm arose in the hall. He had to come out again and again from behind his screen. The man with the shiny buttons carried up more wreaths: four laurel wreaths, a lyre made of violets, a bouquet of roses. He had not arms enough to convey all these tributes, the impresario himself mounted the stage to help him. He hung a laurel wreath round Bibi's neck, he tenderly stroked the black hair—and suddenly as though overcome he bent down and gave the prodigy a kiss, a resounding kiss, square on the mouth. And then the storm became a hurricane. That kiss ran through the room like an electric shock, it went direct to peoples' marrow and made them shiver down their backs. They were carried away by a helpless compulsion of sheer noise. Loud shouts mingled with the hysterical clapping of hands. Some of Bibi's commonplace little friends down there waved their handkerchiefs. But the critic thought: "Of course that kiss had to come—it's a good old gag. Yes, good Lord, if only one did not see through everything quite so clearly—"

And so the concert drew to a close. It began at half past seven and finished at half past eight. The platform was laden with wreaths and two little pots of flowers stood on the lamp-stands of the piano. Bibi played as his last number his *Rhapsodie grecque,* which turned into the Greek national hymn at the end. His fellow-countrymen in the audience would gladly have sung it with him if the company had not been so august. They made up for it with a powerful noise and hullabaloo, a hot-blooded national demonstration. And the aging critic was thinking: "Yes, the hymn had to come too. They have to exploit every vein—publicity cannot afford to neglect any means to its end. I think I'll criticize that as inartistic. But perhaps I am wrong, perhaps that is the most artistic thing of all. What is the artist? A jack-in-the-box. Criticism is on a higher plane. But I can't say that." And away he went in his muddy trousers.

After being called out nine or ten times the prodigy did not come any more from behind the screen but went to his mother and the impresario down in the hall. The audience stood about among the chairs and applauded and pressed forward to see Bibi close at hand. Some of them wanted to see the princess too. Two dense circles formed, one round the prodigy, the other round the princess, and you could actually not tell which of them was receiving more homage. But the court lady was commanded to go over to Bibi; she smoothed down his silk jacket a bit to make it look suitable for a court function, led him by the arm to the princess, and solemnly indicated to him that he was to kiss the royal hand. "How do you do it, child?" asked the princess. "Does it come into your head of itself when you sit down?" "*Oui, madame,*" answered Bibi. To himself he thought: "Oh, what a stupid old princess!" Then he turned round shyly and un-courtier-like and went back to his family.

Outside in the cloak-room there was a crowd. People held up their numbers and received with open arms furs, shawls, and galoshes. Somewhere among her acquaintances the piano-teacher stood making her critique. "He is not very original," she said.

In front of one of the great mirrors an elegant young lady was being arrayed in her evening cloak and fur shoes by her brothers, two lieutenants. She was exquisitely beautiful, with her steel-blue eyes and her clean-cut, well-bred face. A really noble dame. When she was ready she stood waiting for her brothers. "Don't stand so long in front of the glass, Adolf," she said softly to one of them, who could not tear himself away from the sight of his simple, good-looking young features. But Lieutenant Adolf thinks: What cheek! He would button his overcoat in front of the glass, just the same. Then they went out on the street where the arc-lights gleamed cloudily through the white mist. Lieutenant Adolf struck up a little nigger-dance on the frozen snow to keep warm, with his hands in his slanting overcoat pockets and his collar turned up.

A girl with untidy hair and swinging arms, accompanied by a gloomy-faced youth, came out just behind them. A child! she thought. A charming child. But in there he was an awe-inspiring . . . and aloud in a toneless voice she said: "We are all infant prodigies, we artists."

"Well, bless my soul!" thought the old gentleman who had never got further than Augustin on the piano, and whose boil was now concealed by a top hat. "What does all that mean? She sounds very oracular." But the gloomy youth understood. He nodded.

Then they were silent and the untidy-haired girl gazed after the brothers and sister. She rather despised them, but she looked after them until they had turned the corner.

A MOTHER

**James Joyce
1882-1941**

Thomas Mann's "The Infant Prodigy" centers on an exploited child and James Joyce's "A Mother," from *Dubliners* (1914), is about what we now call a "stage mother." Joyce's own mother was an accomplished pianist, his father and himself skillful tenors. Indeed, James was so talented that at one point in his life he entered a competition and would have won the Gold Medal but for his refusal to participate in the sight reading. Literary critics have long noted the importance of music in Joyce's work.

Mr. Holohan, assistant secretary of the *Eire Abu* Society, had been walking up and down Dublin for nearly a month, with his hands and pockets full of dirty pieces of paper, arranging about the series of concerts. He had a game leg and for this his friends called him Hoppy Holohan. He walked up and down constantly, stood by the hour at street corners arguing the point and made notes; but in the end it was Mrs. Kearney who arranged everything.

Miss Devlin had become Mrs. Kearney out of spite. She had been educated in a high-class convent, where she had learned French and music. As she was naturally pale and unbending in manner she made few friends at school. When she came to the age of marriage she was sent out to many houses, where her playing and ivory manners were much admired. She sat amid the chilly circle of her accomplishments, waiting for some suitor to brave it and offer her a brilliant life. But the young men whom she met were ordinary and she gave them no encouragement, trying to console her romantic desires by eating a great deal of Turkish Delight in secret. However, when she drew near the limit and her friends began to loosen their tongues about her, she silenced them by marrying Mr. Kearney, who was a bootmaker on Ormond Quay.

He was much older than she. His conversation, which was serious, took place at intervals in his great brown beard. After the first year of married life, Mrs. Kearney perceived that such a man would wear better than a romantic person, but she never put her own romantic ideas away. He was sober, thrifty and pious; he went to the altar every first Friday, sometimes with her, oftener by himself. But she never weakened in her religion and was a good wife to him. At some party in a strange house when she lifted her eyebrow ever so slightly he stood up to take his leave and, when his cough troubled him, she put the eider-down quilt over his feet and made a strong rum punch. For his part, he was a model father. By paying a small sum every week into a society, he ensured for both his daughters a dowry of one hundred pounds each when they came to the age of twenty-four. He sent the older daughter, Kathleen, to a good convent, where she learned French and music, and afterward paid her fees at the Academy. Every year in the month of July Mrs. Kearney found occasion to say to some friend:

"My good man is packing us off to Skerries for a few weeks."

If it was not Skerries it was Howth or Greystones.

When the Irish Revival began to be appreciable Mrs. Kearney determined to take advantage of her daughter's name and brought an Irish teacher to the house. Kathleen and her sister sent Irish picture postcards to their friends and these friends sent back other Irish picture postcards. On special Sundays, when Mr. Kearney went with his family to the pro-cathedral, a little crowd of people would assemble after mass at the corner of Cathedral Street. They were all friends of the Kearneys—musical friends or Nationalist friends; and, when they had played every little counter of gossip, they shook hands with one another all together, laughing at the crossing of so many hands, and said good-bye to one another in Irish. Soon the name of Miss Kathleen Kearney began to be heard often on people's lips. People said that she was very clever at music and a very nice girl and, moreover, that she was a believer in the language movement. Mrs. Kearney was well content at this. Therefore she was not surprised when one day Mr. Holohan came to her and proposed that her daughter should be the accompanist at a series of four grand concerts which his Society was going to give in the Antient Concert Rooms. She brought him into the drawing-room, made him sit down and brought out the decanter and the silver biscuit-barrel. She entered heart and soul into the details of the enterprise, advised and dissuaded: and finally a contract was drawn up by which Kathleen was to receive eight guineas for her services as accompanist at the four grand concerts.

As Mr. Holohan was a novice in such delicate matters as the wording of bills and the disposing of items for a programme, Mrs. Kearney helped him. She had tact. She knew what *artistes* should go into capitals and what *artistes* should go into small type. She knew that the first tenor would not like to come on after Mr. Meade's comic turn. To keep the audience continually diverted she slipped the doubtful items in between the old favourites. Mr. Holohan called to see her every day to have her advice on some point. She was invariably friendly and advising—homely, in fact. She pushed the decanter towards him, saying:

"Now, help yourself, Mr. Holohan!"

And while he was helping himself she said:

"Don't be afraid! Don't be afraid of it!"

Everything went on smoothly. Mrs. Kearney bought some lovely blush-pink charmeuse in Brown Thomas's to let into the front of Kathleen's dress. It cost a pretty penny; but there are occasions when a little expense is justifiable. She took a dozen of two-shilling tickets for the final concert and sent them to those friends who could not be trusted to come otherwise. She forgot nothing, and, thanks to her, everything that was to be done was done.

The concerts were to be on Wednesday, Thursday, Friday and Saturday. When Mrs. Kearney arrived with her daughter at the Antient Concert Rooms on Wednesday night she did not like the look of things. A few young men, wearing bright blue badges in their coats, stood idle in the vestibule; none of them wore evening dress. She passed by with her daughter and a quick glance through the open door of the hall showed her the cause of the stewards' idleness. At first she wondered had she mistaken the hour. No, it was twenty minutes to eight.

In the dressing-room behind the stage she was introduced to the secretary of the Society, Mr. Fitzpatrick. She smiled and shook his hand. He was a little man, with a white, vacant face. She noticed that he wore his soft brown hat carelessly on the side of his head and that his accent was flat. He held a programme in his hand, and, while he was talking to her, he chewed one end of it into a moist pulp. He seemed to bear disappointments lightly. Mr. Holohan came into the dressing-room every few minutes with reports from the box-office. The *artistes* talked among themselves nervously, glanced from time to time at the mirror and rolled and unrolled their music. When it was nearly half-past eight, the few people in the hall began to express their desire to be entertained. Mr. Fitzpatrick came in, smiled vacantly at the room, and said:

"Well now, ladies and gentlemen. I suppose we'd better open the ball."

Mrs. Kearney rewarded his very flat final syllable with a quick stare of contempt, and then said to her daughter encouragingly:

"Are you ready, dear?"

When she had an opportunity, she called Mr. Holohan aside and asked him to tell her what it meant. Mr. Holohan did not know what it meant. He said that the committee had made a mistake in arranging for four concerts: four was too many.

"And the *artistes*!" said Mrs. Kearney. "Of course they are doing their best, but really they are not good."

Mr. Holohan admitted that the *artistes* were no good but the committee, he said, had decided to let the first three concerts go as they pleased and reserve all the talent for Saturday night. Mrs. Kearney said nothing, but, as the mediocre items followed one another on the platform and the few people in the hall grew fewer and fewer, she began to regret that she had put herself to any expense for such a concert. There was something she didn't like in the look of things and Mr. Fitzpatrick's vacant smile irritated her very much. However, she said nothing and waited to see how it would end. The concert expired shortly before ten, and everyone went home quickly.

The concert on Thursday night was better attended, but Mrs. Kearney saw at once that the house was filled with paper. The audience behaved indecorously, as if the concert were an informal dress rehearsal. Mr. Fitzpatrick seemed to enjoy himself; he was quite unconscious that Mrs. Kearney was taking angry note of his conduct. He stood at the edge of the screen, from time to time jutting out his head and exchanging a laugh with two friends in the corner of the balcony. In the course of the evening, Mrs. Kearney learned that the Friday concert was to be abandoned and that the committee was going to move heaven and earth to secure a bumper house on Saturday night. When she heard this, she sought out Mr. Holohan. She buttonholed him as he was limping out quickly with a glass of lemonade for a young lady and asked him was it true. Yes, it was true.

"But, of course, that doesn't alter the contract," she said. "The contract was for four concerts."

Mr. Holohan seemed to be in a hurry; he advised her to speak to Mr. Fitzpatrick. Mrs. Kearney was now beginning to be alarmed. She called Mr.. Fitzpatrick away from his screen and told him that her daughter had signed for four concerts and that, of course, according to the terms of the contract, she should receive the sum originally stipulated for, whether the society gave the four concerts or not. Mr. Fitzpatrick, who did not catch the point at issue very quickly, seemed unable to resolve the difficulty and said that he would bring the matter before the committee. Mrs. Kearney's anger began to flutter in her cheek and she had all she could do to keep from asking:

"And who is the *Cometty* pray?"

But she knew that it would not be ladylike to do that: so she was silent.

Little boys were sent out into the principal streets of Dublin early on Friday morning with bundles of handbills. Special puffs appeared in all the evening papers, reminding the music-loving public of the treat which was in store for it on the following evening. Mrs. Kearney was somewhat reassured, but she thought well to tell her husband part of her suspicions. He listened carefully and said that perhaps it would be better if he went with her on Saturday night. She agreed. She respected her husband in the same way as she respected the General Post Office, as something large, secure and fixed; and though she knew the small number of his talents she appreciated his abstract value as a male. She was glad that he had suggested coming with her. She thought her plans over.

The night of the grand concert came. Mrs. Kearney, with her husband and daughter, arrived at the Antient Concert Rooms three-quarters of an hour before the time at which the concert was to begin. By ill luck it was a rainy evening. Mrs. Kearney placed her daughter's clothes and music in charge of her husband and went all over the building looking for Mr. Holohan or Mr. Fitzpatrick. She could find neither. She asked the stewards was any member of the committee in the hall and, after a great deal of trouble, a steward brought out a little woman named Miss Beirne to whom Mrs. Kearney explained that she wanted to see one of the secretaries. Miss Beirne expected them any minute and asked could she do anything. Mrs. Kearney looked searchingly at the oldish face which was screwed into an expression of trustfulness and enthusiasm and answered:

"No, thank you!"

The little woman hoped they would have a good house. She looked out at the rain until the melancholy of the wet street effaced all the trustfulness and enthusiasm from her twisted features. Then she gave a little sigh and said:

"Ah, well! We did our best, the dear knows."

Mrs. Kearney had to go back to the dressing-room.

The *artistes* were arriving. The bass and the second tenor had already come. The bass, Mr. Duggan, was a slender young man with a scattered black moustache. He was the son of a hall porter in an office in the city and, as a boy, he had sung prolonged bass notes in the resounding hall. From this humble state he had raised himself until he had become a first-rate *artiste*. He had appeared in grand opera. One night, when an operatic *artiste* had fallen ill, he had undertaken the part of the king in the opera of *Maritana* at the Queen's Theatre. He sang his music with great feeling and volume and was warmly welcomed by the gallery; but, unfortunately, he marred the good impression by wiping his nose in his gloved hand once or twice out of thoughtlessness. He was unassuming and spoke little. He said *yous* so softly that it passed unnoticed and he never drank anything stronger than milk for his voice's sake. Mr. Bell, the second tenor, was a fair-haired little man who competed every year for prizes at the Feis Ceoil. On his fourth trial he had been awarded a bronze medal. He was extremely nervous and extremely jealous of other tenors and he covered his nervous jealousy with an ebullient friendliness. It was his humour to have people know what an ordeal a concert was to him. Therefore when he saw Mr. Duggan he went over to him and asked:

"Are you in it too?"

"Yes," said Mr. Duggan.

Mr. Bell laughed at his fellow-sufferer, held out his hand and said:

"Shake!"

Mrs. Kearney passed by these two young men and went to the edge of the screen to view the house. The seats were being filled up rapidly and a pleasant noise circulated in the auditorium. She came back and spoke to her husband privately. Their conversation was evidently about Kathleen for they both glanced at her often as she stood chatting to one of her Nationalist friends, Miss Healy, the contralto. An unknown solitary woman with a pale face walked through the room. The women followed with keen eyes the faded blue dress which was stretched upon a meagre body. Someone said that she was Madam Glynn, the soprano.

"I wonder where did they dig her up," said Kathleen to Miss Healy. "I'm sure I never heard of her."

Miss Healy had to smile. Mr. Holohan limped into the dressing-room at that moment and the two young ladies asked him who was the unknown woman. Mr. Holohan said that she was Madam Glynn from London. Madam Glynn took her stand in a corner of the room, holding a roll of music stiffly before her and from time to time changing the direction of her startled gaze. The shadow took her faded dress into shelter but fell revengefully into the little cup behind her collar-bone. The noise of the hall became more audible. The first tenor and the baritone arrived together. They were both well dressed, stout and complacent and they brought a breath of opulence among the company.

Mrs. Kearney brought her daughter over to them, and talked to them amiably. She wanted to be on good terms with them but, while she strove to be polite, her eyes followed Mr. Holohan in his limping and devious courses. As soon as she could she excused herself and went out after him.

"Mr. Holohan, I want to speak to you for a moment," she said.

They went down to a discreet part of the corridor. Mrs. Kearney asked him when was her daughter going to be paid. Mr. Holohan said that Mr. Fitzpatrick had charge of that. Mrs. Kearney said that she didn't know anything about Mr. Fitzpatrick. Her daughter had signed a contract for eight guineas and she would have to be paid. Mr. Holohan said that it wasn't his business.

"Why isn't it your business?" asked Mrs. Kearney. "Didn't you yourself bring her the contract? Anyway, if it's not your business it's my business and I mean to see to it."

"You'd better speak to Mr. Fitzpatrick," said Mr. Holohan distantly.

"I don't know anything about Mr. Fitzpatrick," repeated Mrs. Kearney. "I have my contract, and I intend to see that it is carried out."

When she came back to the dressing-room her cheeks were slightly suffused. The room was lively. Two men in outdoor dress had taken possession of the fireplace and were chatting familiarly with Miss Healy and the baritone. They were the *Freeman* man and Mr. O'Madden Burke. The *Freeman* man had come in to say that he could not wait for the concert as he had to report the lecture which an American priest was giving in the Mansion House. He said they were to leave the report for him at the *Freeman* office and he would see that it went in. He was a grey-haired man, with a plausible voice and careful manners. He held an extinguished cigar in his hand and the aroma of cigar smoke floated near him. He had not intended to stay a moment because concerts and *artistes* bored him considerably but he remained leaning against the mantelpiece. Miss Healy stood in front of him, talking and laughing. He was old enough to suspect one reason for her politeness but young enough in spirit to turn the moment to account. The warmth, fragrance and colour of her body appealed to his senses. He was pleasantly conscious that the bosom which he saw rise and fall slowly beneath him rose and fell at that moment for him, that the laughter and fragrance and wilful glances were his tribute. When he could stay no longer he took leave of her regretfully.

"O'Madden Burke will write the notice," he explained to Mr. Holohan, "and I'll see it in."

"Thank you very much, Mr. Hendrick," said Mr. Holohan. "You'll see it in, I know. Now, won't you have a little something before you go?"

"I don't mind," said Mr. Hendrick.

92

The two men went along some tortuous passages and up a dark staircase and came to a secluded room where one of the stewards was uncorking bottles for a few gentlemen. One of these gentlemen was Mr. O'Madden Burke, who had found out the room by instinct. He was a suave, elderly man who balanced his imposing body, when at rest, upon a large silk umbrella. His magniloquent western name was the moral umbrella upon which he balanced the fine problem of his finances. He was widely respected.

While Mr. Holohan was entertaining the *Freeman* man Mrs. Kearney was speaking so animatedly to her husband that he had to ask her to lower her voice. The conversation of the others in the dressing-room had become strained. Mr. Bell, the first item, stood ready with his music but the accompanist made no sign. Evidently something was wrong. Mr. Kearney looked straight before him, stroking his beard, while Mrs. Kearney spoke into Kathleen's ear with subdued emphasis. From the hall came sounds of encouragement, clapping and stamping of feet. The first tenor and the baritone and Miss Healy stood together, waiting tranquilly, but Mr. Bell's nerves were greatly agitated because he was afraid the audience would think that he had come late.

Mr. Holohan and Mr. O'Madden Burke came into the room. In a moment Mr. Holohan perceived the hush. He went over to Mrs. Kearney and spoke with her earnestly. While they were speaking the noise in the hall grew louder. Mr. Holohan became very red and excited. He spoke volubly, but Mrs. Kearney said curtly at intervals:

"She won't go on. She must get her eight guineas."

Mr. Holohan pointed desperately towards the hall where the audience was clapping and stamping. He appealed to Mr. Kearney and to Kathleen. But Mr. Kearney continued to stroke his beard and Kathleen looked down, moving the point of her new shoe: it was not her fault. Mrs. Kearney repeated:

"She won't go on without her money."

After a swift struggle of tongues Mr. Holohan hobbled out in haste. The room was silent. When the strain of the silence had become somewhat painful Miss Healy said to the baritone:

"Have you seen Mrs. Pat Campbell this week?"

The baritone had not seen her but he had been told that she was very fine. The conversation went no further. The first tenor bent his head and began to count the links of the gold chain which was extended across his waist, smiling and humming random notes to observe the effect on the frontal sinus. From time to time everyone glanced at Mrs. Kearney.

The noise in the auditorium had risen to a clamour when Mr. Fitzpatrick burst into the room, followed by Mr. Holohan, who was panting. The clapping and stamping in the hall were punctuated by whistling. Mr. Fitzpatrick held a few banknotes in his hand. He counted out four into Mrs. Kearney's hand and said she would get the other half at the interval. Mrs. Kearney said:

"This is four shillings short."

But Kathleen gathered in her skirt and said: "Now, Mr. Bell," to the first item, who was shaking like an aspen. The singer and the accompanist went out together. The noise in the hall died away. There was a pause of a few seconds; and then the piano was heard.

The first part of the concert was very successful except for Madam Glynn's item. The poor lady sang Killarney in a bodiless gasping voice, with all the old-fashioned mannerisms of intonation and pronunciation which she believed lent elegance to her singing. She looked as if she had been resurrected from an old stage-wardrobe and the cheaper parts of the hall made fun of her high wailing notes. The first tenor and the contralto, however, brought down the house. Kathleen played a selection of Irish airs which was generously applauded. The first part closed with a stirring patriotic recitation delivered by a young lady who arranged amateur theatricals. It was deservedly applauded; and, when it was ended, the men went out for the interval, content.

All this time the dressing-room was a hive of excitement. In one corner were Mr. Holohan, Mr. Fitzpatrick, Miss Beirne, two of the stewards, the baritone, the bass, and Mr. O'Madden Burke. Mr. O'Madden Burke said it was the most scandalous exhibition he had ever witnessed. Miss Kathleen Kearney's musical career was ended in Dublin after that, he said. The baritone was asked what did he think of Mrs. Kearney's conduct. He did not like to say anything. He had been paid his money and wished to be at peace with men. However, he said that Mrs. Kearney might have taken the *artistes* into consideration. The stewards and the secretaries debated hotly as to what should be done when the interval came.

"I agree with Miss Beirne," said Mr. O'Madden Burke. "Pay her nothing."

In another corner of the room were Mrs. Kearney and her husband, Mr. Bell, Miss Healy and the young lady who had to recite the patriotic piece. Mrs. Kearney said that the committee had treated her scandalously. She had spared neither trouble nor expense and this was how she was repaid.

They thought they had only a girl to deal with and that, therefore, they could ride roughshod over her. But she would show them their mistake. They wouldn't have dared to have treated her like that if she had been a man. But she would see that her daughter got her rights: she wouldn't be fooled. If they didn't pay her to the last farthing she would make Dublin ring. Of course she was sorry for the sake of the *artistes*. But what else could she do? She appealed to the second tenor, who said he thought she had not been well treated. Then she appealed to Miss Healy. Miss Healy wanted to join the other group but she did not like to do so because she was a great friend of Kathleen's and the Kearneys had often invited her to their house.

As soon as the first part was ended Mr. Fitzpatrick and Mr. Holohan went over to Mrs. Kearney and told her that the other four guineas would be paid after the committee meeting on the following Tuesday and that, in case her daughter did not play for the second part, the committee would consider the contract broken and would pay nothing.

"I haven't seen any committee," said Mrs. Kearney angrily. "My daughter has her contract. She will get four pounds eight into her hand or a foot she won't put on that platform."

"I'm surprised at you, Mrs. Kearney," said Mr. Holohan. "I never thought you would treat us this way."

"And what way did you treat me?" asked Mrs. Kearney.

Her face was inundated with an angry colour and she looked as if she would attack someone with her hands.

"I'm asking for my rights," she said.

"You might have some sense of decency," said Mr. Holohan.

"Might I, indeed? . . . And when I ask when my daughter is going to be paid I can't get a civil answer."

She tossed her head and assumed a haughty voice:

"You must speak to the secretary. It's not my business. I'm a great fellow fol-the-diddle-I-do."

"I thought you were a lady," said Mr. Holohan, walking away from her abruptly.

After that Mrs. Kearney's conduct was condemned on all hands: everyone approved of what the committee had done. She stood at the door, haggard with rage, arguing with her husband and daughter, gesticulating with them. She waited until it was time for the second part to begin in the hope that the secretaries would approach her. But Miss Healey had kindly consented to play one or two accompaniments. Mrs. Kearney had to stand aside to allow the baritone and his accompanist to pass up to the platform. She stood still for an instant like an angry stone image and, when the first notes of the song struck her ear, she caught up her daughter's cloak and said to her husband:

"Get a cab!"

He went out at once. Mrs. Kearney wrapped the cloak round her daughter and followed him. As she passed through the doorway she stopped and glared into Mr. Holohan's face.

"I'm not done with you yet," she said.

"But I'm done with you," said Mr. Holohan.

Kathleen followed her mother meekly. Mr. Holohan began to pace up and down the room, in order to cool himself for he felt his skin on fire.

"That's a nice lady!" he said. "O, she's a nice lady!"

"You did the proper thing, Holohan," said Mr. O'Madden Burke, poised upon his umbrella in approval.

FLUTE DREAM

Hermann Hesse
1887-1962

Hermann Hesse had a musical mother who inspired in him a lifelong love of music. Hermann's half-brother Theodor was a musician too, and the writer himself studied violin as a youth. Hesse's writings owe much to music both in form and style. The novel *Steppenwolf* (1927) has been called a "sonata in prose." "Flute Dream" (1919), printed here, strains toward a lyricism recalling romantic music.

᯽

"Here," said my father, handing me a small ivory flute, "take this and don't forget your old father when you are entertaining people in foreign lands with your playing. It is now high time for you to see the world and gain knowledge. I had this flute made for you because you don't like any other kind of work and always just want to sing. Only be sure always to choose bright, cheery songs, otherwise it would be a pity about the gift God has given you."

My dear father understood little about music, he was a scholar; he thought all I had to do was blow into the pretty little flute and that would be that. I did not wish to undeceive him, and so I gave him my thanks, put the flute in my pocket, and took my departure.

Our valley was familiar to me only as far as the big farm mill; and so beyond that the world began, and it pleased me greatly. A bee, tired from flying about, had lighted on my sleeve; I took her with me so that later on at my first resting place I would have a messenger ready to send back home with my greetings.

Woods and meadows accompanied me on my way and the river ran merrily beside me; I saw that the world was little different from my home. The trees and flowers, the ears of corn, and the hazel bushes spoke to me, I sang their songs with them and they understood me just as at home; the singing wakened my bee, she crept slowly up to my shoulder, flew off and circled twice around me with her deep, sweet buzzing, then steered straight as an arrow back toward home.

Presently a young girl came strolling out of the woods carrying a basket on her arm and wearing a broad shade hat of straw on her blond head.

"Grüss Gott," I said to her, "where are you off to?"

"I'm taking the harvesters their dinner," she said, walking beside me. "And where are you going today?"

"I am going out into the world, my father sent me. He thinks I ought to give concerts on the flute, but I don't really know how, I shall have to learn first."

"Well now. And what can you really do? Everyone has to be able to do something, after all."

"Nothing special. I can sing songs."

"What kind of songs do you sing?"

"You know, all kinds of songs, for the morning and the evening, and for all the trees and the animals and the flowers. Now, for example, I could sing a pretty song about a young girl coming out of the woods and taking the harvesters their dinner."

"Could you really? Then go ahead and sing it!"

"Yes, but what's your name?"

"Brigitte."

Then I sang a song about the beautiful Brigitte in her straw hat and what she had in her basket, and how all the flowers stared at her, and the blue bindweed in the garden hedge reached out after her, and all the other particulars. She paid strict attention and said it was good. And when I told her I was hungry, she raised the lid of her basket and got out a piece of bread. I took a bite of it, continuing to walk rapidly, and she said: "You mustn't run while you're eating. One thing after the other." And so we sat down in the grass and I ate my bread, and she clasped her brown hands around her knees and looked at me.

"Will you sing something else for me?" she asked when I had finished.

"Of course I will. What shall it be?"

"About a girl whose darling ran away from her and she is sad."

"No, I can't do that. I don't know what that would be like, and anyway one oughtn't to be so sad. I must only sing bright, cheery songs, my father said. I'll sing to you about the cuckoo bird or the butterfly."

"Then you know nothing at all about love?" she asked.

"About love? Oh, yes I do. That is the most beautiful thing of all."

I began at once and sang about the sunbeam that has fallen in love with the red poppy blossoms and how it sports with them and is filled with joy. And about the female finch when she is waiting for the male, and when he comes she flies away and pretends to be terrified. I sang further about the girl with brown eyes and about the youth who comes along and sings and is rewarded with a piece of bread; but now he does not want any more bread, he wants a kiss from the girl and wants to look into her brown eyes, and he will go on singing and will not stop until she begins to smile and shuts his mouth with her lips.

Then Brigitte bent over and shut my mouth with her lips and closed her eyes and then opened them again, and I looked into the close-up, brown-golden stars in which I saw myself and a few white meadow flowers reflected.

"The world is very beautiful," I said. "My father was quite right. Now I will help you carry your basket and we will take it to your people."

I picked up her basket and we walked on, her footsteps ringing with mine and her merriment matching my own, and the forest whispered gently and coolly from the mountain heights; I had never wandered with so much joy, I continued to sing gaily for a while until I had to stop from sheer superabundance; there were just too many songs coming from valley and mountain, from grass and trees and river and underbrush, all the whisperings and the stories.

Then I had to reflect: If I could simultaneously understand and sing all these thousands of songs of the world, about the grass and flowers and people and clouds and about everything, the leafy forests and the pine forests and all the animals, and also about the distant seas and mountains and the stars and the moon, and if all this could resound and sing inside me at once, then I would be God Almighty and each new song would take its place in the sky as a star.

But while I was thinking this, perfectly still inside, filled with wonder because such a thing had never come into my mind before, Brigitte stopped and held me back by the handle of the basket.

"Now I must go up this way," she said. "Our people are up there in the field. And you, where are you going? Will you come with me?"

"No, I cannot come with you. I must go out into the world. My best thanks for the bread, Brigitte, and for the kiss. I will think of you."

She took her dinner basket, and across it she once more bent her eyes upon me in the brown shadow, and her lips clung to mine and her kiss was so sweet and good that I almost grew sad from sheer gladness. Then I hastily called farewell and walked quickly off down the road.

The girl climbed slowly up the mountainside, and under the hanging foliage of the beech trees at the forest's edge she stopped and gazed after me, and when I signaled to her, waving my hat over my head, she nodded once and disappeared into the shadow of the beeches, as silent as a picture.

I, however, went on my way absorbed in my own thoughts until the road turned a corner.

There stood a mill and beside the mill a boat lay in the water and in it sat a solitary man who seemed to have been waiting just for me, for as I touched my hat to him and climbed aboard, the boat immediately began to move and ran downstream. I sat amidships and the man sat in the stern at the helm, and when I asked him where we were going he raised his head and stared at me with veiled gray eyes.

"Wherever you like," he said in a low tone. "Downstream and into the ocean, or to the great cities, you have your choice. It all belongs to me."

"It all belongs to you? Then you are the King?"

"Perhaps," he said. "And you are a poet, it seems. Then sing me a song as we travel."

I pulled myself together. Fear filled me because of the solemn gray man and because our boat moved so fast and silently down the river. I sang about the river, which carries boats and mirrors the sun and boils up on the rocky shores and is happy when it completes its wanderings.

The man's face remained expressionless, and when I stopped singing he nodded as silent as a dreamer, and then all at once to my astonishment he began to sing himself, and he too sang of the river and of the river's journey through the valleys, and his song was more beautiful and more powerful than mine, but in it everything sounded quite different.

The river, as he sang of it, rushed down from the hills like a roistering vandal, dark and wild; with gnashing teeth it fought against the constraint of mills and arching bridges; it loathed every boat it had to carry, and in its waves and long green waterweed it smilingly cradled the white corpses of the drowned.

All this pleased me not at all, and yet the sound of it was so beautiful and mysterious that I became wholly confused and fell silent in my distress. If what this subtle, clever old bard was singing in his muted voice was true, then all my songs were only nonsense and silly child's play. Then the world at bottom was not good and bright like God's own heart, but dark and desperate, evil and somber, and when the woods rustled, it was not from joy but from pain.

We voyaged on and the shadows lengthened, and each time I began to sing, it sounded less assured and my voice grew fainter, and each time the strange singer would answer me with a song that made the world ever more enigmatic and sorrowful and me ever more oppressed and sad.

My soul ached and I lamented not having stayed on shore with the flowers or with beautiful Brigitte, and to console myself in the growing dusk I began to sing again in a loud voice and I sang amid the red glow of evening the song of Brigitte and her kisses.

Then twilight came and I fell silent, and the man at the helm sang, and he too sang of love and the pleasures of love, of brown eyes and of blue eyes, of moist red lips, and his impassioned singing above the darkling flood was beautiful and moving, but in his song love too had become dark and terrifying and a deadly mystery for which men groped, mad and bleeding in their misery, and with which they tortured and killed one another.

I gave ear and grew as weary and troubled as though I had already been underway for years and had traveled through nothing but sorrow and misery. I felt a constant faint chilly stream of sorrow and anguish creeping across to me from the stranger, and into my heart.

"Well then, life is not the highest and best," I cried at last, bitterly, "but death is. Then I beseech you, sorrowful King, sing me a song of death!"

The man at the helm now sang about death, and his singing was more beautiful than anything I had ever heard. But even death was not the highest and best, even in death there was no comfort. Death was life, and life was death, and they were locked together in an eternal, mad love-battle, and this was the final word and the meaning of the world, and thence came a radiance that could glorify all misery, and thence came a shadow that troubled all joy and beauty and shrouded them in darkness. But from out of this darkness, joy burned more intimately and more beautifully, and love had a deeper glow within this night.

I listened, and had become perfectly still; there was no more will in me save that of this strange man. His glance rested on me calmly and with a certain sad kindliness, and his gray eyes were full of the sorrow and the beauty of the world. He smiled at me and then I took heart and pleaded in my misery: "Oh, let us put about, you! I am fearful here in the dark and I want to turn back and go where I can find Brigitte, or home to my father."

The man stood up and pointed into the night, and the lantern shone bright on his thin, determined face. "There is no way back," he said solemnly and gently. "One must continue to go forward if one wants to fathom the world. And you have already had what is best and finest from the girl with the brown eyes, and the farther you are from her the better and finer it will be. But no matter, sail on, wherever you wish. I will give you my place at the helm!"

I was in deathly despair and yet I saw that he was right. Full of yearning, I thought of Brigitte and of my home and of everything that had so recently been near and bright and my own, and that I had now lost. But now I must take the stranger's place and man the helm, so it must be.

Therefore, I got up in silence and stepped through the boat toward the pilot's seat, and the man came toward me silently, and as we were passing he looked fixedly into my face and handed me his lantern.

But when I was seated at the helm and had placed the lantern beside me, I was alone in the boat. I recognized with a deep shudder that the man had disappeared, and yet I was not surprised. I had had a premonition. It seemed to me that the beautiful day of wandering and Brigitte and my father and my homeland had been only dreams and that I was old and sorrowful and had already been voyaging forever and ever on this nocturnal river.

I knew that I must not call the man, and recognition of the truth came over me like a chill.

To make sure of what I already suspected, I leaned out over the water and lifted the lantern, and out of the black watery mirror a face peered up at me, a face with severe and solemn features and gray eyes, an old knowing face, and it was I.

And since no way led back, I voyaged forth over the dark waters deeper into the night.

MR. REGINALD PEACOCK'S DAY

Katherine Mansfield
1888-1923

Katherine Mansfield had a difficult time choosing between literary and musical careers. She studied cello seriously with the idea of becoming a professional musician, but after discouragement from her father turned to writing. Taking Anton Chekhov as a model, she became one of the acknowledged master stylists in the short story form. "Mr. Reginald Peacock's Day" is from *Bliss and Other Stories* (1920), the volume which brought her recognition.

❧

If there was one thing that he hated more than another it was the way she had of waking him in the morning. She did it on purpose, of course. It was her way of establishing her grievance for the day, and he was not going to let her know how successful it was. But really, really, to wake a sensitive person like that was positively dangerous! It took him hours to get over it—simply hours. She came into the room buttoned up in an overall, with a handkerchief over her head—thereby proving that she had been up herself and slaving since dawn—and called in a low, warning voice: "Reginald!"

"Eh! What! What's that? What's the matter?"

"It's time to get up; it's half-past eight." And out she went, shutting the door quietly after her, to gloat over her triumph, he supposed.

He rolled over in the big bed, his heart still beating in quick, dull throbs, and with every throb he felt his energy escaping him, his—his inspiration for the day stifling under those thudding blows. It seemed that she took a malicious delight in making life more difficult for him than—Heaven knows—it was, by denying him his rights as an artist, by trying to drag him down to her level. What was the matter with her? What the hell did she want? Hadn't he three times as many pupils now as when they were first married, earned three times as much, paid for every stick and stone that they possessed, and now had begun to shell out for Adrian's kindergarten? . . . And had he ever reproached her for not having a penny to her name? Never a word—never a sign! The truth was that once you married a woman she became insatiable, and the truth was that nothing was more fatal for an artist than marriage, at any rate until he was well over forty. . . . Why had he married her? He asked himself this question on an average about three times a day, but he never could answer it satisfactorily. She had caught him at a weak moment, when the first plunge into reality had bewildered and overwhelmed him for a time. Looking back, he saw a pathetic, youthful creature, half child, half wild untamed bird, totally incompetent to cope with bills and creditors and all the sordid details of existence. Well—she had done her best to clip his wings, if that

106

was any satisfaction for her, and she could congratulate herself on the success of this early morning trick. One ought to wake exquisitely, reluctantly, he thought, slipping down in the warm bed. He began to imagine a series of enchanting scenes which ended with his latest, most charming pupil putting her bare, scented arms round his neck, and covering him with her long, perfumed hair. "Awake, my love!" . . .

As was his daily habit, while the bath water ran, Reginald Peacock tried his voice.

When her mother tends her before the laughing mirror,
Looping up her laces, tying up her hair,

he sang, softly at first, listening to the quality, nursing his voice until he came to the third line:

Often she thinks, were this wild thing wedded . . .

and upon the word "wedded" he burst into such a shout of triumph that the tooth-glass on the bathroom shelf trembled and even the bath tap seemed to gush stormy applause. . . .

Well, there was nothing wrong with his voice, he thought, leaping into the bath and soaping his soft, pink body all over with a loofah shaped like a fish. He could fill Covent Garden with it! "*Wedded,*" he shouted again, seizing the towel with a magnificent operatic gesture, and went on singing while he rubbed as though he had been Lohengrin tipped out by an unwary Swan and drying himself in the greatest haste before that tiresome Elsa came along. . . .

Back in his bedroom, he pulled the blind up with a jerk, and standing upon the pale square of sunlight that lay upon the carpet like a sheet of cream blotting-paper, he began to do his exercises—deep breathing, bending forward and back, squatting like a frog and shooting out his legs—for if there was one thing he had a horror of it was of getting fat, and men in his profession had a dreadful tendency that way. However, there was no sign of it at present. He was, he decided, just right, just in good proportion. In fact, he could not help a thrill of satisfaction when he saw himself in the glass, dressed in a morning coat, dark grey trousers, grey socks and a black tie with a silver thread in it. Not that he was vain—he couldn't stand vain men—no; the sight of himself gave him a thrill of purely artistic satisfaction. "*Violà tout!*" said he, passing his hand over his sleek hair.

That little, easy French phrase blown so lightly from his lips, like a whiff of smoke, reminded him that someone had asked him again, the evening before, if he was English. People seemed to find it impossible to believe that he hadn't some Southern blood. True, there was an emotional quality in his singing that had nothing of the John Bull in it. . . . The door-handle rattled and turned round and round. Adrian's head popped through.

"Please, father, mother says breakfast is quite ready, please."

"Very well," said Reginald. Then, just as Adrian disappeared: "Adrian!"

"Yes, father."

"You haven't said 'good morning.' "

A few months ago Reginald had spent a week-end in a very aristocratic family, where the father received his little sons in the morning and shook hands with them. Reginald thought the practice charming, and introduced it immediately, but Adrian felt dreadfully silly at having to shake hands with his own father every morning. And why did his father always sort of sing to him instead of talk? . . .

In excellent temper, Reginald walked into the dining-room and sat down before a pile of letters, a copy of the *Times*, and a little covered dish. He glanced at the letters and then at his breakfast. There were two thin slices of bacon and one egg.

"Don't you want any bacon?" he asked.

"No, I prefer a cold baked apple. I don't feel the need of bacon every morning."

Now, did she mean that there was no need for him to have bacon every morning, either, and that she grudged having to cook it?

"If you don't want to cook the breakfast," said he, "why don't you keep a servant? You know we can afford one, and you know how I loathe to see my wife doing the work. Simply because all the women we have had in the past have been failures, and utterly upset my regime, and made it almost impossible for me to have any pupils here, you've given up trying to find a decent woman. It's not impossible to train a servant—is it? I mean, it doesn't require genius?"

"But I prefer to do the work myself; it makes life so much more peaceful. . . . Run along, Adrian darling, and get ready for school."

"Oh no, that's not it!" Reginald pretended to smile. "You do the work yourself, because, for some extraordinary reason, you love to humiliate me. Objectively, you may not know that, but, subjectively, it's the case." This last remark so delighted him that he cut open an envelope as gracefully as if he had been on the stage. . . .

"DEAR MR. PEACOCK,

I feel I cannot go to sleep until I have thanked you again for the wonderful joy your singing gave me this evening. Quite unforgettable. You make me wonder, as I have not wondered since I was a girl, if this is *all*. I mean, if this ordinary world is *all*. If there is not, perhaps, for those of us who understand, divine beauty and richness awaiting us if we only have the *courage* to see it And to make it ours. . . . The house is so quiet. I wish you were here now that I might thank you in person. You are doing a great thing. You are teaching the world to escape from life!

Yours, most sincerely,
ÆNONE FELL.

P.S.—I am in every afternoon this week. . . ."

The letter was scrawled in violet ink on thick, handmade paper. Vanity, that bright bird, lifted its wings again, lifted them until he felt his breast would break.

"Oh well, don't let us quarrel," said he, and actually flung out a hand to his wife.

But she was not great enough to respond.

"I must hurry and take Adrian to school," said she. "Your room is quite ready for you."

Very well—very well—let there be open war between them! But he was hanged if he'd be the first to make it up again!

He walked up and down his room, and was not calm again until he heard the outer door close upon Adrian and his wife. Of course, if this went on, he would have to make some other arrangement. That was obvious. Tied and bound like this, how could he help the world to escape from life? He opened the piano and looked up his pupils for the morning. Miss Betty Brittle, the Countess Wilkowska and Miss Marian Morrow. They were charming, all three.

Punctually at half-past ten the door-bell rang. He went to the door. Miss Betty Brittle was there, dressed in white, with her music in a blue silk case.

"I'm afraid I'm early," she said, blushing and shy, and she opened her big blue eyes very wide. "Am I?"

"Not at all, dear lady. I am only too charmed," said Reginald. "Won't you come in?"

"It's such a heavenly morning," said Miss Brittle. "I walked across the Park. The flowers were too marvellous."

"Well, think about them while you sing your exercises," said Reginald, sitting down at the piano. "It will give your voice colour and warmth."

Oh, what an enchanting idea! What a *genius* Mr. Peacock was. She parted her pretty lips, and began to sing like a pansy.

"Very good, very good, indeed," said Reginald, playing chords that would waft a hardened criminal to heaven. "Make the notes round. Don't be afraid. Linger over them, breathe them like a perfume."

How pretty she looked, standing there in her white frock, her little blond head tilted, showing her milky throat.

"Do you ever practise before a glass?" asked Reginald. "You ought to, you know; it makes the lips more flexible. Come over here."

They went over to the mirror and stood side by side.

"Now sing—moo-e-koo-e-oo-e-a!"

But she broke down, and blushed more brightly than ever.

"Oh," she cried, "I can't. It makes me feel so silly. It makes me want to laugh. I do look so absurd!"

"No, you don't. Don't be afraid," said Reginald, but laughed, too, very kindly. "Now, try again!"

The lesson simply flew, and Betty Brittle quite got over her shyness.

"When can I come again?" she asked, tying the music up again in the blue silk case. "I want to take as many lessons as I can just now. Oh, Mr. Peacock, I *do* enjoy them so much. May I come the day after to-morrow?"

"Dear lady, I shall be only too charmed," said Reginald, bowing her out.

Glorious girl! And when they had stood in front of the mirror, her white sleeve had just touched his black one. He could feel—yes, he could actually feel a warm glowing spot, and he stroked it. She loved her lessons. His wife came in.

"Reginald, can you let me have some money? I must pay the dairy. And will you be in for dinner to-night?"

"Yes, you know I'm singing at Lord Timbuck's at half-past nine. Can you make me some clear soup, with an egg in it?"

"Yes. And the money, Reginald. It's eight and sixpence."

"Surely that's very heavy—isn't it?"

"No, it's just what it ought to be. And Adrian must have milk."

There she was—off again. Now she was standing up for Adrian against him.

"I have not the slightest desire to deny my child a proper amount of milk," said he. "Here is ten shillings."

The door-bell rang. He went to the door.

"Oh," said the Countess Wilkowska, "the stairs. I have not a breath." And she put her hand over her heart as she followed him into the music-room. She was all in black, with a little black hat with a floating veil—violets in her bosom.

"Do not make me sing exercises, to-day," she cried, throwing out her hands in her delightful foreign way. "No, to-day, I want only to sing songs. . . . And may I take off my violets? They fade so soon."

"They fade so soon—they fade so soon," played Reginald on the piano.

"May I put them here?" asked the Countess, dropping them in a little vase that stood in front of one of Reginald's photographs.

"Dear lady, I should be only too charmed!"

She began to sing, and all was well until she came to the phrase: "You love me. Yes, I *know* you love me!" Down dropped his hands from the keyboard, he wheeled round, facing her.

"No, no; that's not good enough. You can do better than that," cried Reginald ardently. "You must sing as if you were in love. Listen; let me try and show you." And he sang.

"Oh, yes, yes. I see what you mean," stammered the little Countess. "May I try it again?"

"Certainly. Do not be afraid. Let yourself go. Confess yourself. Make proud surrender!" he called above the music. And she sang.

"Yes; better that time. But I still feel you are capable of more. Try it with me. There must be a kind of exultant defiance as well—don't you feel?" And they sang together. Ah! now she was sure she understood. "May I try once again?"

"You love me. Yes, I *know* you love me."

The lesson was over before that phrase was quite perfect. The little foreign hands trembled as they put the music together.

"And you are forgetting your violets," said Reginald softly.

"Yes, I think I will forget them," said the Countess, biting her underlip. What fascinating ways these foreign women have!

"And you will come to my house on Sunday and make music?" she asked.

"Dear lady, I shall be only too charmed!" said Reginald.

> *Weep ye no more, sad fountains*
> *Why need ye flow so fast?*

sang Miss Marian Morrow, but her eyes filled with tears and her chin trembled.

"Don't sing just now," said Reginald. "Let me play it for you." He played so softly.

"Is there anything the matter?" asked Reginald. "You're not quite happy this morning."

No, she wasn't; she was awfully miserable.

"You don't care to tell me what it is?"

It really was nothing particular. She had those moods sometimes when life seemed almost unbearable.

"Ah, I know," he said; "if I could only help!"

"But you do; you do! Oh, if it were not for my lessons I don't feel I could go on."

"Sit down in the arm-chair and smell the violets and let me sing to you. It will do you just as much good as a lesson."

Why weren't all men like Mr. Peacock?

"I wrote a poem after the concert last night—just about what I felt. Of course, it wasn't *personal*. May I send it to you?"

"Dear lady, I should be only too charmed!"

By the end of the afternoon he was quite tired and lay down on a sofa to rest his voice before dressing. The door of his room was open. He could hear Adrian and his wife talking in the dining room.

"Do you know what that teapot reminds me of, Mummy? It reminds me of a little sitting-down kitten."

"Does it, Mr. Absurdity?"

Reginald dozed. The telephone bell woke him.

"Ænone Fell is speaking. Mr. Peacock, I have just heard that you are singing at Lord Timbuck's to-night. Will you dine with me, and we can go on together afterwards?" And the words of his reply dropped like flowers down the telephone.

"Dear lady, I should be only too charmed."

What a triumphant evening! The little dinner *tête-à-tête* with Ænone Fell, the drive to Lord Timbuck's in her white motor-car, when she thanked him again for the unforgettable joy. Triumph upon triumph! And Lord Timbuck's champagne simply flowed.

"Have some more champagne, Peacock," said Lord Timbuck. Peacock, you notice—not Mr. Peacock—but Peacock, as if he were one of them. And wasn't he? He was an artist. He could sway them all. And wasn't he teaching them all to escape from life? How he sang! And as he sang, as in a dream he saw their feathers and their flowers and their fans, offered to him, laid before him, like a huge bouquet.

"Have another glass of wine, Peacock."

112

"I could have any one I liked by lifting a finger," thought Peacock, positively staggering home.

But as he let himself into the dark flat his marvellous sense of elation began to ebb away. He turned up the light in the bedroom. His wife lay asleep, squeezed over to her side of the bed. He remembered suddenly how she had said when he had told her he was going out to dinner: "You might have let me know before!" And how he had answered: "Can't you possibly speak to me without offending against even good manners?" It was incredible, he thought, that she cared so little for him—incredible that she wasn't interested in the slightest in his triumphs and his artistic career. When so many women in her place would have given their eyes. . . . Yes, he knew it. . . . Why not acknowledge it? . . . And there she lay, an enemy, even in her sleep. . . . Must it ever be thus? he thought, the champagne still working. Ah, if we only were friends, how much I could tell her now! About this evening; even about Timbuck's manner to me, and all that they said to me and so on and so on. If only I felt that she was here to come back to—that I could confide in her—and so on and so on.

In his emotion he pulled off his evening boot and simply hurled it in the corner. The noise woke his wife with a terrible start. She sat up, pushing back her hair. And he suddenly decided to have one more try to treat her as a friend, to tell her everything, to win her. Down he sat on the side of the bed, and seized one of her hands. But of all those splendid things he had to say, not one could he utter. For some fiendish reason, the only words he could get out were: "Dear lady, I should be so charmed—so charmed!"

THE KING'S FAVOR

Stephen Crane
1871-1900

Stephen Crane's precocious talent produced two great novels: *Maggie: A Girl of the Streets* (1893) and, to be sure, *The Red Badge of Courage* (1894). Crane also penned some of America's classic and familiar short stories, including "The Open Boat," "The Bride Comes to Yellow Sky," and "The Blue Hotel." How remarkable for a writer who lived only twenty-nine years! "The King's Favor" (1891) is the amusing story of a male singer and a black African King.

The lives of all musicians do not glide on in a quiet flow of melody and unpaid music bills. It is popularly supposed that a musician is a long-haired individual who does nothing more exciting than fall in love with his loveliest pupil, dine on mutton chops and misery all his life; and finally become famous as a composer, after the name on his tombstone has been nearly obliterated by the moss and mould of years.

Mr. Albert G. Thies, a prominent New York tenor, proves by his history that such is not always the case. He has had adventures in many strange lands. The crowned heads of Europe and the furred backs of Africa have both taken a hand in chasing him from their dominions; the first, as an alleged political conspirator; the second, as a choice morsel of diet. He has sung before crowned heads and before heads in dilapidated old hats; before the gilded, tasseled boots of the German hussar and the ponderous, wooden sabots of the Hollandese peasant. In fact, he has had as varied an existence as a soldier of fortune. The frozen ice-fields of the North have made him cold and the scorched sands of the desert have made iced lemonade an absolute necessity.

About four years ago, Mr. Thies was giving a series of evenings of song in the principal cities of the British colonies in South Africa. In the height of a successful season, he was told that old King Cetewayo, the famous Zulu chief, had sent a request for a private musicale. The king was then a prisoner in the hands of the British. His dark-skinned *impis* had gone down, the red and purple of the waving plumes had fallen beneath the Enfield rifles of the scarlet-coated visitors from the sea. Cetewayo's captors did all in their power to make his captivity as comfortable as possible. He, with his wives, occupied a large and commodious farm-house, and was dealt out liberal allowances of provisions and supplies by the government. They even possessed a piano though, of course, it was of no use except as a means of recreation and wholesome amusement to the fair Mursala, one of the king's wives. She was very muscular; she was six-feet-two-inches high; and she played the piano by main strength. The hand-organ grinders of America, playing different tunes in chorus, would have felt insignificant if they could have listened to Mrs. Cetewayo. Her mode of amusement caused some discomfort in the family circle. If the three others had shown a like propensity for contrasting their dark fingers with the ivory keys, I fear there would have been direful murder done in that household. But the king had paid sixteen cows for Mursala, so she was a valuable piece of property; she had an intrinsic worth; a face value, although the last would never be noted except by a Zulu in an advanced stage of barbarism. And she must be allowed to disturb the entire vicinity without reproach, or she might take herself off to the dim recesses of her native jungle; and her dark fingers never more mingle in the wool of her imperial lord and master; and he be at a dead loss in cows.

Mr. Thies, accompanied by an English friend and a Hottentot interpreter, appeared before the king. Cetewayo sat on the floor, in front of his four wives. He arose and received the singer with gracious dignity. After they had exchanged the usual compliments, through the interpreter, Mr. Thies went to the piano. Mursala had caused sad havoc in the instrument, but the singer did not allow that to disconcert him. He sang numbers of songs. He did not choose highly classical music, but sang the simple English ballads and American popular songs. The interpreter explained the words of each number after it was rendered. The king was delighted. He demanded to hear some of the pieces over and over again.

For the last of the programme Mr. Thies chose an inspiring war song. There was no need of an interpreter then; the king recognized at once the sounds of battle, the clatter and din of war, and the cries of victory.

His eye, grown sullen and down-cast from years of captivity, again flashed, and his chest heaved. He was again a great chief, leading his hundreds of brown-bodied warriors, snake-like through the rustling grass to where the red coats and bayonets of the stolid, calm Britons glimmered and shone in the sunlight. He heard the swift rush of hundreds of naked feet, as his warriors swept down on the immovable British square, and writhed and twisted about it like a monstrous serpent. He heard the low muttered war-chant of his followers, sounding to his enemies in the distance as the most ominous and dreadful of forebodings; the great, wild cry of battle as his swarthy demons dyed their spears in the white man's blood; the yells and curses of the Britons as they went down, blanched and pale and bloody, to death. He saw the ghastly faces and gory bodies of his enemies lie thick amongst the brown grass.

When the music ceased, he drew a long deep breath. He associated closely the singer, his own thoughts of battle, and the music.

He stood up and extended his royal hand. "Thou art a great warrior, oh, son of a wise father. Come with me, and we two will drive these English dogs into the sea."

Mr. Thies modestly declined to drive his half of several millions of people into anything.

The king was surprised that a great warrior who could stir people's hearts in such a manner would not accept the partnership. He thought he could get his people to rise once more for one great final struggle could they but hear the inspiring voice of this mighty warrior from an unknown land, whose warriors had defeated the red-coats in many battles. But he did not allow his disappointment to affect his attitude toward his guest. The musician stood high in the king's favor.

Suddenly a thought struck his imperial majesty. He would confer upon the great stranger the highest honor known to his race.

"Hearken, oh warrior, son of many warriors, the fallen king loves you," said Cetewayo, waving his hand graciously, "I, even I, king of the Zulus. And it becomes a great king to give honor to his friend, aye, even to as much as twenty cows. Then, oh great stranger, take Mursala, my wife, to be your wife, to follow you to the land of the setting sun and keep your hut and tend your cows until she die."

When the interpreter put the king's kindness and condescension into English, a solemn hush fell upon the two white men. The king and his four wives gazed expectantly.

The silence was horrible. Mr. Thies moved his feet restlessly and felt very uncomfortable. The Englishman, with his head down, laughed in an insane manner.

The king detected the giggle. He stood up and glanced fiercely at them. Was this the way to treat the gift of a monarch? His brow grew dark. He was a prisoner but he looked formidable. Standing six-feet-four-inches high, his massive shoulders and long, sinewy arms showed him to be indeed the king who had led his people in so many desperate battles. The two friends felt that it was an evil hour for them. They turned to the interpreter and implored him, by all he held sacred, to smooth the thing over some way and let them escape the royal displeasure. They begged him to make it known to Cetewayo that an American gentleman's views on connubial bliss were a little queer and old-fashioned, and differed from the prevailing modes of the jungle *elite*. Mr. Thies urged him to thank the monarch heartily and say that it would be Mr. Thies' pleasure to send a red and white sun-umbrella and a toy pistol to the king, from Capetown, the moment of his arrival there. The

Englishman expressed his great desire to forward a pair of suspenders and an opera-glass by the first Hottentot express. The king could not be propitiated by these munificent offers. He smiled faintly. The two friends saw their advantage and followed it up with the promise of a jack-knife and a bottle of red ink. The great monarch smiled decidedly and irrevocably. When Mr. Thies heaped on, so to speak, a pack of cards and a silk handkerchief, the Englishman responding with a dozen clay pipes and a banjo, his imperial majesty became gleeful. They commenced to feel safe. The king grew cheerful and pleasant. His conversation became as courtly and affable as it had been in the first part of the interview. They considered it a good time to retreat and so made their adieus. The king seemed very sorry to have Mr. Thies leave. He inquired anxiously if he could not be counted on to change his mind about the insurrection scheme. Mr. Thies, however, assured him that no considerations could induce him to devote his talents to the extermination of the whites of Africa. So the old king bowed his head as if his last hope of revenge was taken from him, and reluctantly bade adieu. The two whites backed out the door. The last sight of Cetewayo was as he sat calm and immovable, with his stern old face set with the rigidity of a bronze cast, only the eyes seeming to say that his hope of being once more the ruler of a nation was gone forever.

When they reached open air, Mr. Thies heaved a sigh which is said to have shaken the more tender of the young sprouts on certain of the banyan trees, adjacent to him. Mursala, mayhap, pressed her face against the pane, and bade a sad farewell as the horses clattered down the road.

Mr. Thies always speaks of this adventure as the narrowest escape of his life. Daniel, mingling in a social way with the denizens of the den, could never have experienced the sensations that the singer did, as he stood before the king and felt, somehow, that he must refuse the royal gift.

Mr. Thies returned to America safely and was very glad to put several thousand miles of water between him and the lovely Zulu. He has resolved upon a course of action when called to sing before savage kings. He will send a little circular with a blank to be filled in. The questions will be something as follows: 1—"Are you married?" 2—"How many?" 3—"Have you a natural affection for your wives?" 4—"Could any offer induce you to part with one?"

These questions being answered satisfactorily, Mr. Thies feels that he can trust himself.

A DEATH IN THE DESERT

Willa Cather
1873-1947

Willa Cather's short stories about musicians would in themselves fill a substantial volume. Cather became especially interested in music after her college years when, living in Pittsburgh, she made friends with a newspaper music critic. "A Death in the Desert" is from *The Troll Garden* (1905), her first successful book.

Everett Hilgarde was conscious that the man in the seat across the aisle was looking at him intently. He was a large, florid man, wore a conspicuous diamond solitaire upon his third finger, and Everett judged him to be a traveling salesman of some sort. He had the air of an adaptable fellow who had been about the world and who could keep cool and clean under almost any circumstances.

The "High Line Flyer," as this train was derisively called among railroad men, was jerking along through the hot afternoon over the monotonous country between Holdridge and Cheyenne. Besides the blond man and himself the only occupants of the car were two dusty, bedraggled-looking girls who had been to the Exposition at Chicago, and who were earnestly discussing the cost of their first trip out of Colorado. The four uncomfortable passengers were covered with a sediment of fine, yellow dust which clung to their hair and eyebrows like gold powder. It blew up in clouds from the bleak, lifeless country through which they passed, until they were one color with the sagebrush and sandhills. The gray-and-yellow desert was varied only by occasional ruins of deserted towns, and the little red boxes of station houses, where the spindling trees and sickly vines in the blue-grass yards made little green reserves fenced off in that confusing wilderness of sand.

As the slanting rays of the sun beat in stronger and stronger through the car windows, the blond gentleman asked the ladies' permission to remove his coat, and sat in his lavender striped shirt sleeves, with a black silk handkerchief tucked carefully about his collar. He had seemed interested in Everett since they had boarded the train at Holdridge, and kept glancing at him curiously and then looking reflectively out of the window, as though he were trying to recall something. But wherever Everett went someone was almost sure to look at him with that curious interest, and it had ceased to embarrass or annoy him. Presently the stranger, seeming satisfied with his observation, leaned back in his seat, half-closed his eyes, and began softly to whistle the "Spring Song" from *Proserpine*, the cantata that a dozen years before had made its young composer famous in a night. Everett had heard that air on guitars in Old Mexico, on mandolins at college glees, on cottage organs in New

122

England hamlets, and only two weeks ago he had heard it played on sleighbells at a variety theater in Denver. There was literally no way of escaping his brother's precocity. Adriance could live on the other side of the Atlantic, where his youthful indiscretions were forgotten in his mature achievements, but his brother had never been able to outrun *Proserpine*, and here he found it again in the Colorado sand hills. Not that Everett was exactly ashamed of *Proserpine*: only a man of genius could have written it, but it was the sort of thing that a man of genius outgrows as soon as he can.

Everett unbent a trifle and smiled at his neighbor across the aisle. Immediately the large man rose and, coming over, dropped into the seat facing Hilgarde, extending his card.

"Dusty ride, isn't it? I don't mind it myself; I'm used to it. Born and bred in de briar patch, like Br'er Rabbit. I've been trying to place you for a long time; I think I must have met you before."

"Thank you," said Everett, taking the card; "my name is Hilgarde. You've probably met my brother, Adriance; people often mistake me for him."

The traveling man brought his hand down upon his knee with such vehemence that the solitaire blazed.

"So I was right after all, and if you're not Adriance Hilgarde, you're his double. I thought I couldn't be mistaken. Seen him? Well, I guess! I never missed one of his recitals at the Auditorium, and he played the piano score of *Proserpine* through to us once at the Chicago Press Club. I used to be on the *Commercial* there before I began to travel for the publishing department of the concern. So you're Hilgarde's brother, and here I've run into you at the jumping-off place. Sounds like a newspaper yarn, doesn't it?"

The traveling man laughed and offered Everett a cigar, and plied him with questions on the only subject that people ever seemed to care to talk to Everett about. At length the salesman and the two girls alighted at a Colorado way station, and Everett went on to Cheyenne alone.

The train pulled into Cheyenne at nine o'clock, late by a matter of four hours or so; but no one seemed particularly concerned at its tardiness except the station agent, who grumbled at being kept in the office overtime on a summer night. When Everett alighted from the train he walked down the platform and stopped at the track crossing, uncertain as to what direction he should take to reach a hotel. A phaeton stood near the crossing, and a woman held the reins. She was dressed in white, and her figure was clearly silhouetted against the cushions, though it was too dark to see her face.

Everett had scarcely noticed her, when the switch engine came puffing up from the opposite direction, and the headlight threw a strong glare of light on his face. Suddenly the woman in the phaeton uttered a low cry and dropped the reins. Everett started forward and caught the horse's head, but the animal only lifted its ears and whisked its tail in impatient surprise. The woman sat perfectly still, her head sunk betweeen her shoulders and her handkerchief pressed to her face. Another woman came out of the depot and hurried toward the phaeton, crying, "Katharine, dear, what is the matter?"

Everett hesitated a moment in painful embarrassment, then lifted his hat and passed on. He was accustomed to sudden recognitions in the most impossible places, especially by women, but this cry out of the night had shaken him.

While Everett was breakfasting the next morning, the headwaiter leaned over his chair to murmur that there was a gentleman waiting to see him in the parlor. Everett finished his coffee and went in the direction indicated, where he found his visitor restlessly pacing the floor. His whole manner betrayed a high degree of agitation, though his physique was not that of a man whose nerves lie near the surface. He was something below medium height, square-shouldered and solidly built. His thick, closely cut hair was beginning to show gray about the ears, and his bronzed face was heavily lined. His square brown hands were locked behind him, and he held his shoulders like a man conscious of responsibilities; yet, as he turned to greet Everett, there was an incongruous diffidence in his address.

"Good morning, Mr. Hilgarde," he said, extending his hand; "I found your name on the hotel register. My name is Gaylord. I'm afraid my sister startled you at the station last night, Mr. Hilgarde, and I've come around to apologize."

"Ah! The young lady in the phaeton? I'm sure I didn't know whether I had anything to do with her alarm or not. If I did, it is I who owe the apology."

The man colored a little under the dark brown of his face.

"Oh, it's nothing you could help, sir. I fully understand that. You see, my sister used to be a pupil of your brother's, and it seems you favor him; and when the switch engine threw a light on your face it startled her."

Everett wheeled about in his chair. "Oh! *Katharine* Gaylord! Is it possible! Now it's you who have given me a turn. Why, I used to know her when I was a boy. What on earth—"

"Is she doing here?" said Gaylord, grimly filling out the pause.

"You've got at the heart of the matter. You knew my sister had been in bad health for a long time?"

"No, I had never heard a word of that. The last I knew of her she was singing in London. My brother and I correspond infrequently and seldom get beyond family matters. I am deeply sorry to hear this. There are more reasons why I am concerned than I can tell you."

The lines in Charley Gaylord's brow relaxed a little.

"What I'm trying to say, Mr. Hilgarde, is that she wants to see you. I hate to ask you, but she's so set on it. We live several miles out of town, but my rig's below, and I can take you out anytime you can go."

"I can go now, and it will give me real pleasure to do so," said Everett, quickly. "I'll get my hat and be with you in a moment."

When he came downstairs Everett found a cart at the door, and Charley Gaylord drew a long sigh of relief as he gathered up the reins and settled back into his own element.

"You see, I think I'd better tell you something about my sister before you see her, and I don't know just where to begin. She traveled in Europe with your brother and his wife, and sang at a lot of his concerts; but I don't know just how much you know about her."

"Very little, except that my brother always thought her the most gifted of his pupils, and that when I knew her she was very young and very beautiful and turned my head sadly for a while."

Everett saw that Gaylord's mind was quite engrossed by his grief. He was wrought up to the point where his reserve and sense of proportion had quite left him, and his trouble was the one vital thing in the world. "That's the whole thing," he went on, flicking his horses with the whip.

"She was a great woman, as you say, and she didn't come of a great family. She had to fight her own way from the first. She got to Chicago, and then to New York, and then to Europe, where she went up like lightning, and got a taste for it all; and now she's dying here like a rat in a hole, out of her own world, and she can't fall back into ours. We've grown apart, some way—miles and miles apart—and I'm afraid she's fearfully unhappy."

"It's a very tragic story that you are telling me, Gaylord," said Everett. They were well out into the country now, spinning along over the dusty plains of red grass, with the ragged-blue outline of the mountains before them.

"Tragic!" cried Gaylord, starting up in his seat, "my God, man, nobody will ever know how tragic. It's a tragedy I live with and eat with and sleep with, until I've lost my grip on everything. You see she had made a good bit of money, but she spent it all going to health resorts. It's her lungs, you know. I've got money enough to send her anywhere, but the doctors all say it's no use. She hasn't the ghost of a chance. It's just getting through the days now. I had no notion she was half so bad before she came to me. She just wrote that she was all run down. Now that she's here. I think she'd be happier anywhere under the sun, but she won't leave. She says it's easier to let go of life here, and that to go East would be dying twice. There was a time when I was a brakeman with a run out of Bird City, Iowa, and she was a little thing I could carry on my shoulder, when I could get her everything on earth she wanted, and she hadn't a wish my $80 a month didn't cover; and now, when I've got a little property together, I can't buy her a night's sleep!"

Everett saw that, whatever Charley Gaylord's present status in the world might be, he had brought the brakeman's heart up the ladder with him, and the brakeman's frank avowal of sentiment. Presently Gaylord went on:

"You can understand how she has outgrown her family. We're all a pretty common sort, railroaders from away back. My father was a conductor. He died when we were kids. Maggie, my other sister, who lives with me, was a telegraph operator here while I was getting my grip on things. We had no education to speak of. I have to hire a stenographer because I can't spell straight—the Almighty couldn't teach me to spell. The things that make up life to Kate are all Greek to me, and there's scarcely a point where we touch any more, except in our recollections of the old times when we were all young and happy together, and Kate sang in a church choir in Bird City. But I believe, Mr. Hilgarde, that if she can see just one person like you, who knows about the things and people she's interested in, it will give her about the only comfort she can have now."

The reins slackened in Charley Gaylord's hand as they drew up before a showily painted house with many gables and a round tower. "Here we are," he said, turning to Everett, "and I guess we understand each other."

They were met at the door by a thin, colorless woman, whom Gaylord introduced as "my sister, Maggie." She asked her brother to show Mr. Hilgarde into the music room, where Katharine wished to see him alone.

When Everett entered the music room he gave a little start of surprise, feeling that he had stepped from the glaring Wyoming sunlight into some New York studio that he had always known. He wondered which it was of those countless studios, high up under the roofs, over banks and shops and wholesale houses, that this room resembled, and he looked incredulously out of the window at the gray plain that ended in the great upheaval of the Rockies.

The haunting air of familiarity about the room perplexed him. Was it a copy of some particular studio he knew, or was it merely the studio atmosphere that seemed so individual and poignantly reminiscent here in Wyoming? He sat down in a reading chair and looked keenly about him. Suddenly his eye fell upon a large photograph of his brother above the piano. Then it all became clear to him: this was veritably his brother's room. If it were not an exact copy of one of the many studios that Adriance had fitted up in various parts of the world, wearying of them and leaving almost before the renovator's varnish had dried, it was at least in the same tone. In every detail Adriance's taste was so manifest that the room seemed to exhale his personality.

Among the photographs on the wall there was one of Katharine Gaylord, taken in the days when Everett had known her, and when the flash of her eye or the flutter of her skirt was enough to set his boyish heart in a tumult. Even now he stood before the portrait with a certain degree of embarrassment. It was the face of a woman already old in her first youth, thoroughly sophisticated and a trifle hard, and it told of what her brother had called her fight. The camaraderie of her frank, confident eyes was qualified by the deep lines about her mouth and the curve of the lips, which was both sad and cynical. Certainly she had more good will than confidence toward the world, and the bravado of her smile could not conceal the shadow of an unrest that was almost discontent. The chief charm of the woman, as Everett had known her, lay in her superb figure and in her eyes, which possessed a warm, life-giving quality like the sunlight; eyes which glowed with a sort of perpetual *salutat* to the world. Her head, Everett remembered as peculiarly well-shaped and proudly poised. There had been always a little of the imperatrix about her, and her pose in the photograph revived all his old impressions of her unattachedness, of how absolutely and valiantly she stood alone.

Everett was still standing before the picture, his hands behind him and his head inclined, when he heard the door open. A very tall woman advanced toward him, holding out her hand. As she started to speak, she coughed slightly; then, laughing, said, in a low, rich voice, a trifle husky: "You see I make the traditional Camille entrance—with the cough. How good of you to come, Mr. Hilgarde."

Everett was acutely conscious that while addressing him she was not looking at him at all, and, as he assured her of his pleasure in coming, he was glad to have an opportunity to collect himself. He had not reckoned upon the ravages of a long illness. The long, loose folds of her white gown had been especially designed to conceal the sharp outlines of her emaciated body, but the stamp of her disease was there; simple and ugly and obtrusive, a pitiless fact that could not be disguised or evaded. The splendid shoulders were stooped, there was a swaying unevenness in her gait, her arms seemed disproportionately long, and her hands were transparently white and cold to the touch. The changes in her face were less obvious; the proud carriage of the head, the warm, clear eyes, even the delicate flush of color in her cheeks, all defiantly remained, though they were all in a lower key—older, sadder, softer.

She sat down upon the divan and began nervously to arrange the pillows. "I know I'm not an inspiring object to look upon, but you must be quite frank and sensible about that and get used to it at once, for we've no time to lose. And if I'm a trifle irritable you won't mind?—for I'm more than usually nervous."

"Don't bother with me this morning, if you are tired," urged Everett. "I can come quite as well tomorrow."

"Gracious, no!" she protested, with a flash of that quick, keen humor that he remembered as a part of her. "It's solitude that I'm tired to death of—solitude and the wrong kind of people. You see, the minister, not content with reading the prayers for the sick, called on me this morning. He happened to be riding by on his bicycle and felt it his duty to stop. Of course, he disapproves of my profession, and I think he takes it for granted that I have a dark past. The funniest feature of his conversation is that he is always excusing my own vocation to me—condoning it, you know—and trying to patch up my peace with my conscience by suggesting possible noble uses for what he kindly calls my talent."

Everett laughed. "Oh! I'm afraid I'm not the person to call after such a serious gentleman—I can't sustain the situation. At my best I don't reach higher than low comedy. Have you decided to which one of the noble uses you will devote yourself?"

Katharine lifted her hands in a gesture of renunciation and exclaimed: "I'm not equal to any of them, not even the least noble. I didn't study that method."

She laughed and went on nervously: "The parson's not so bad. His English never offends me, and he has read Gibbon's *Decline and Fall*, all five volumes, and that's something. Then, he has been to New York, and that's a great deal. But how we are losing time! Do tell me about New York; Charley says you're just on from there. How does it look and taste and smell just now? I think a whiff of the Jersey ferry would be as flagons of cod-liver oil to me. Who conspicuously walks the Rialto now, and what does he or she wear? Are the trees still green in Madison Square, or have they grown brown and dusty? Does the chaste Diana on the Garden Theatre still keep her vestal vows through all the exasperating changes of weather? Who has your brother's old studio now, and what misguided aspirants practice their scales in the rookeries about Carnegie Hall? What do people go to see at the theaters, and what do they eat and drink there in the world nowadays? You see, I'm homesick for it all, from the Battery to Riverside. Oh, let me die in Harlem!" She was interrupted by a violent attack of coughing, and Everett, embarrassed by her discomfort, plunged into gossip about the professional people he had met in town during the summer and the musical outlook for the winter. He was diagraming with his pencil, on the back of an old envelope he found in his pocket, some new mechanical device to be used at the Metropolitan in the production of the *Rheingold*, when he became conscious that she was looking at him intently, and that he was talking to the four walls.

Katharine was lying back among the pillows, watching him through half-closed eyes, as a painter looks at a picture. He finished his explanation vaguely enough and put the envelope back in his pocket. As he did so she said, quietly: "How wonderfully like Adriance you are!" and he felt as though a crisis of some sort had been met and tided over.

He laughed, looking up at her with a touch of pride in his eyes that made them seem quite boyish. "Yes, isn't it absurd? It's almost as awkward as looking like Napoleon—but, after all, there are some advantages. It has made some of his friends like me, and I hope it will make you."

Katharine smiled and gave him a quick, meaning glance from under her lashes. "Oh, it did that long ago. What a haughty, reserved youth you were then, and how you used to stare at people and then blush and look cross if they paid you back in your own coin. Do you remember that night when you took me home from a rehearsal and scarcely spoke a word to me?"

"It was the silence of admiration," protested Everett, "very crude and boyish, but very sincere and not a little painful. Perhaps you suspected something of the sort? I remember you saw fit to be very grown-up and worldly."

"I believe I suspected a pose; the one that college boys usually affect with singers—'an earthen vessel in love with a star,' you know. But it rather surprised me in you, for you must have seen a good deal of your brother's pupils. Or had you an omnivorous capacity, and elasticity that always met the occasion?"

"Don't ask a man to confess the follies of his youth," said Everett, smiling a little sadly: "I am sensitive about some of them even now. But I was not so sophisticated as you imagined. I saw my brother's pupils come and go, but that was about all. Sometimes I was called on to play accompaniments, or to fill out a vacancy at a rehearsal, or to order a carriage for an infuriated soprano who had thrown up her part. But they never spent any time on me, unless it was to notice the resemblance you speak of."

"Yes," observed Katharine, thoughtfully, "I noticed it then, too; but it has grown as you have grown older. That is rather strange, when you have lived such different lives. It's not merely an ordinary family likeness of feature, you know, but a sort of interchangeable individuality; the suggestion of the other man's personality in your face—like an air transposed to another key. But I'm not attempting to define it; it's beyond me; something altogether unusual and a trifle—well, uncanny," she finished, laughing.

"I remember," Everett said seriously, twirling the pencil between his fingers and looking, as he sat with his head thrown back, out under the red window blind which was raised just a little, and as it swung back and forth in the wind revealed the glaring panorama of the desert—a blinding stretch of yellow, flat as the sea in dead calm, splotched here and there with deep purple shadows; and, beyond, the ragged-blue outline of the mountains and the peaks of snow, white as the white clouds—"I remember, when I was a little fellow I used to be very sensitive about it. I don't think it exactly displeased me, or that I would have had it otherwise if I could, but it seemed to me like a birthmark, or something not to be lightly spoken of. People were naturally always fonder of Ad than of me, and I used to feel the chill of reflected light pretty often. It came into even my relations with my mother. Ad went abroad to study when he was absurdly young, you know, and mother was all broken

130

up over it. She did her whole duty by each of us, but it was sort of generally understood among us that she'd have made burnt offerings of us all for Ad any day. I was a little fellow then, and when she sat alone on the porch in the summer dusk she used sometimes to call me to her and turn my face up in the light that streamed out through the shutters and kiss me, and then I always knew she was thinking of Adriance."

"Poor little chap," said Katharine, and her tone was a trifle huskier than usual. "How fond people have always been of Adriance! Now tell me the latest news of him. I haven't heard, except through the press, for a year or more. He was in Algeria then, in the valley of the Chelif, riding horseback night and day in an Arabian costume, and in his usual enthusiastic fashion he had quite made up his mind to adopt the Mohammedan faith and become as nearly an Arab as possible. How many countries and faiths has he adopted, I wonder? Probably he was playing Arab to himself all the time. I remember he was a sixteenth-century duke in Florence once for weeks together."

"Oh, that's Adriance," chuckled Everett. "He is himself barely long enough to write checks and be measured for his clothes. I didn't hear from him while he was an Arab; I missed that."

"He was writing an Algerian suite for the piano then; it must be in the publisher's hands by this time. I have been too ill to answer his letter, and have lost touch with him."

Everett drew a letter from his pocket. "This came about a month ago. It's chiefly about his new opera, which is to be brought out in London next winter. Read it at your leisure."

"I think I shall keep it as a hostage, so that I may be sure you will come again. Now I want you to play for me. Whatever you like; but if there is anything new in the world, in mercy let me hear it. For nine months I have heard nothing but 'The Baggage Coach Ahead' and 'She Is My Baby's Mother.' "

He sat down at the piano, and Katharine sat near him, absorbed in his remarkable physical likeness to his brother and trying to discover in just what it consisted. She told herself that it was very much as though a sculptor's finished work had been rudely copied in wood. He was of a larger build than Adriance, and his shoulders were broad and heavy, while those of his brother were slender and rather girlish. His face was of the same oval mold, but it was gray and darkened about the mouth by continual shaving. His eyes were of the same inconstant April color, but they were reflective and rather dull; while Adriance's were always points of highlight, and always meaning another thing than the thing they meant yesterday. But it was hard to see why this earnest man should so continually suggest that lyric, youthful face that was as gay as his was grave. For Adriance, though he was ten years the elder, and though his hair was streaked with silver, had the face of a boy of twenty, so mobile that it told his thoughts before he could put them into words. A contralto, famous for the extravagance of her vocal methods and of her affections, had once said to him that the shepherd boys who sang in the Vale of Tempe must certainly have looked like young Hilgarde; and the comparison had been appropriated by a hundred shyer women who preferred to quote.

As Everett sat smoking on the veranda of the Inter-Ocean House that night, he was a victim to random recollections. His infatuation for Katharine Gaylord, visionary as it was, had been the most serious of his boyish love affairs, and long disturbed his bachelor dreams. He was painfully timid in everything relating to the emotions, and his hurt had withdrawn him from the society of women. The fact that it was all so done and dead and far behind him, and that the woman had lived her life out since then, gave him an oppressive sense of age and loss. He bethought himself of something he had read about "sitting by the hearth and remembering the faces of women without desire," and felt himself an octogenarian.

He remembered how bitter and morose he had grown during his stay at his brother's studio when Katharine Gaylord was working there, and how he had wounded Adriance on the night of his last concert in New York. He had sat there in the box while his brother and Katharine were called back again and again after the last number, watching the roses go up over the footlights until they were stacked half as high as the piano, brooding, in his sullen boy's heart, upon the pride those two felt in each other's work—spurring each other to their best and beautifully contending in song. The footlights had seemed a hard, glittering line drawn sharply between their life and his; a circle of flame set about those splendid children of genius. He walked back to his hotel alone and sat in his window staring out on Madison Square until long after midnight, resolving to beat no more at doors that he could never enter and realizing more keenly than ever before how far this glorious world of beautiful creations lay from the paths of men like himself. He told himself that he had in common with this woman only the baser uses of life.

Everett's week in Cheyenne stretched to three, and he saw no prospect of release except through the thing he dreaded. The bright, windy days of the Wyoming autumn passed swiftly. Letters and telegrams came urging him to hasten his trip to the coast, but he resolutely postponed his business engagements. The mornings he spent on one of Charley Gaylord's ponies, or fishing in the mountains, and in the evenings he sat in his room writing letters or reading. In the afternoon he was usually at his post of duty. Destiny, he reflected, seems to have very positive notions about the sort of parts we are fitted to play. The scene changes and the compensation varies, but in the end we usually find that we have played the same class of business from first to last. Everett had been a stopgap all his life. He remembered going through a looking glass labyrinth when he was a boy and trying gallery after gallery, only at every turn to bump his nose against his own face—which, indeed, was not his own, but his brother's. No matter what his mission, east or west, by land or sea, he was sure to find himself employed in his brother's business, one of the tributary lives which helped to swell the shining current of Adriance Hilgarde's. It was not the first time that his duty had been to comfort, as best he could, one of the broken things his brother's imperious speed had cast aside and forgotten. He made no attempt to analyze the situation or to state it in exact terms; but he felt Katharine Gaylord's need for him, and he accepted it as a commission from his brother to help this woman to die. Day by day he felt her demands on him grow more imperious, her need for him grow more acute and positive; and day by day he felt that in his peculiar relation to her his own individuality played a smaller and smaller part. His power to minister to her comfort, he saw, lay solely in his link with his brother's life. He understood all that his physical resemblance meant to her. He knew that she sat by him always watching for some common trick of gesture, some familiar play of expression, some illusion of light and shadow, in which he should seem wholly Adriance. He knew that she lived upon this and that her disease fed upon it; that it sent shudders of remembrance through her and that in the exhaustion which followed this turmoil of her dying senses, she slept deep and sweet and dreamed of youth and art and days in a certain old Florentine garden, and not of bitterness and death.

The question which most perplexed him was, "How much shall I know? How much does she wish me to know?" A few days after his first meeting with Katharine Gaylord, he had cabled his brother to write her. He had merely said that she was mortally ill; he could depend on Adriance to say the right thing—that was a part of his gift. Adriance always said not only the right thing, but the opportune, graceful, exquisite thing. His phrases took the color of the moment and the then-present condition, so that they never savored of perfunctory compliment or frequent usage. He always caught the lyric essence of the moment, the poetic suggestion of every situation. Moreover, he usually did the right thing, the opportune, graceful, exquisite thing—except, when he did very cruel things—bent upon making people happy when their existence touched his, just as he insisted that his material environment should be beautiful; lavishing upon those near him all the warmth and radiance of his rich nature, all the homage of the poet and troubadour, and, when they were no longer near, forgetting—for that also was a part of Adriance's gift.

Three weeks after Everett had sent his cable, when he made his daily call at the gaily painted ranch house, he found Katharine laughing like a schoolgirl. "Have you ever thought," she said, as he entered the music room, "how much these seances of ours are like Heine's 'Florentine Nights,' except that I don't give you an opportunity to monopolize the conversation as Heine did?" She held his hand longer than usual, as she greeted him, and looked searchingly up into his face. "You are the kindest man living; the kindest," she added, softly.

Everett's gray face colored faintly as he drew his hand away, for he felt that this time she was looking at him and not at a whimsical caricature of his brother. "Why, what have I done now?" he asked, lamely. "I can't remember having sent you any stale candy or champagne since yesterday."

She drew a letter with a foreign postmark from between the leaves of a book and held it out, smiling. "You got him to write it. Don't say you didn't, for it came direct, you see, and the last address I gave him was a place in Florida. This deed shall be remembered of you when I am with the just in Paradise. But one thing you did not ask him to do, for you didn't know about it. He has sent me his latest work, the new sonata, the most ambitious thing he has ever done, and you are to play it for me directly, though it looks horribly intricate. But first for the letter; I think you would better read it aloud to me."

Everett sat down in a low chair facing the window seat in which she reclined with a barricade of pillows behind her. He opened the letter, his lashes half-veiling his kind eyes, and saw to his satisfaction that it was a long one—wonderfully tactful and tender, even for Adriance, who was tender with his valet and his stable boy, with his old gondolier and the beggar-women who prayed to the saints for him.

134

The letter was from Granada, written in the Alhambra, as he sat by the fountain of the Patio di Lindaraxa. The air was heavy with the warm fragrance of the South and full of the sound of splashing, running water, as it had been in a certain old garden in Florence, long ago. The sky was one great turquoise, heated until it glowed. The wonderful Moorish arches threw graceful blue shadows all about him. He had sketched an outline of them on the margin of his notepaper. The subtleties of Arabic decoration had cast an unholy spell over him, and the brutal exaggerations of Gothic art were a bad dream, easily forgotten. The Alhambra itself had, from the first, seemed perfectly familiar to him, and he knew that he must have trod that court, sleek and brown and obsequious, centuries before Ferdinand rode into Andalusia. The letter was full of confidences about his work, and delicate allusions to their old happy days of study and comradeship, and of her own work, still so warmly remembered and appreciatively discussed everywhere he went.

As Everett folded the letter he felt that Adriance had divined the thing needed and had risen to it in his own wonderful way. The letter was consistently egotistical and seemed to him even a trifle patronizing, yet it was just what she had wanted. A strong realization of his brother's charm and intensity and power came over him; he felt the breath of that whirlwind of flame in which Adriance passed, consuming all in his path, and himself even more resolutely than he consumed others. Then he looked down at this white, burnt-out brand that lay before him. "Like him, isn't it?" she said, quietly.

"I think I can scarcely answer his letter, but when you see him next you can do that for me. I want you to tell him many things for me, yet they can all be summed up in this: I want him to grow wholly into his best and greatest self, even at the cost of the dear boyishness that is half his charm to you and me. Do you understand me?"

"I know perfectly well what you mean," answered Everett, thoughtfully. "I have often felt so about him myself. And yet it's difficult to prescribe for those fellows; so little makes, so little mars."

Katharine raised herself upon her elbow, and her face flushed with feverish earnestness. "Ah, but it is the waste of himself that I mean; his lashing himself out on stupid and uncomprehending people until they take him at their own estimate. He can kindle marble, strike fire from putty, but is it worth what it costs him?"

"Come, come," expostulated Everett, alarmed at her excitement. "Where is the new sonata? Let him speak for himself."

He sat down at the piano and began playing the first movement, which was indeed the voice of Adriance, his proper speech. The sonata was the most ambitious work he had done up to that time and marked the transition from his purely lyric vein to a deeper and nobler style. Everett played intelligently and with that sympathetic comprehension which seems peculiar to a certain lovable class of men who never accomplish anything in particular. When he had finished he turned to Katharine.

"How he has grown!" she cried. "What the three last years have done for him! He used to write only the tragedies of passion; but this is the tragedy of the soul, the shadow coexistent with the soul. This is the tragedy of effort and failure, the thing Keats called hell. This is my tragedy, as I lie here spent by the racecourse, listening to the feet of the runners as they pass me. Ah, God! The swift feet of the runners!"

She turned her face away and covered it with her straining hands. Everett crossed over to her quickly and knelt beside her. In all the days he had known her she had never before, beyond an occasional ironical jest, given voice to the bitterness of her own defeat. Her courage had become a point of pride with him, and to see it going sickened him.

"Don't do it," he gasped. "I can't stand it. I really can't, I feel it too much. We mustn't speak of that; it's too tragic and too vast."

When she turned her face back to him there was a ghost of the old, brave, cynical smile on it, more bitter than the tears she could not shed. "No, I won't be so ungenerous; I will save that for the watches of the night when I have no better company. Now you may mix me another drink of some sort. Formerly, when it was not *if* I should ever sing Brunnhilde, but quite simply when I *should* sing Brunnhilde, I was always starving myself and thinking what I might drink and what I might not. But broken music boxes may drink whatsoever they list, and no one cares whether they lose their figure. Run over that theme at the beginning again. That, at least, is not new. It was running in his head when we were in Venice years ago, and he used to drum it on his glass at the dinner table. He had just begun to work it out when the late autumn came on, and the paleness of the Adriatic oppressed him, and he decided to go to Florence for the winter, and lost touch with the theme during his illness. Do you remember those frightful days? All the people who have loved him are not strong enough to save him from himself! When I got word from Florence that he had been ill I was in Nice filling a concert engagement. His wife was hurrying to him from Paris, but I reached him first. I arrived at dusk, in a terrific storm.

They had taken an old palace there for the winter, and I found him in the library—a long, dark room full of old Latin books and heavy furniture and bronzes. He was sitting by a wood fire at one end of the room, looking, oh, so worn and pale!—as he always does when he is ill, you know. Ah, it is so good that you *do* know! Even his red smoking jacket lent no color to his face. His first words were not to tell me how ill he had been, but that that morning he had been well enough to put the last strokes to the score of his *Souvenirs d'Automne*. He was as I most like to remember him: so calm and happy and tired; not gay, as he usually is, but just contented and tired with that heavenly tiredness that comes after a good work done at last. Outside, the rain poured down in torrents, and the wind moaned for the pain of all the world and sobbed in the branches of the shivering olives and about the walls of that desolated old palace. How that night comes back to me! There were no lights in the room, only the wood fire which glowed upon the hard features of the bronze Dante, like the reflection of purgatorial flames, and threw long black shadows about us; beyond us it scarcely penetrated the gloom at all. Adriance sat staring at the fire with the weariness of all his life in his eyes, and of all the other lives that must aspire and suffer to make up one such life as his. Somehow the wind with all its world-pain had got into the room, and the cold rain was in our eyes, and the wave came up in both of us at once—that awful, vague, universal pain, that cold fear of life and death and God and hope—and we were like two clinging together on a spar in mid-ocean after the shipwreck of everything. Then we heard the front door open with a great gust of wind that shook even the walls, and the servants came running with lights, announcing that Madam had returned, '*and in the book we read no more than night.*' "

She gave the old line with a certain bitter humor, and with the hard, bright smile in which of old she had wrapped her weakness as in a glittering garment. That ironical smile, worn like a mask through so many years, had gradually changed even the lines of her face completely, and when she looked in the mirror she saw not herself, but the scathing critic, the amused observer and satirist of herself. Everett dropped his head upon his hand and sat looking at the rug. "How much you have cared!" he said.

"Ah, yes, I cared," she replied, closing her eyes with a long-drawn sigh of relief; and lying perfectly still, she went on: "You can't imagine what a comfort it is to have you know how I cared, what a relief it is to be able to tell it to someone. I used to want to shriek it out to the world in the long nights when I could not sleep. It seemed to me that I could not die with it. It demanded some sort of expression. And now that you know, you would scarcely believe how much less sharp the anguish of it is."

Everett continued to look helplessly at the floor. "I was not sure how much you wanted me to know," he said.

"Oh, I intended you should know from the first time I looked into your face, when you came that day with Charley. I flatter myself that I have been able to conceal it when I chose, though I suppose women always think that. The more observing ones may have seen, but discerning people are usually discreet and often kind, for we usually bleed a little before we begin to discern. But I wanted you to know; you are so like him that it is almost like telling him himself. At least, I feel now that he will know some day, and then I will be quite sacred from his compassion, for we none of us dare pity the dead. Since it was what my life has chiefly meant, I should like him to know. On the whole I am not ashamed of it. I have fought a good fight."

"And has he never known at all?" asked Everett, in a thick voice.

"Oh! Never at all in the way that you mean. Of course, he is accustomed to looking into the eyes of women and finding love there; when he doesn't find it there he thinks he must have been guilty of some discourtesy and is miserable about it. He has a genuine fondness for everyone who is not stupid or gloomy, or old or preternaturally ugly. Granted youth and cheerfulness, and a moderate amount of wit and some tact, and Adriance will always be glad to see you coming around the corner. I shared with the rest; shared the smiles and the gallantries and the droll little sermons. It was quite like a Sunday-school picnic; we wore our best clothes and a smile and took our turns. It was his kindness that was hardest. I have pretty well used my life up at standing punishment."

"Don't; you'll make me hate him," groaned Everett.

Katharine laughed and began to play nervously with her fan. "It wasn't in the slightest degree his fault; that is the most grotesque part of it. Why, it had really begun before I ever met him. I fought my way to him, and I drank my doom greedily enough."

Everett rose and stood hesitating. "I think I must go. You ought to be quiet, and I don't think I can hear any more just now."

She put out her hand and took his playfully. "You've put in three weeks at this sort of thing, haven't you? Well, it may never be to your glory in this world, perhaps, but it's been the mercy of heaven to me, and it ought to square accounts for a much worse life than yours will ever be."

Everett knelt beside her, saying, brokenly: "I stayed because I wanted to be with you, that's all. I have never cared about other women since I met you in New York when I was a lad. You are a part of my destiny, and I could not leave you if I would."

She put her hands on his shoulders and shook her head. "No, no; don't tell me that. I have seen enough of tragedy, God knows. Don't show me any more just as the curtain is going down. No, no, it was only a boy's fancy, and your divine pity and my utter pitiableness have recalled it for a moment. One does not love the dying, dear friend. If some fancy of that sort had been left over from boyhood, this would rid you of it, and that were well. Now go, and you will come again tomorrow, as long as there are tomorrows, will you not?" She took his hand with a smile that lifted the mask from her soul, that was both courage and despair, and full of infinite loyalty and tenderness, as she said softly:

> For ever and for ever, farewell, Cassius;
> If we do meet again, why, we shall smile;
> If not, why then, this parting was well made.

The courage in her eyes was like the clear light of a star to him as he went out.

On the night of Adriance Hilgarde's opening concert in Paris Everett sat by the bed in the ranch house in Wyoming, watching over the last battle that we have with the flesh before we are done with it and free of it forever. At times it seemed that the serene soul of her must have left already and found some refuge from the storm, and only the tenacious animal life were left to do battle with death. She labored under a delusion at once pitiful and merciful, thinking that she was in the Pullman on her way to New York, going back to her life and her work. When she aroused from her stupor it was only to ask the porter to waken her half an hour out of Jersey City, or to remonstrate with him about the delays and the roughness of the road. At midnight Everett and the nurse were left alone with her. Poor Charley Gaylord had lain down on a couch outside the door. Everett sat looking at the sputtering night lamp until it made his eyes ache. His head dropped forward on the foot of the bed, and he sank into a heavy, distressful slumber. He was dreaming of Adriance's concert in Paris, and of Adriance, the troubadour, smiling and debonair, with his boyish face and the touch of silver gray in his hair. He heard the applause and he saw the roses going up over the footlights until they were stacked half as high as the piano, and the petals fell and scattered, making crimson splotches on the floor.

Down this crimson pathway came Adriance with his youthful step, leading his prima donna by the hand; a dark woman this time, with Spanish eyes.

The nurse touched him on the shoulder; he started and awoke. She screened the lamp with her hand. Everett saw that Katharine was awake and conscious, and struggling a little. He lifted her gently on his arm and began to fan her. She laid her hands lightly on his hair and looked into his face with eyes that seemed never to have wept or doubted. "Ah, dear Adriance, dear, dear," she whispered.

Everett went to call her brother, but when they came back the madness of art was over for Katharine.

Two days later Everett was pacing the station siding, waiting for the westbound train. Charley Gaylord walked beside him, but the two men had nothing to say to each other. Everett's bags were piled on the truck, and his step was hurried and his eyes were full of impatience, as he gazed again and again up the track, watching for the train. Gaylord's impatience was not less than his own; these two, who had grown so close, had now become painful and impossible to each other, and longed for the wrench of farewell.

As the train pulled in Everett wrung Gaylord's hand among the crowd of alighting passengers. The people of a German opera company, en route to the coast, rushed by them in frantic haste to snatch their breakfast during the stop. Everett heard an exclamation in a broad German dialect, and a massive woman whose figure persistently escaped from her stays in the most improbable places rushed up to him, her blond hair disordered by the wind, and glowing with joyful surprise she caught his coat sleeve with her tightly gloved hands.

"*Herr Gott*, Adriance, *lieber Freund*," she cried, emotionally.

Everett quickly withdrew his arm and lifted his hat, blushing. "Pardon me, madam, but I see that you have mistaken me for Adriance Hilgarde. I am his brother," he said quietly, and turning from the crestfallen singer, he hurried into the car.

140

OLYMPIANS

Kenneth Burke
1897-

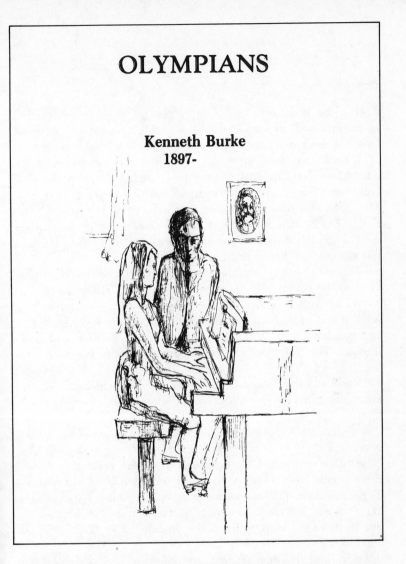

One of America's greatest literary philosophers, Kenneth Burke served several publications as music critic in the late '20s and '30s. More recently, he admits to tinkering "shame-facedly at the piano . . ., [making] up lame pieces now and then." "Olympians," from his collection of stories *The White Oxen* (1924), draws on his special musical knowledge.

After the Wilsons moved from Edgewood, their house was left empty for nearly two months; at the end of this time it was occupied by a Mr. Beck, who put a little black and gold sign in his window, "J. J. Beck, Instructor in Music." Also, Mr. Beck joined the Methodist Church on Braddock Avenue, and gave five dollars to the local ball team. When asked to become affiliated with the gymnasium, Mr. Beck said they were doing invaluable good towards the upbuilding of healthy American manhood, but that he personally was denied all violent exertion, owing to cardiac rheumatism. He gave full assurance of his moral support, however.

Within a year Mr. Beck had convinced everyone that he was an asset to the community. As a member of the Christian Entertainment Committee he had applied himself with an earnestness that was not easily forgotten, and already he had piloted seven little girls and two boys safely through Czerny, both elementary and intermediate. The Howardell's eldest daughter, Dorothy, was even playing the "Valse" by Durand, and the "Scarf Dance" by somebody, but she had taken lessons before Mr. Beck taught her, and was unusually gifted anyhow. Besides, she was older, now being nearly fifteen.

A disagreeable incident took place in the basement of the church once, when a chapter of the Boy Scouts was being organized. One little ruffian nominated Mr. Beck as scout-master, causing a subdued titter to pass around the room; but he was afterwards reprimanded by the minister, and his own father as well. A younger and sturdier man was elected scout-master, of course, and no further mention was made of the matter. It is even doubtful if Mr. Beck ever got wind of it.

Aside from this one incident, which was of no importance as it was occasioned by a mere child, Mr. Beck was treated everywhere with consideration and respect. The minister's wife used to invite him now and then to speak at one of her teas on "The Appreciation of Music," or "Music as a Factor in Education," or some such subject, where he always charmed his audience with his astonishing modesty, a certain lovable shyness, and a wealth of anecdotes taken from the lives of great musicians. And nothing is more illustrative of his goodness of heart than the fact that, although he was by far the best musician in the community, he refused to hear of replacing the church organist.

Perhaps the quality which went farthest towards Mr. Beck's popularity was this pathetic modesty of his. Although he knew so *much*, he seemed to be continually apologizing for his presence. One might almost say that he was timid. When he was introduced to anyone, he stuttered noticeably, and retired from a conversation as soon as was possible within the bounds of politeness. He was tall and thin, which with his ailment, the cardiac rheumatism, gave him a very *fragile* appearance, so that one would inevitably treat him with a kind of tenderness almost without knowing it. As a result Mr. Beck always brought with him into the room an air of peace and mildness, and anyone who talked to him for any length of time was left with an impression of how lovely life can be if we but choose to make it so.

So that Mr. Beck was sweetly and inexorably removed from the class of eligible men, and looked upon as a kindly institution. With an unquestioning docility, he walked in the path that was laid out for him, shielded his failing soul with umbrella and galoshes, kept it sufficiently warm with the horrible respect of his acquaintances. The facts of his own flesh and blood, however, caused him to suffer a mild degradation, which made all of his contacts with life awkward for him. This was the cause of his timidity, or his *fragility*.

All of which agitations culminated when he was teaching the Howardell's eldest daughter, little Dorothy, who was now nearly fifteen, and was his favourite pupil.

Three time a week she came here with her music-roll, corrected her *expressivos*, practised her fourth finger, and when Mr. Beck praised her, fed her joyous little ego with satisfaction. To Dorothy, Mr. Beck was simply a nervous "Good morning, Dorothy," a pulling of a chair up beside her at the piano, and a voice in her ear that made suggestions, with a queer licking sound in its throat after it swallowed. To Dorothy, none of this was especially pleasant, but it must be gone through before one can play before visitors, and was therefore beyond question. Miss Sweeny was a Catholic, while father said that the teachers down-town charged too much. Then again, she really preferred Mr. Beck in a way. For Mr. Beck meant music to her; the taking of lessons was clearly associated with Mr. Beck; when she went to Mr. Beck, she was performing one of the functions of all the music students in her Sunday-school class.

This morning Dorothy was with him again, had come out of the first spring day and into the dark parlour with the picture of a man with side-whiskers over the piano. One of the windows was open a little, so that the spring air, and the soft noises outside, and the notes of Dorothy's "Witches' Revel" had commingled in a way that caused Mr. Beck to feel a mild and uncertain despair.

A few houses farther up the street, some boys were playing marbles, shooting against the curb-stone; while directly beyond, the Wrights' washerwoman was standing in the doorway, leaning, her bare arms crossed gloriously on her breasts. The grass on the front lawns was soppy with the last of the melting snow. Dorothy had finished. "I want you to learn that well, Dorothy. . . . You know, you are my favourite pupil."

Dorothy was his favourite pupil. Dorothy his favourite pupil, and it was spring! That urge, then, was to awaken in them? The tender urge which lends poignancy to "The Barcarolle" and perpetuates the funny little grasshoppers? Were Dorothy and Mr. Beck to *sing* together? Mr. Beck's heart, already weakened as it was by rheumatism, fluttered irregularly with affirmation. The Olympian was rising within him, along with the sap in the trees outside. Apollo was stirring; Balder . . . But Dorothy had fastened her music-roll; she was leaving. "Good morning, Dorothy."

The next time Dorothy came for her music lesson, Mr. Beck felt strangely unfit. She stepped into the parlour, laid her hat and coat on the settee, and sat down at the piano. She was now ready for the voice to buzz in her ear, and make the funny licking sound when it swallowed. But Mr. Beck experienced a sudden fling of insolence. "It is going to be a wonderful spring, Dorothy." He was comforted with the tenderness of his own voice.

Dorothy spread out the "Dance of the Elves" before her. "Yes, Mr. Beck," she answered, obediently. Mr. Beck understood fatally that she had not responded. Somehow or other, he had expected something of her. There was a pause; Dorothy glanced with unconscious significance at the piano. Mr. Beck found something strangely disproportionate. It was as though he were walking arm in arm with a midget, or riding a puppy-dog on his back.

"Let me play you something, Dorothy." The piano became a lovable instrument. Dorothy arose from the stool with a puzzled "Yes, do, Mr. Beck." He seated himself in the place she had left; it was warmed! He ran a scale, and was astonished that it was so *brilliant* a scale. "I shall play a little *Albumblatt* of Beethoven."

Here was he, and here was the piano; he felt very professional; yet he was trembling as he began to play.

He was elated by the daintiness of its arabesques. Then came a miniature *crescendo*, with its insistent bass, followed immediately by a clean chromatic descent in triplets. It transformed again into the arabesques, and was finished. . . . Mr. Beck left the piano with a feeling of surprise. He had taught this piece probably fifty times in his life, and never realized until now that it was so neat and white. Dorothy broke in with a dutiful "How fine it was, Mr. Beck," and that was all gone, too. Without spirit, he gave her her lesson.

After Dorothy had left, Mr. Beck was frank to himself about any number of things. The scene he had just been through made him weak with humiliation. And to have played for her; as though he had stood beneath her window as a *troubadour*.

Out of this unaccountable disgust, Mr. Beck tried to reach a determination. He must annihilate Dorothy from his head. For at best he could only awake her out of a dead sleep; at best prepare her for some coarse, brutal youth.

It was late, and they were returning in a street-car. Dorothy was trying to hold her eyes open, lulled by the low groan of the motor. In another fifteen minutes, thank God, Mr. Beck would leave her at her doorstep; she would go to bed without cleaning her teeth. Mr. Beck sat beside her, his eyes working over the other occupants of the car. Everyone was dull, and detestable. But in Mr. Beck there was still a disturbance from his memory of the opera. The duet is so *bold*; the voice of a man and woman in harmonization, adapting themselves to each other, intertwining. The car jerked and groaned through the deserted streets. And they passed dark houses, shutting away all manner of things; houses that stood out frankly and openly, but within their walls, what slinking possibilities; houses with black corridors, with furniture and people in the shadows. These were sleeping houses, and as secret as caves.

GUITAR

Langston Hughes
1902-1967

One critic has noted that Langston Hughes's pages "throb with the abrupt rhythm of popular music." Hughes is remembered best as a writer who rendered "blues" in poetry but, as we can see from the story "Guitar" (1930), he also captured it in prose. Hughes once gave the following summary of his own work: "My writing has been largely concerned with the depicting of Negro life in America."

Throw yo' arms around me, baby,
Like de circle round de sun!
Baby, throw yo' arms around me
Like de circle round de sun,
An' tell yo' pretty papa
How you want yo' lovin' done!

Jimboy was home. All the neighborhood could hear his rich low baritone voice giving birth to the blues. On Saturday night he and Annjee went to bed early. On Sunday night Aunt Hager said: "Put that guitar right up, less'n it's hymns you plans on playin'. An' I don't want too much o' them, 'larmin' the white neighbors."

But this was Monday, and the sun had scarcely fallen below the horizon before the music had begun to float down the alley, over back fences and into kitchen-windows where nice white ladies sedately washed their supper dishes.

Did you ever see peaches
Growin' on a watermelon vine?
Says did you ever see peaches
On a watermelon vine?
Did you ever see a woman
That I couldn't get for mine.

Long, lazy length resting on the kitchen-door-sill, back against the jamb, feet in the yard, fingers picking his sweet guitar, left hand holding against his finger-board the back of an old pocket-knife, sliding the knife upward, downward, getting thus weird croons and sighs from the vibrating strings:

O, I left ma mother
An' I cert'ly can leave you.
Indeed I left ma mother
An' I cert'ly can leave you.
For I'd leave any woman
That mistreats me like you do.

148

Jimboy, remembering brown-skin mamas in Natchez, Shreve-port, Dallas; remembering Creole women in Baton Rouge, Loui-siana:

> O, yo' windin' an' yo' grindin'
> Don't have no effect on me,
> Babe, yo' windin' an' yo' grindin'
> Don't have no 'fect on me,
> 'Cause I can wind an' grind
> Like a monkey round a cocoanut-tree!

Then Harriett, standing under the ripening apple tree, in the back yard, chiming in:

> Now I see that you don't want me,
> So it's fare thee, fare thee well!
> Lawd, I see that you don't want me,
> So it's fare—thee—well!
> I can still get plenty lovin',
> An you can go to—Kansas City!

"O, play it, sweet daddy Jimboy!" She began to dance.

Then Hager, from her seat on the edge of the platform covering the well, broke out: "Here, madam! Stop that prancin'! Bad enough to have all this singin' without turnin' de yard into a show-house." But Harriett kept on, her hands picking imaginary cherries out of the stars, her hips speaking an earthly language quite their own.

"You got it, kid," said Jimboy, stopping suddenly, then fingering his instrument for another tune. "You do it like the stage women does. You'll be takin' Ada Walker's place if you keep on."

"Wha! Wha! . . . You chillen sho can sing!" Tom Johnson shouted his compliments from across the yard. And Sarah, beside him on the bench behind their shack, added: "Minds me o' de ole plantation times, honey! It sho do."

"Unhuh! Bound straight fo' de devil, that's what they is," Hager returned calmly from her place beside the pump. "You an' Harriett both—singin' an' dancin' this stuff befo' these chillens here." She pointed to Sandy and Willie-Mae, who sat on the ground with their backs against the chicken-box. "It's a shame!"

"I likes it," said Willie-Mae.

"Me too," the little boy agreed.

"Naturally you would—none o' you-all's converted yet," countered the old woman to the children as she settled back against the pump to listen to some more.

The music rose hoarse and wild:

> *I wonder where ma easy rider's gone?*
> *He done left me, put ma new gold watch in pawn.*

It was Harriett's voice in plaintive moan to the night sky. Jimboy had taught her that song, but a slight, clay-colored brown boy who had hopped bells at the Clinton Hotel for a couple of months, on his way from Houston to Omaha, discovered its meaning to her. Puppy-love, maybe, but it had hurt when he went away, saying nothing. And the guitar in Jimboy's hands echoed that old pain with an even greater throb than the original ache itself possessed.

Approaching footsteps came from the front yard.

"Lord, I can hear you-all two blocks away!" said Annjee, coming around the house, home from work, with a bundle of food under her left arm. "Hello! How are you daddy? Hello, ma! Gimme a kiss Sandy. . . . Lord, I'm hot and tired and almost played out. This late just getting from work! . . . Here, Jimboy, come on in and eat some of these nice things the white folks had for supper." She stepped across her husband's outstretched legs into the kitchen. "I brought a mighty good piece of cold ham for you, hon', from Mis' Rice's."

"All right, sure, I'll be there in a minute," the man said, but he went on playing *Easy Rider*, and Harriett went on singing, while the food was forgotten on the table until long after Annjee had come outdoors again and sat down in the cool, tired of waiting for Jimboy to come in to her.

Off and on for nine years, ever since he had married Annjee, Jimboy and Harriett had been singing together in the evening. When they started, Harriett was a little girl with braided hair, and each time that her roving brother-in-law stopped in Stanton, he would amuse himself by teaching her the old Southern songs, the popular rag-time ditties, and the hundreds of varying verses of the blues that he would pick up in the big dirty cities of the South. The child, with her strong sweet voice (colored folks called it alto) and her racial sense of rhythm, soon learned to sing the songs as well as Jimboy. He taught her the *parse me la*, too, and a few other movements peculiar to Southern Negro dancing, and sometimes together they went through the buck and wing and a few taps. It

150

was all great fun, and innocent fun except when one stopped to think, as white folks did, that some of the blues lines had, not only double, but triple meanings, and some of the dance steps required very definite movements of the hips. But neither Harriett nor Jimboy soiled their minds by thinking. It was music, good exercise—and they loved it.

"Do you know this one, Annjee?" asked Jimboy, calling his wife's name out of sudden politeness because he had forgotten to eat her food, had hardly looked towards her in the darkness where she sat plump on a kitchen-chair in the yard, apart from the others, with her back to the growing corn in the garden. Softly he ran his fingers, light as a breeze, over his guitar strings, imitating the wind rustling through the long leaves of the corn. A rectangle of light from the kitchen-door fell into the yard striking sidewise across the healthy orange-yellow of his skin above the unbuttoned neck of his blue laborer's shirt.

"Come on, sing it with us, Annjee," he said.

"I don't know it," Annjee replied, with a lump in her throat, and her eyes on the silhouette of his long, muscular, animal-hard body. She loved Jimboy too much, that's what was the matter with her! She knew there was nothing between him and her young sister except the love of music, yet he might have dropped the guitar and left Harriett in the yard for a little while to come eat the nice cold slice of ham she had brought him. She hadn't seen him all day long. When she went to work in the morning, he was still in bed—and now the blues claimed him.

In the starry blackness the singing notes of the guitar became a plaintive hum, like a breeze in a grove of palmettos; became a low moan, like the wind in a forest of live-oaks strung with long strands of hanging moss. The voice of Annjee's golden, handsome husband on the door-step rang high and far away, lonely-like, crying with only the guitar, not his wife, to understand; crying grotesquely, crying absurdly in the summer night:

> I got a mule to ride.
> I got a mule to ride.
> Down in the South somewhere
> I got a mule to ride.

Then asking the questions as an anxious, left-lonesome girl-sweetheart would ask it:

151

You say you goin' North.
You say you goin' North.
How 'bout yo' . . . lovin' gal?
You say you goin' North.

Then sighing in rhythmical despair:

O, don't you leave me here.
Babe, don't you leave me here.
Dog-gone yo' comin' back!
Said don't you leave me here.

On and on the song complained, man-verses and woman-verses, to the evening air in stanzas that Jimboy had heard in the pine-woods of Arkansas from the lumber-camp workers; in other stanzas that were desperate and dirty like the weary roads where they were sung; and in still others that the singer created spontaneously in his own mouth then and there:

O, I done made ma bed,
Says I done made ma bed.
Down in some lonesome grave
I done made ma bed.

It closed with a sad eerie twang.

"That's right decent," said Hager. "Now I wish you-all'd play some o' ma pieces like *When de Saints Come Marchin' In* or *This World Is Not Ma Home*—something Christian from de church."

"Aw, mama, it's not Sunday yet," said Harriett.

"Sing *Casey Jones*," called old man Tom Johnson. "That's ma song."

So the ballad of the immortal engineer with another mama in the Promised Land rang out promptly in the starry darkness, while everybody joined in the choruses.

"Aw, pick it, boy," yelled the old man. "Can't nobody play like you."

And Jimboy remembered when he was a lad in Memphis that W.C. Handy had said: "You ought to make your living out of that, son," But he hadn't followed it up—too many things to see, too many places to go, too many other jobs.

"What song do you like, Annjee?" he asked, remembering her presence again.

"O, I don't care. Any ones you like. All of 'em are pretty." She was pleased and petulant and a little startled that he had asked her.

"All right, then," he said. "Listen to me":

> Here I is in de mean ole jail.
> Ain't got nobody to go ma bail.
> Lonesome an' sad an' chain gang bound—
> Ever' friend I had's done turned me down.

"That's sho it!" shouted Tom Johnson in great sympathy. "Now, when I was in de Turner County Jail . . ."

"Shut up yo' mouth!" squelched Sarah, jabbing her husband in the ribs.

The songs went on, blues, shouts, jingles, old hits: *Bon Bon Buddy, The Chocolate Drop; Wrap Me in Your Big Red Shawl; Under the Old Apple Tree; Turkey in the Staw*—Jimboy and Harriett breaking the silence of the small-town summer night until Aunt Hager interrupted:

"Yo all better wind up, chillens, 'cause I wants to go to bed. I ain't used to stayin' 'wake so late, nohow. Play something kinder decent, there, son, fo' you stops."

Jimboy, to tease the old woman, began to rock and moan like an elder in the Sanctified Church, patting both feet at the same time as he played a hymn-like lugubrious tune with a dancing overtone:

> Tell me, sister,
> Tell me, brother,
> Have you heard de latest news?

Then seriously as if he were about to announce the coming of the Judgment:

> A woman down in Georgia
> Got her two sweet-men confused.

How terrible! How sad! moaned the guitar.

> One knocked on de front do',
> One knocked on de back—

Sad, sad . . . sad, sad! said the music.

153

Now that woman down in Georgia's
Door-knob is hung with black.

O, play the funeral march boy! while the guitar laughed a dirge.

An' de hearse is comin' easy
With two rubber-tired hacks!

Followed by a long-drawn out, churchlike:

Amen . . . !

Then with rapid glides, groans, and shouts the instrument screamed of a sudden in profane frenzy, and Harriett began to ball-the-jack, her arms flopping like the wings of a headless pigeon, the guitar strings whining in ecstasy, the player rocking gaily to the urgent music, his happy mouth crying: "Tack 'em down, gal! Tack 'em on down, Harrie!"

But Annjee had risen.

"I wish you'd come in and eat the ham I brought you," she said as she picked up her chair and started towards the house. "And you, Sandy! Get up from under that tree and go to bed." She spoke roughly to the little fellow, whom the songs had set a-dreaming. Then to her husband: "Jimboy, I wish you'd come in."

The man stopped playing, with a deep vibration of the strings that seemed to echo through the whole world. Then he leaned his guitar against the side of the house and lifted straight up in his hairy arms Annjee's plump, brown-black little body while he kissed her as she wriggled like a stubborn child, her soft breasts rubbing his hard body through the coarse blue shirt.

"You don't like my old songs do you, baby? You don't want to hear me sing 'em," he said, laughing. "Well, that's all right. I like you, anyhow, and I like your ham, and I like your kisses, and I like everything you bring me. Let's go in and chow down." And he carried her into the kitchen, where he sat with her on his knees as he ate the food she so faithfully had brought him from Mrs. J. J. Rice's dinner-table.

Outside, Willie-Mae went running home through the dark. And Harriett pumped a cool drink of water for her mother, then helped her to rise from her low seat. Sandy aiding from behind, with both hands pushing firmly in Aunt Hager's fleshy back. Then the three of them came into the house and glanced, as they passed through the kitchen, at Annjee sitting on Jimboy's lap with both arms tight around his neck.

"Looks like you're clinging to the Rock of Ages," said Harriett to her sister. "Be sure you don't slip, old evil gal!"

But at midnight when the owl that nested in a tree near the corner began to hoot, they were all asleep—Annjee and Jimboy in one room, Harriett and Hager in another, with Sandy on the floor at the foot of his grandmother's bed. Far away on the railroad line a whistle blew, lonesome and long.

A GLIMPSE

Edith Wharton
1862-1937

Edith Wharton, the first woman to receive an honorary Litt.D. from Yale University, was also the first to win *two* Pulitzer Prizes for writing. Her polished style and command of fictional structure was influenced both by reading Continental literature and her friendship with Henry James, in whose work she found congenial models. "A Glimpse" (1932), for example, exhibits the so-called "Jamesian observer," a character through whom the story of the two symbiotic musicians is told.

❧

1

As John Kilvert got out of the motor at the Fusina landing stage, and followed his neat suitcases on board the evening boat for Venice, he growled to himself inconsequently: "Always on wheels! When what I really want is to walk—"

To walk? How absurd! Would he even have known how to, any longer? In youth he had excelled in the manly exercises then fashionable: lawn tennis, racquets, golf and the rest. He had even managed, till well over forty, to combine the more violent of these with his busy life of affairs in New York, and since then, with devout regularity and some success, had conformed to the national ritual of golf. But the muscles used for a mere walk were probably long since atrophied, and, indeed, so little did this modest form of exercise enter into the possibilities of his life that in his sudden outburst he had used the word metaphorically, meaning that all at once his existence seemed to him too cushioned, smooth and painless—he didn't know why.

Perhaps it was the lucky accident of finding himself on board the wrong boat—the unfashionable boat; an accident caused by the chauffeur's having mistaken a turn soon after they left Padua, missed the newly opened "*auto-strada*," and slipped through reed-grown byways to the Fusina waterside. It was a hot Sunday afternoon in September, and a throng of dull and dingy-looking holiday makers were streaming across the gangplank onto the dirty deck, and settling down with fretful babies, withered flowers, and baskets stuffed with provisions from the mainland on the narrow uncomfortable bench along the rail. Perhaps it was that—at any rate the discomfort did not annoy John Kilvert; on the contrary, it gave him a vague glow of satisfaction. Camping for an hour on this populous garlicky boat would be almost the equivalent of walking from Padua to Fusina instead of gliding there in the commodious Fiat he had hired at Milan. And to begin with, why had he hired it? Why hadn't the train been good enough for him? What was the matter with him, anyhow? . . . He hadn't meant to include Venice in his holiday that summer. He had settled down in Paris to do some systematic sightseeing in the Ile-de-France: French church architecture was his hobby, he had collected a library on the subject, and liked going on archaeological trips (also in a commodious motor, with a pause for lunch at the most reputed restaurants) in company with a shy shabby French archaeologist who could guide and explain, and save him the labor of reading all the books he bought. But he concealed his archaeological interests from most of his American friends because they belonged to a cosmopolitan group who thought that motors were made for speeding, not sight-seeing, and that Paris existed merely to launch new fashions, new plays and new restaurants, for rich and easily bored Americans. John Kilvert, at fifty-five, had accepted this point of view with the weary tolerance which had long since replaced indignation in his moral make-up.

And now, after all, his plans had been upset by a telegram from Sara Roseneath, insisting that he should come to Venice at once to help her about her fancy dress for the great historical ball which was to be given at the Ducal Palace (an unheard-of event, looming in cosmopolitan society far higher than declarations of war, or peace treaties). And he had started.

But why, again—why? Sara Roseneath was an old friend, of course; an old love. He had been half disposed to marry her once, when she was Sara Court; but she had chosen a richer man, and now that she was widowed, though he had no idea of succeeding to the late Roseneath, he and she had drifted into a semisentimental friendship, occasionally went on little tours together, and were expected by their group to foregather whenever they were both in New York, or when they met in Paris or London. A safe, prudent arrangement, gradually fading into an intimacy scarcely calmer than the romance that went before. It was all she wanted of the emotional life (practical life being so packed with entertainments, dressmakers, breathless travel and all sorts of fashionable rivalries); and it was all he had to give in return for what she was able to offer. What held him, then? Partly habit, a common stock of relations and allusions, the knowledge that her exactions would never be more serious than this urgent call to help her to design a fancy dress—and partly, of course, what survived in her, carefully preserved by beauty doctors and gymnastic trainers, of the physical graces which had first captured him.

Nevertheless he was faintly irritated with both himself and her for having suffered this journey to be imposed on him. Of course it was his own fault; if he had refused to come she would have found half a dozen whippersnappers to devise a fancy dress for her. And she would not have been really angry; only gently surprised and disappointed. She would have said: "I thought I could *always* count

159

on you in an emergency!" An emergency—this still handsome but middle-aged woman, to whom a fancy ball represented an event! There is no frivolity, he thought, like that of the elderly. . . . Venice in September was a place wholly detestable to him, and that he should be summoned there to assist a spoilt woman in the choice of a fancy dress shed an ironic light on the contrast between his old ambitions and his present uses. The whole affair was silly and distasteful, and he wished he could shake off his social habits and break once and for all with the trivial propinquities which had created them. . . .

The slatternly woman who sat crammed close against him moved a little to readjust the arm supporting her sleep-drunken baby, and her elbow pressed uncomfortably against Kilvert's ribs. He got up and wandered forward. As the passengers came on board he had noticed two people—a man and a woman—whose appearance singled them out from the workaday crowd. Not that they fitted in with his standard of personal seemliness; the woman was bareheaded with blown hair, untidy and turning gray, and the man, in worn shapeless homespun, with a short beard turning gray also, was as careless in dress and bearing as his companion. Still, blowsy and shabby as they were, they were evidently persons of education and refinement, and Kilvert, having found a corner for himself in the forward part of the boat, began to watch them with a certain curiosity.

First he speculated about their nationality; but that was hard to determine. The woman was dusky, almost swarthy, under her sunburn; her untidy hair was still streaked with jet, and the eyes under her dense black eyebrows were of a rich burning brown. The man's eyes were gray, his nose was straight, his complexion and hair vaguely pepper and salt, like his clothes. He had taken off his stalking cap, disclosing thick hair brushed back carelessly from a high wide forehead. His brow and his high cheekbones were burnt to a deeper bronze than his companion's, but his long nervous hands showed whiter at the wrists than hers. For the rest, they seemed of about the same age, and though there was no trace of youth about either of them their vigorous maturity seemed to give out a strong emotional glow. Such had been Kilvert's impression as they came on board, hurriedly, almost precipitately, after all the other passengers were seated. The woman had come first, and the man, after a perceptible interval, had scrambled over the side as the boat was actually beginning to put off. Where had they come from, Kilvert wondered, why such haste and such agitation? They had no luggage, no wraps, the woman, gloveless and cloakless, apparently had not even a hat.

For a while Kilvert had lost them in the crowd; but now, going forward, he found them wedged between the prow of the boat and the low skylight of the forward cabin. They had not found seats, but they seemed hardly aware of it; the woman was perched on the edge of the closed skylight, the man, facing her, leaned against the side of the boat, his hands braced against the rail. Both turned their backs to the low misty line along the horizon that was rapidly defining itself as a distant view of Venice. Kilvert's first thought was: "I don't believe they even know where they are."

A fat passenger perched on a coil of rope had spied the seat which Kilvert had left, and the latter was able to possess himself of the vacated rope. From where he sat he was only a few yards from the man and woman he had begun to watch; just too far to catch their words, or even to make quite sure of the language they were speaking (he wavered between Hungarian and Austrian German smattered with English), but near enough to observe the play of their facial muscles and the corresponding gestures of their dramatic bodies.

Husband and wife? No—he dismissed the idea as it shaped itself. They were too acutely aware of each other, what each said (whatever its import might be) came to the other with too sharp an impact of surprise for habit to have dulled their intercourse. Lovers, then—as he and Sara had once been, for a discreet interval? Kilvert winced at the comparison. He tried, but in vain, to picture Sara Roseneath and himself, in the hour of their rapture, dashing headlong and hatless on board a dirty boat crowded with perspiring work people, and fighting out the last phase of their amorous conflict between coils of tarry rope and bulging baskets of farm produce. In fact there had been no conflict; he and Sara had ceased their sentimental relations without shedding of blood. But then they had only strolled around the edge of the crater, picking flowers, while these two seemed writhing in its depths.

As Kilvert settled himself on his coil of rope their conversation came to an end. The man walked abruptly away, striding the length of the crowded deck (in his absorption he seemed unaware of the obstacles in his advance), while the woman, propped against her precarious ledge, remained motionless, her eyes fixed, her rough gray head, with the streaks of wavy jet, bowed as under a crushing thought. "They've quarreled," Kilvert said to himself with a half-envious pang.

The woman sat there for several minutes. Her only motion was to clasp and unclasp her long sunburnt fingers. Kilvert noticed that her hands, which were large for her height, had the same nervous suppleness as the man's; high-strung intellectual hands, as eloquent as her burning brown eyes. As she continued to sit alone their look deepened from feverish fire to a kind of cloudy resignation, as though to say that now the worst was over. "Ah, quarreled irremediably—" Kilvert thought, disappointed.

Then the man came back. He forced his way impatiently through the heaped-up bags and babies, regained his place at his companion's side, and stood looking down at her, sadly but not resignedly. An unappeased entreaty was in his gaze. Kilvert became aware that the struggle was far from being over, and his own muscles unconsciously braced themselves for the renewal of the conflict. "He won't give up—he *won't* give up!" he exulted inwardly.

The man lowered his head above his companion, and spoke to her in pressing inaudible tones. She listened quietly, without stirring, but Kilvert noticed that her lower lip trembled a little. Was her mouth beautiful? He was not yet sure. It had something of the sinuous strength of her long hands, and the complexity of its curves made it a matchless vehicle for the expression of irony, bitterness and grief. An actress's mouth, perhaps; overelastic, subtly drawn, capable of being beautiful or ugly as her own emotions were. It struck Kilvert that her whole face, indeed her whole body, was like that: a vehicle, an instrument, a language rather than a plastic fact. Kilvert's interest deepened to excitement as he watched her.

She began to speak, at first very low and gravely; then more eagerly, passionately, passing (as he imagined) from pleading, from tenderness and regret, to the despair of an accepted renouncement. "Ah, don't tempt me—don't begin it all over again!" her eyes and lips seemed to be saying in tortured remonstrance, as his gray head bent above her and their urgent whispers were interwoven. . . .

Kilvert felt that he was beginning to understand the situation. "She's married—unhappily married. That must be it. And everything draws her to this man, who is her predestined mate . . . but some terrible obstacle lies between them. Her husband, her children, perhaps some obligation of his that he wants to forget, but that she feels compelled, for his own sake, to remind him of, though she does so at the cost of her very life—ah, yes, she's bleeding to death for him! And they've been off, spending a last day together in some quiet place, to talk it all over for the last time; and he won't take her refusal for an answer—and by God, I wouldn't either!"

Kilvert inwardly shrieked, kindled to a sudden forgotten vehemence of passion by the mute display of it before him. "When people need each other as desperately as those two do—not mere instinct-driven infants, but a mature experienced man and woman—the gods ought to let them come together, no matter how much it costs, or for how short a time it is! And that's what he's saying to her; by heaven, he's saying: 'I thought I could stand it, but I can't.'"

To Kilvert's surprise his own eyes filled with tears; they came so thick that he had to pull out his handkerchief and wipe them away. What was he mourning—the inevitable break between these two anguished people, or some anguish that he himself had once caught a glimpse of, and missed? There had been that gray-eyed Russian girl, the governess of his sister's children; with her he had very nearly sounded the depths. He remembered one long walk with her in the summer woods, the children scampering ahead. . . . At a turn when they were out of sight, he and she had suddenly kissed and clung to each other. . . . But his sister's children's governess? Did he mean to marry her? He asked himself that through a long agitated night—recalled the chapter in "Resurrection" where Prince Nekludov paces his room, listening to the drip of the spring thaw in the darkness outside—and was off by the earliest train the next morning, and away to Angkor and Bali the following week. A man can't be too careful—or *can* he? Who knows? He still remembered the shuddering ebb of that night's emotions. . . .

"But what a power emotion is!" he reflected. "I could lift mountains still if I could feel as those two do about anything. I suppose all the people worth remembering—lovers or poets or inventors—have lived at white-heat level, while we crawl along in the temperate zone." Once more he concentrated his attention on the couple facing him. The woman had risen in her turn. She walked away a few steps, and stood leaning against the rail, her gaze fixed on the faint horizon line that was shaping itself into wavering domes and towers. What did that distant view say to her? Perhaps it symbolized the life she must go back to, the duties, sacrifices, daily weariness from which this man was offering her an escape. She knew all that; she saw her fate growing clearer and clearer before her as the boat advanced through the summer twilight; in half an hour more the crossing would be over, and the gangplank run out to the quay.

The man had not changed his position; he stood where she had left him, as though respecting the secrecy of her distress, or else perhaps too worn out, too impoverished in argument, to resume the conflict. His eyes were fixed on the ground; he looked suddenly years older—a baffled and beaten man. . . .

The woman turned her head first. Kilvert saw her steal a furtive glance at her companion. She detached her hands from the rail, and half moved toward him; then she stiffened herself, resumed her former attitude, and addressed her mournful sunken profile to the contemplation of Venice. . . . But not for long; she looked again; her hands twitched, her face quivered, and suddenly she swept about, rejuvenated, and crossed the space between herself and her companion. He stared at her touch on his arm, and looked at her, bewildered, reproachful, while she began to speak low and rapidly, as though all that was left to be said must be crowded into the diminishing minutes before the boat drew alongside the quay. "Ah, how like a woman!" Kilvert groaned, all his compassion transferred to the man. "Now she's going to begin it all over again—just as he'd begun to resign himself to the inevitable!"

Yet he envied the man on whom this intolerable strain was imposed. "How she must love him to torture him so!" he ejaculated. "She looks ten years younger since she's come back to him. Anything better than to spend these last minutes apart from him . . . nothing that he may be suffering counts a single instant in comparison with that. . . ." He saw the man's brow darken, his eyebrows jut out almost savagely over his suffering bewildered eyes, and his lips open to utter a word, a single word, that Kilvert could not hear, but of which he traced the passage on the woman's face as if it had been the sting of a whip. She paled under her deep sunburn, her head dropped, she clung to her companion desolately, almost helplessly, and for a minute they neither spoke nor looked at each other. Then Kilvert saw the man's hand steal toward hers and clasp it as it still lay on his arm. He spoke again, more softly, and her head sank lower, but she made no answer. They both looked exhausted with the struggle.

Two men who had been sitting nearby got up and began to collect their bags and baskets. One of the couple whom Kilvert was watching pointed out to the other the seats thus vacated, and the two moved over and sat down on the narrow board. Dusk was falling, and Kilvert could no longer see their faces distinctly; but he noticed that the man had slipped his arm about his companion, not so much to embrace as to support her. She smiled a little at his touch and leaned back, and they sat silent, their worn faces half averted from one another, as though they had reached a point beyond entreaties and arguments. Kilvert watched them in an agony of participation. . . .

Now the boat was crossing the Grand Canal; the dusky palaces glimmered with lights, lamplit prows flashed out from the side canals, the air was full of cries and guttural hootings. On board the boat the passengers were all afoot, assembling children and possessions, rummaging for tickets, chattering and pushing. Kilvert sat quiet. He knew the boat would first touch near the railway station, where most of the passengers would probably disembark, before it carried him to his own landing place at the Piazzetta. The man and woman sat motionless also; he concluded with satisfaction that they would probably land at the Piazzetta, and that there he might very likely find some one waiting for him—some friend of Mrs. Roseneath's or a servant sent to meet him—and might just conceivably discover who his passionate pilgrims were.

But suddenly the man began to speak again, quickly, vehemently, in less guarded tones. He was speaking Italian now, easily and fluently, though it was obvious from his intonation that it was not his native tongue. "You promised—you promised!" Kilvert heard him reiterate, no doubt made reckless by the falling darkness and the hurried movements of the passengers. The woman's lips seemed to shape a "no" in reply; but Kilvert could not be sure. He knew only that she shook her head once or twice, softly, resignedly. Then the two lapsed once more into silence, and the man leaned back and stared ahead of him.

The boat had drawn close to her first landing stage, and the gangplank was being run out. The couple sat listlessly watching it, still avoiding each other's eyes. The people who were getting off streamed by them, chattering and jostling each other, lifting children and baskets of fowls over their heads. The couple watched. . . .

And then, suddenly, as the last passengers set foot on the quay, and the whistle for departure sounded, the woman sprang up, forced her way between the sailors who had their hands on the gangplank, and rushed ashore without a backward glance or gesture. The man, evidently taken by surprise, started to his feet and tried to follow; but a bewildered mother clutching a baby blocked his way, the bell rang, and the gangplank was already being hauled onto the boat. . . . The man drew back baffled, and stood straining his eyes after the fugitive; but she had already vanished in the dispersing throng.

As Kilvert's gaze followed her he felt as if he too were straining his eyes in the pursuit of some rapture just glimpsed and missed. It might have been his own lost destiny mocking him in the flight of this haggard woman stumbling away distraught from her last hope of youth and freedom. Kilvert saw the man she had forsaken raise his hand to his eyes with a vague hopeless gesture, then give his shoulders a shake and stand leaning aginst the rail, unseeing, unhearing. "It's the end," Kilvert muttered to himself.

The boat was now more than half empty, and as they swung back into the Grand Canal he was tempted to go up to the solitary traveler and say a word to him—perhaps only ask him for a light, or where the boat touched next. But the man's face was too closed, too stricken; Kilvert did not dare intrude on such a secrecy of suffering. At the Piazzetta the man, who had taken up his place near the gangplank, was among the first to hurry ashore, and in the confusion and the cross play of lights Kilvert for a moment lost sight of him. But his tall gray head reappeared again above the crowd just as Kilvert himself was greeted by young Harry Breck, Mrs. Roseneath's accomplished private secretary. Kilvert seized the secretary's arm. "Look here! Who's that man over there? The tall fellow with gray hair and reddish beard . . . stalking cap . . . there, ahead of you," Kilvert gasped incoherently, clutching the astonished Breck, who was directing one of Mrs. Roseneath's gondoliers toward his luggage.

"Tall man—where?" Young Breck, swinging round, lifted himself on his tiptoes to follow the other's gesture.

"There—over there! Don't you see? The man with a stalking cap—"

"That? I can't be certain at this distance; but it looks like Brand, the cellist, don't it? Want to speak to him? No? All right. Anyhow, I'm not so sure. . . ."

They went down the steps to the gondola.

2

"That would account for their hands," Kilvert suddenly thought, rousing himself to wave away a second offering of *langoustines à la Vénitienne*. He looked down Mrs. Roseneath's shining dinner table, trying to force himself to a realization of the scene; but the women's vivid painted heads, the men's polished shirt fronts, the gliding gondoliers in white duck and gold-fringed sashes, handing silver dishes down the table, all seemed as remote and unrelated to reality as the great Tiepolesque fresco which formed the background of the scene. Before him Kilvert could see only a middle-aged life-worn man and woman torn with the fullness of human passion. "If he's a musician, so is she, probably," he thought; and this evocation of their supple dramatic hands presented itself as a new clue to their identity.

He did not know why he was so anxious to find out who they were. Indeed, some secret apprehension half held him back from pressing his inquiries. "Brand the cellist—" From young Breck's tone it would seem that the name was well-known among musicians. Kilvert racked his memories; but music and musicians were not prominent in them, and he could not discover any association with the name of Brand—or any nationality either, since it might have been at home anywhere from Edinburgh to Oslo.

Well, all this brooding was really morbid. Was it possible that he would stoop to gather up gossip about this couple, even if he succeeded in finding out who they were? No! All he wanted was to identify them, to be able to call them by name, and then enshrine them in some secret niche of memory in all their tragic isolation. "Musicians' hands—that's it," he murmured.

But the problem would not let him rest, and after dinner, forsaking the groups who were scattering and forming again down the length of the great frescoed salon, he found a pretext for joining Breck on the balcony.

"That man I pointed out as I left the boat—you said he was a musician?"

"When? Oh, as you were leaving the boat? Well, he looked uncommonly like Julian Brand. You've never heard him? Not much in that line, are you? Thought not. They gave you a cigar, I hope?" he added, suddenly remembering his duties.

Kilvert waved that away too. "I'm not particularly musical. But his head struck me. They were sitting near me on the boat."

"They? Who?" queried Breck absently, craning his head back toward the salon to make sure that the liqueurs were being handed.

"This man. He was with a woman, very dark, black hair turning gray, splendid eyes—dreadfully badly dressed, and not young, but tingling. Something gypsy-like about her. Who was she, do you suppose? They seemed very intimate."

"Love making, eh?"

"No. Much more—more *intimate* than that. Hating and loving and despairing all at once," stammered Kilvert, reluctant to betray himself to such ears, yet driven by the irresistible need to find out what he could from this young fool. "They weren't husband and wife, either, you understand."

Breck laughed. "Obviously! You said they were intimate."

"Well, who was she then—the woman? Can you tell me?"

Breck wrinkled his brows retrospectively. He saw so many people in the course of a day, his uncertain frown seemed to plead. "Splendid eyes, eh?" he repeated, as if to gain time.

"Well, burning—"

"Ah, burning," Breck echoed, his eyes on the room. "But I must really. . . . Here. Count Dossi's the very man to tell you," he added, hurrying away in obedience to a signal from Mrs. Roseneath.

The small, dry waxen-featured man who replaced him was well-known to Kilvert, and to all cosmopolitan idlers. He was an Anglo-Italian by birth, with a small foothold in Rome, where he spent the winter months, drifting for the rest of the year from one center of fashion to another, and gathering with impartial eye and indefatigable memory the items of a diary which, he boasted, could not safely be published till fifty years after his death. Count Dossi bent on Kilvert his coldly affable glance. "Who has burning eyes?" he asked. "I came out here in search of a light, but hadn't hoped to find one of that kind." He produced a cigarette, and continued, as he held it to Kilvert's lighter: "There are not so many incandescent orbs left in the world that one shouldn't be able to identify them."

Kilvert shrank from exposing the passionate scene on the boat to Count Dossi's disintegrating scrutiny; yet he could not bear to miss the chance of tracing the two who had given him so strange a cross section of their souls. He tried to appear indifferent, and slightly ironical. "There are still some. . . ."

"Oh, no doubt. A woman, I suppose?"

Kilvert nodded. "But neither young nor beautiful—by rule, at least."

"Who is beautiful, by rule? A plaster cast at best. But your lady interests me. Who is she? I know a good many people. . . ."

Kilvert, tempted, began to repeat his description of the couple, and Count Dossi, meditatively twisting his cigarette, listened with a face wrinkled with irony. "Ah, that's interesting," he murmured, as the other ended. "Musicians' hands, you say?"

"Well, I thought—"

"You probably thought rightly. I should say Breck's guess was correct. From your description the man was almost certainly Brand, the cellist. He was to arrive about this time for a series of concerts with Margaret Aslar. You've heard the glorious Margaret? Yes, it must have been Brand and Aslar. . . ." He pinched his lips in a dry smile. "Very likely she crossed over to Fusina to meet him. . . ."

"To meet him? But I should have thought they'd been together for hours. They were in the thick of a violent discussion when they came on board. . . . They looked haggard, worn out . . . and so absorbed in each other that they hardly knew where they were."

Dossi nodded appreciatively. "No, they wouldn't—they wouldn't! The foolish things. . . ."

"Ah—they care so desperately for each other?" Kilvert murmured.

Dossi lifted his thin eyebrows. "Care—? They care frantically for each other's music; they can't get on without each other—in that respect."

"But when I saw them they were not thinking about anybody's music; they were thinking about each other. They were desperate . . . they . . . they. . . ."

"Ah, just so! Fighting like tigers, weren't they?"

"Well, one minute, yes—and the next, back in each other's arms, almost."

"Of course! Can't I see them? They were probably quarreling about which of their names should come first on the program, and have the biggest letters. And Brand's weak; I back Margaret to come out ahead . . . you'll see when the bills are posted up." He chuckled at the picture, and was turning to re-enter the room when he paused to say: "But, by the way, they're playing here tomorrow night, aren't they? Yes; I'm sure our hostess told me this afternoon that she'd finally captured them. They don't often play in private houses—Margaret hates it, I believe. But when Mrs. Roseneath sets her heart on anything she's irresistible." With a nod and smile he strolled back into the long salon where the guests were dividing into groups about the bridge tables.

Kilvert continued to lean on the stone balustrade and look down into the dark secret glitter of the canal. He was fairly sure that Dossi's identification of the mysterious couple was correct; but of course his explanation of their quarrel was absurd. A child's quarrel over toys and spangles! That was how people of the world interpreted the passions of great artists. Kilvert's heart began to beat excitedly at the thought of seeing and hearing his mysterious couple. And yet—supposing they turned out to be mere tawdry *cabotins*?. Would it not be better to absent himself from the concert and nurse his dream? It was odd how Dossi's tone dragged down those vivid figures to the level of the dolls about Mrs. Roseneath's bridge tables.

169

3

Kilvert had not often known his hostess to be in the field as early as ten in the morning. But this was a field day, almost as important as the day of the fancy ball, since two or three passing royalties (and not in exile either) had suddenly signified their desire to be present at her musical party that evening; and Mrs. Roseneath, on such occasions, had the soldier's gift of being in the saddle at dawn. But when Kilvert—his own *café au lait* on the balcony barely dispatched—was summoned to her room by an agitated maid, he found the mistress even more agitated.

"They've chucked—they've chucked for tonight! The devils—they won't come!" Mrs. Roseneath cried out, waving a pale hand toward a letter lying on her brocaded bedspread.

"But do take a mouthful of tea, madam," the maid intervened, proffering a tray.

"Tea? How can I take tea? Take it away! It's a catastrophe, John—a catastrophe . . . and Breck's such a helpless fool when it comes to anything beyond getting people together for bridge," Mrs. Roseneath lamented, sinking back discouraged among her pillows.

"But who's chucked? The Prince and Princess?"

"Lord, no! They're all coming, the King is too, I mean. And *he's* musical, and has stayed over on purpose. . . . It's Aslar, of course, and Brand. . . . Her note is perfectly insane. She says Brand's disappeared, and she's half crazy, and can't play without him."

"Disappeared—the cellist?"

"Oh, for heaven's sake, read the note, and don't just stand there and repeat what I say! Where on earth am I to get other performers for this evening, if you don't help me?"

Kilvert stared back blankly. "I don't know."

"You don't know? But you must know! Oh, John, you must go instantly to see her. You're the only person with brains—the only one who'll know how to talk to such people. If I offered to double the fee, do you suppose—?"

"Oh, no, no!" Kilvert protested indignantly, without knowing why.

"Well, what I'd already agreed to give is colossal," Mrs. Roseneath sighed, "so perhaps it's not that, after all. John, darling, you must go and see her at once! You'll know what to say. She must keep her engagement, she must telegraph, she must send a motor after him; if she can't find *him*, she must get hold of another cellist. None of these people will know if it's Brand or not. I'll lie about it if I have to. Oh, John, ring for the gondola! Don't lose an instant . . . say anything you like, use any argument . . . only make her see it's her duty!" Before the end of the sentence he was out of her door, borne on the rush of Mrs. Roseneath's entreaties down the long marble flights to the gondola. . . .

Kilvert was in the mood to like the shabbiness, the dinginess almost, of the little hotel on an obscure canal to which the gondola carried him. He liked even the slit of untidy garden, in which towels were drying on a sagging rope, the umbrella stand in imitation of rustic woodwork, the slatternly girl with a shawl over her head delivering sea urchins to the black-wigged landlady. This was the way real people lived, he thought, glancing at a crumby dining room glimpsed through glass doors. He thought he would find a pretext for moving there the next day from the Palazzo, and very nearly paused to ask the landlady if she could take him in. But his errand was urgent, and he went on.

The room into which he was shown was small, and rather bare. A worn cashmere shawl had been thrown over the low bed in a hasty attempt to convert it into a divan. The center front was filled by a grand piano built on a concert stage scale, and looking larger than any that Kilvert had ever seen. Between it and the window stood a woman in a frayed purple-silk dressing gown, her tumbled grayish hair streaked with jet tossed back from her drawn dusky face. She had evidently not noticed Kilvert the previous evening on the boat, for the glance she turned on him was unrecognizing. Obviously she resented his intrusion. "You come from Mrs. Roseneath, don't you? About tonight's concert? I said you could come up in order to get it over sooner. But it's no use whatever—none! Please go back and tell her so."

She was speaking English now, with a slightly harsh yet rich intonation, and an accent he could not quite place, but guessed to be partly Slavonic. He stood looking at her in an embarrassed silence. He was not without social adroitness, or experience in exercising it; but he felt as strongly as she evidently did that his presence was an intrusion. "I don't believe I know how to talk to real people," he reproached himself inwardly.

"Before you send me away," he said at length, "you must at least let me deliver Mrs. Roseneath's message of sympathy."

Margaret Aslar gave a derisive shrug. "Oh, sympathy—!"

He paused a moment, and then ventured: "Don't you need it? On the boat yesterday evening I rather thought you did."

She turned toward him with a quick swing of her whole body. "The boat yesterday evening? You were there?"

"I was sitting close to you. I very nearly had the impertinence to go up to you and tell you I was—sorry."

She received this in a wondering silence. Then she dropped down on the piano stool, and rested her thin elbows on the closed lid of the instrument, and her drooping head on her hands. After a moment she looked up and signed to him to take the only chair. "Put the music on the floor," she directed. Kilvert obeyed.

"You were right—I need pity, I need sympathy," she broke out, her burning eyes on his.

"I wish I could give you something more—give you real help, I mean."

She continued to gaze at him intently. "Oh, if you could bring him back to me!" she exclaimed, lifting her prayerful hands with the despair of the mourning women in some agonizing Deposition.

"I would if I could—if you'd tell me how," Kilvert murmured.

She shook her head, and sank back into her weary attitude at the piano. "What nonsense I'm talking! He's gone for good, and I'm a desolate woman."

Kilvert had by this time entirely forgotten the object of his visit. All he felt was a burning desire to help this stricken Ariadne.

"Are you sure I couldn't find him and bring him back—if you gave me a clue?"

She sat silent, her face plunged in her long tortured hands. Finally she looked up again to murmur: "No. I said things he can never forgive—"

"But if you tell him that, perhaps he will," suggested Kilvert.

She looked at him questioningly, and then gave a slight laugh. "Ah, you don't know—you don't know either of us!"

"Perhaps I could get to, if you'd help me; if you could tell me, for instance, without breach of confidence, the subject of that painful discussion you were having yesterday—a lovers' quarrel, shall we call it?"

She seemed to catch only the last words, and flung them back at him with a careless sneer. "Lovers' quarrel? Between *us*? Do you take us for children?" She swept her long arms across the piano lid, as if it were an open keyboard. "Lovers' quarrels are pastry *éclairs*. Brand and I are artists, Mr.—Mr.—"

"Kilvert."

"I've never denied his greatness as an artist—never! And he knows it. No living cellist can touch him. I've heard them all, and

172

I know. But, good heavens, if you think that's enough for him!"

"Such praise from you—"

She laughed again. "One would think so! Praise from Margaret Aslar! But no—! You say you saw us yesterday on the boat. I'd gone to Fusina to meet him—really in the friendliest spirit. He'd been off on tour in Poland and Hungary; I hadn't seen him for weeks. And I was so happy, looking forward to our meeting so eagerly. I thought it was such a perfect opportunity for talking over our Venetian programs, tonight's, and our two big concerts next week. Wouldn't you have thought so too? He arrived half an hour before the boat started, and his first word was: 'Have you settled the programs?' After that—well, you say you saw us."

"But he was awfully glad to see you; I saw that, at any rate."

"Oh, yes; awfully glad! He thought that after such a separation I'd be like dough in his hands—accept anything, agree to anything! I had settled the programs; but when he'd looked them over, he just handed them back to me with that sort of *sotto voce* smile he has, and said: 'Beautiful—perfect. But I thought it was understood that we were to appear together?' "

"Well—wasn't it?" Kilvert interjected, beginning to flounder.

She glanced at him with a shrug. "When Brand smiles like that it means: 'I see you've made out the whole program to your own advantage. It's really a piano solo from one end to the other.' That's what he means. Of course it isn't, you understand, but the truth is that nowadays he has come to consider me simply as an accompanist, and would like to have our tour regarded as a series of cello concerts, so that he's furious when I don't subordinate myself entirely."

Kilvert listened in growing bewilderment. He knew very little about artists, except that they were odd and unaccountable. He would have given all his possessions to be one himself; but he wasn't, and he had never felt his limitations more keenly than at this moment. Still, he argued with himself, fundamentally we're all made of the same stuff, and this splendid fury is simply a woman in love, who's afraid of having lost her lover. He tried to puruse the argument on those lines.

"After all—suppose you were to subordinate yourself, or at least affect to? Offer to let him make out your next few programs, I mean . . . if you know where he's to be found, I could carry your message. . . ."

"Let him give a cello tour with 'Mrs. J. Margaret Aslar at the piano'—in small type, at the bottom of the page? Ah," she cried, swept to her feet by a great rush of Sybilline passion, *"That's* what you think of my playing, is it? I always knew fashionable people could barely distinguish a barrel organ from a Steinway—but I didn't know they confused the players as well as the instruments."

Kilvert felt suddenly reassured by her unreasonableness. "I wasn't thinking of you as a player—but only as a woman."

"A woman? Any woman, I suppose?"

"A woman in love *is* 'any woman.' A man in love is 'any man.' If you tell your friend that all that matters is your finding him again, he'll put your name back on the program wherever you want it."

Margaret Aslar, leaning back against the piano, stood looking down at him sternly. "Have you *no* respect for art?" she exclaimed.

"Respect for art? But I venerate it—in all its forms!" Kilvert stammered, overwhelmed.

"Well, then—you ought to try to understand its interpreters. We're instruments, you see. Mr.—Mr.—"

"Kilvert."

"We're the pipes the god plays on—not mere servile eyes or ears, like all the rest of you! And whatever branch of art we're privileged to represent, that we must uphold, we must defend—even against the promptings of our own hearts. Brand has left me because he won't recognize that *my* branch is higher, is more important, than his. In his infatuated obstinacy he won't admit what all the music of all the greatest composers goes to show; that the piano ranks above the cello. And yet it's so obvious, isn't it? I could have made my career as a great pianist without him—but where would he as a cellist be without me? Ah, let him try—let him try! That's what I've always told him. If he thinks any girl of twenty, because she has long eyelashes, and pretends to swoon whenever he plays his famous Beethoven adagio, can replace an artist who is his equal; but his equal in a higher form of art—" She broke off, and sank down again on the piano stool. "Our association has made him; but he won't admit it. He won't admit that the cello has no life of its own without the piano. Well, let him see how he feels as number four in a string quartet! Because that's what he'll have to come to now."

Kilvert felt himself out of his depth in this tossing sea of technical resentments. He might have smiled at it in advance, as a display of artistic fatuity; but now he divined, under the surface commotion, something nobler, something genuine and integral. "I've never before met a mouthpiece of the gods," he thought, "and I don't believe I know how to talk to them."

174

And then, with a start, he recalled the humble purpose of his mission, and that he was there, not as the answering mouthpiece of divinity, but only as Mrs. Roseneath's. After all, it was hard on her to have her party wrecked for a whim. He looked at Margaret Aslar with a smile.

"You have a wonderful opportunity of proving your argument to your friend this very evening. Everybody in Venice is coming to hear you at Mrs. Roseneath's. You have simply to give a piano recital to show that you need no one to help you."

She gazed at him in a sort of incredulous wonder, and slowly an answering smile stole over her grave lips. "Ah, he'd see *then*—he'd see!" She seemed to be looking beyond Kilvert's shoulder, at a figure unseen by him, to whom she flung out her ironic challenge. "Let him go off, and do as much himself! Let him try to cram a house to bursting, and get ten recalls, with a stammering baby at the piano!" She put up her hands to her tossed hair. "I've grown gray at this work—and so has he! Twenty years ago we began. And every gray hair is a string in the perfect instruments that time has made of us. That's what a man never sees—never remembers! Ah, just let him try; let him have his lesson now, if he wants to!"

Kilvert sprang up, as if swept to his feet on the waves of her agitation. "You will come then, won't you? And the program? Can I go back and say you'll have it ready in an hour or two? I hate to bother you; but, you see, Mrs. Roseneath's in suspense—I must hurry back now with your promise."

"My promise?" Margaret Aslar confronted him with a brow of tragic wonderment. Her face reminded him of a wind-swept plain with cloud shadows rushing over it. "My promise—to play tonight without Brand? But my poor Mr.—Mr.—"

"Kilvert."

"Are you serious? Really serious? Do you really suppose that a tree torn up by the roots and flung to the ground can give out the same music as when it stands in the forest by its mate, and the wind rushes through their branches? I couldn't play a note tonight. I must bury my old self first—the self made out of Brand and Margaret Aslar. Tell Mrs. Roseneath I'm sorry—tell her anything you like. Tell her I'm burying a friend; tell her that Brand's dead—and he *is* dead, now that he's lost me. Tell her I must watch by him to-night. . . ."

She stood before Kilvert with lifted arms, in an attitude of sculptural desolation; then she turned away and went and leaned in the window, as unconscious of his presence as if he had already left.

Kilvert wanted to speak, to argue, urge, entreat; but a kind of awe, a sense of her inaccessibility, restrained him. What plea of expediency would weigh anything in the scales of such anger and such sorrow? He stood waiting for a while, trying to think of something to say; but no words came, and he slipped out and closed the door on the greatest emotional spectacle he had ever witnessed.

The whirr of wings was still in his ears when he reached the door of the hotel and began to walk along the narrow street leading to the nearest *traghetto*. A few yards from the door he almost stumbled against a man who, turning a corner, stopped abruptly in his path. They looked at each other in surprise, and Kilvert stammered, "You're Mr. Brand?"

The other smiled and nodded. He had the delicately shaded smile of a man who seldom laughs, and its kindly disenchanted curve betrayed a hint of recognition. "Yes. I saw you yesterday on the Fusina boat, didn't I?"

Kilvert glanced up and down the narrow deserted *calle*. He seemed, for the first time in his life, to have his hand on the wheels of destiny, and the contact scorched his palm. He had forgotten all about Mrs. Roseneath and the concert. He was still in the presence of the woman upstairs in the shabby hotel, and his only thought was: "He's come back to her!"

Brand's eyes were resting on him with a glance of amiable curiosity, and he was conscious that, in that narrow lane, they were actually obstructing each other's passage, and that his business was to draw aside, bow and pass on. But something suddenly impelled him to speak. "My name's Kilvert. I've just come from Madame Aslar's."

Brand nodded again; he seemed neither surprised nor put off by the half-confidential tone of the remark.

"Ah? I supposed so," he agreed affably.

"Now, why did he suppose so?" Kilvert wondered; and, feeling that the onus of explaining was on his side, he added, collecting himself: "I'm staying with Mrs. Roseneath, and she sent me as—as an ambassador, to reason with Madame Aslar, to do what I could to persuade her . . ."

Brand looked genuinely surprised. "Reason with her?" he echoed, as though faintly amused at anyone's attempting so impossible a task.

"About the concert tonight at Mrs. Roseneath's."

"Oh, the devil! At Mrs. Roseneath's? I'd forgotten all about it! Is Margaret going to play?"

The two men looked at each other a moment, as if attempting to measure the situation; then Kilvert took a plunge. "Of course not. She refused absolutely."

The other gave a low whistle. "Refused? What's up now? Why 'of course'?"

It was Kilvert's turn to sound his surprise. "But without you—she says she'll never play a note without you!"

The musician answered with a wondering glance. His lips were grave, but the disenchanted smile in the depths of his eyes turned into a faint glimmer of satisfaction. "Play without me? Of course she won't—she *can't*! I'm glad she's admitted it for once." He scrutinized Kilvert with quiet irony. "I suppose our lives have no secrets for you, if you've been talking with Margaret. I came back, of course, because we must get through our Venetian engagements somehow. After that—"

"Oh," Kilvert interrupted passionately, "don't say: 'After that'!"

Brand gave a careless shrug. "After that, I shall come back again; I shall keep on coming back; always for the same reason, I suppose."

"If you could see her as she is now, you'd need no other reason than herself!"

The musician repeated his shrug, this time with a gesture of retrospective weariness. "If only she'd leave me alone about that Polish girl! As if a man couldn't have a chance accompanist without . . . her fatal mistake is always mixing the eternal with the transient. But every woman does that, I suppose. Oh, well, we're chained to each other by something we love better than ourselves; and she knows it. She knows I'll always come back—I'll always have to." He stood looking at Kilvert as if this odd burst of confidence had suddenly turned them into old friends. "Do you know what program she's settled on for tonight?" he added wearily, as he turned toward the door of the hotel.

POLDI

Carson McCullers
1917-1967

Carson McCullers began piano lessons at the age of five, practiced incessantly, and wanted at first to become a *Wunderkind*, the title of one of her early short stories. She was sent to New York by her family to study at Juilliard, but instead went to Columbia and New York University to learn to write. "Poldi" (published in 1940) was written for one of her classes. It is the bittersweet love story of a doting young man and his unreciprocating cellist girlfriend.

When Hans was only a block from the hotel a chill rain began to fall, draining the color from the lights that were just being turned on along Broadway. He fastened his pale eyes on the sign reading COLTON ARMS, tucked a sheet of music under his overcoat, and hurried on. By the time he stepped inside the dingily marbled lobby his breath was coming in sharp pants and the sheet of music was crumpled.

Vaguely he smiled at a face before him. "Third floor—this time."

You could always tell how the elevator boy felt about the permanent people of the hotel. When those for whom he had the most respect stepped out on their floors he always held the door open for an extra moment in an attitude of unctuousness. Hans had to jump furtively so that the sliding doors would not nip his heels.

Poldi—

He stood hesitantly in the dim corridor. From the end came the sound of a cello—playing a series of descending phrases that tumbled over each other helter skelter like a handful of marbles dropped downstairs. Stepping down to the room with the music he stood for a moment just outside the door. A wobbly lettered notice was pinned there by a thumbtack.

Poldi Klein
Please Do Not Disturb While Practicing

The first time he had seen that, he recalled, there had been an E before the ING of practicing.

The heat seemed to be very low; the folds of his coat smelled wet and let out little whiffs of coldness. Crouching over the half warm radiator that stood by the end window did not relieve him.

Poldi—I've waited for a long time. And many times I've walked outside until you're through and thought about the words I wish to say to you. Gott! How pretty—like a poem or a little song by Schumann. Start like that. Poldi—

His hand crept along the rusty metal. Warm, she always was. And if he held her it would be so that he would want to bite his tongue in two.

180

Hans, you know the others have meant nothing to me. Joseph, Nikolay, Harry—all the fellows I've known. And this Kurt *only three times she couldn't* that I've talked about this last week—Poof! They all are nothing.

It came to him that his hands were crushing the music. Glancing down he saw that the brutally colored back sheet was wet and faded, but that the notation inside was undamaged. Cheap stuff. Oh well—

He walked up and down the hall, rubbing his pimply forehead. The cello whirred upward in an unclear arpeggio. That concerto—the Castelnuovo-Tedesco— How long was she going to keep on practicing? Once he paused and stretched out his hand toward the door knob. No, that time he had gone in and she had looked—and looked and told him—

The music rocked lushly back and forth in his mind. His fingers jerked as he tried to transcribe the orchestral score to the piano. She would be leaning forward now, her hands gliding over the fingerboard.

The sallow light from the window left most of the corridor dim. With a sudden impulse he knelt down and focussed his eye to the keyhole.

Only the wall and the corner; she must be by the window. Just the wall with its string of staring photographs—Casals, Piatigorsky, the fellow she liked best back home, Heifetz—and a couple of valentines and Christmas cards tucked in between. Nearby was the picture called Dawn of the barefooted woman holding up a rose with the dingy pink paper party hat she had gotten last New Year cocked over it.

The music swelled to a crescendo and ended with a few quick strokes. Ach! The last one a quarter tone off. Poldi—

He stood up quickly and, before the practicing should continue, knocked on the door.

"Who is it?"

"Me—H—Hans."

"All right. You can come in."

She sat in the fading light of the court window, her legs sprawled broadly to clench her cello. Expectantly she raised her eyebrows and let her bow droop to the floor.

His eyes fastened on the trickles of rain on the window glass. "I—I just came in to show you the new popular song we're playing tonight. The one you suggested."

She tugged at her skirt that had slid up above her stocking rolls and the gesture drew his gaze. The calves of her legs bulged out and there was a short run in one stocking. The pimples on his forehead deepened in color and he stared furtively at the rain again.

"Did you hear me practicing outside?"

"Yes."

"Listen, Hans, did it sound spiritual—did it sing and lift you to a higher plane?"

Her face was flushed and a drop of perspiration dribbled down the little gully between her breasts before disappearing under the neck of her frock. "Ye-es."

"I think so. I believe my playing has deepened much in the last month." Her shoulders shrugged expansively. "Life does that to me—it happens every time something like this comes up. Not that it's ever been like this before. It's only after you've suffered that you can play."

"That's what they claim."

She stared at him for a moment as though seeking a stronger confirmation, then curved her lips down petulantly. "That wolf, Hans, is driving me crazy. You know that Fauré thing—in E—well it takes in that note over and over and nearly drives me to drink. I get to dreading that E—it stands out something awful."

"You could have it shifted?"

"Well—but the next thing I take up would probably be in that key. No, that won't do any good. Besides, it costs something and I'd have to let them have my cello for a few days and what should I use? Just what, I ask you?"

When he made money she could get—"I don't notice it so much."

"It's a darn shame, I think. People who play like Hell can have good cellos and I can't even have a decent one. It's not right for me to put up with a wolf like that. It damages my playing—anybody can tell you that. How should I get any tone from that cheese box?"

A phrase from a sonata he was learning weaved itself in and out of his mind. "Poldi—" What was it now? *I love you love you.*

"And for what do I bother anyway—this lousy job we have?" With a dramatic gesture she got up and balanced her instrument in the corner of the room. When she switched on the lamp the bright circle of light made shadows follow the curves of her body.

"Listen, Hans, I'm so restless till I could scream."

The rain splashed on the window. He rubbed his forehead and watched her walk up and down the room. All at once she caught sight of the run in her stockings and, with a hiss of displeasure, spat on the end of her finger and bent over to transfer the wetness to the bottom of the run.

182

"Nobody has such a time with stockings as cellists. And for what? A room in a hotel and five dollars for playing trash three hours every night in the week. A pair of stockings twice every month I have to buy. And if at night I just rinse out the feet the tops run just the same."

She snatched down a pair of stockings that hung side by side with a brassiere in the window and, after peeling off the old ones, began to pull them on. Her legs were white and traced with dark hairs. There were blue veins near the knees. "Excuse me—you don't mind, do you? You seem to me like my little brother back home. And we'll get fired if I start wearing things like that down to play."

He stood at the window and looked at the rain blurred wall of the next building. Just opposite him was a milk bottle and a jar of mayonnaise on a window ledge. Below, someone had hung some clothes out to dry and forgotten to take them in; they flapped dismally in the wind and rain. A little brother—Jesus!

"And dresses," she went on impatiently. "All the time getting split at the seams because of having to stretch your knees out. But at that it's better than it used to be. Did you know me when everybody was wearing those short skirts—and I had such a time being modest when I played and still keeping with the style? Did you know me then?"

"No," Hans answered. "Two years ago the dresses were about like they are now."

"Yes, it was two years ago we first met, wasn't it?"

"You were with Harry after the con—"

"Listen, Hans." She leaned forward and looked at him urgently. She was so close that her perfume came sharp to his nostrils. "I've just been about crazy all day. It's about him, you know."

"Wh—Who?"

"You understand well enough—him—Kurt! How, Hans, he loves me, don't you think so?"

"Well—but Poldi—how many times have you seen him. You hardly know each other." He turned away from her at the Levin's when she was praising his work and—

"Oh, what does it matter if I've only been with him three times. I should worry. But the look in his eyes and the way he spoke about my playing. Such a soul he has. It comes out in his music. Have you ever heard the Beethoven funeral march sonata played so well as he did it that night?"

"It was good—"

"He told Mrs. Levin my playing had so much temperament."

He could not look at her; his grey eyes kept their focus on the rain.

"So gemütlich he is. Ein Edel Mensch! But what can I do? Huh, Hans?"

"I don't know."

"Quit looking so pouty. What would you do?"

He tried to smile. "Have—have you heard from him—he telephoned you or written?"

"No—but I'm sure it's just his delicateness. He wouldn't want me to feel offended or turn him down."

"Isn't he engaged to marry Mrs. Levin's daughter next spring?"

"Yes. But it's a mistake. What would he want with a cow like her?"

"But Poldi—"

She smoothed down the back of her hair, holding her arms above her head so that her broad breasts stood out tautly and the muscles of her underarms flexed beneath the thin silk of her dress. "At his concert, you know, I had a feeling he was playing just to me. He looked straight at me every time he bowed. That's the reason he didn't answer my letter—he's so afraid he'll hurt someone and then he can always tell me what he means in his music."

The adams-apple jutting from Hans' thin neck moved up and down as he swallowed. "You wrote to him?"

"I had to. An artist cannot subdue the greatest of the things that come to her."

"What did you say?"

"I told him how much I love him—that was ten days ago—a week after I saw him first at the Levins'."

"And you heard nothing?"

"No. But can't you see how he feels? I knew it would be that way so day before yesterday I wrote another note telling him not to worry—that I would always be the same."

Hans vaguely traced his hairline with his slender fingers. "But Poldi—there have been so many others—just since I've known you." He got up and put his finger on the photograph next to Casals'.

The face smiled at him. The lips were thick and topped by a dark moustache. On the neck there was a little round spot. Two years ago she had pointed it out to him so many times, telling him that the hicky where his violin rested used always to be so angry-red. And how she used to stroke it with her finger. How she had called it Fiddler's Ill Luck—and how between them it had gotten down to simply his Zilluck. For several moments he stared at that vague

184

splotch on the picture, wondering if it had been photographed or was simply the smudge from the number of times she had pointed it out to him.

The eyes stared at him sharp seeing and dark. Hans' knees felt weak; he sat down again.

"Tell me, Hans, he loves—don't you think so? You think really that he loves me but is only waiting until he feels it's best to reply—you think so?"

A thin haze seemed to cover everything in the room. "Yes," he said slowly.

Her expression changed. "Hans!"

He leaned forward, trembling.

"You—you look so queer. Your nose is wiggling and your lips shake like you are ready to cry. What—"

Poldi—

A sudden laugh broke into her question. "You look like a peculiar little cat my Papa used to have."

Quickly he moved toward the window so that his face was turned away from her. The rain still slithered down the glass, silvery, half opaque. The lights of the next building were on; they shone softly through the grey twilight. Ach! Hans bit his lips. In one of the windows it looked like—like a woman—Poldi in the arms of a big man with dark hair. And on the window sill looking in, beside the bottle of milk and the mayonnaise jar, was a little yellow cat out in the rain. Slowly Hans' bony knuckles rubbed his eyelids.

POWERHOUSE

Eudora Welty
1909-

Like Carson McCullers, Eudora Welty is a writer from the deep South. After a post-secondary Midwestern and New York City education, Miss Welty returned to her native Mississippi to live and work. "Powerhouse" (1941), one of her most celebrated stories, was inspired by a performance of the late jazz pianist Fats Waller.

Powerhouse is playing!

He's here on tour from the city—"Powerhouse and His Keyboard"—"Powerhouse and His Tasmanians"—think of the things he calls himself! There's no one in the world like him. You can't tell what he is. "Nigger man"?—he looks more Asiatic, monkey, Jewish, Babylonian, Peruvian, fanatic, devil. He has pale gray eyes, heavy lids, maybe horny like a lizard's, but big glowing eyes when they're open. He has African feet of the greatest size, stomping, both together, on each side of the pedals. He's not coal black—beverage colored—looks like a preacher when his mouth is shut, but then it opens—vast and obscene. And his mouth is going every minute: like a monkey's when it looks for something. Improvising, coming on a light and childish melody—*smooch*—he loves it with his mouth.

Is it possible that he could be this! When you have him there performing for you, that's what you feel. You know people on a stage—and people of a darker race—so likely to be marvelous, frightening.

This is a white dance. Powerhouse is not a show-off like the Harlem boys, not drunk, not crazy—he's in a trance; he's a person of joy, a fanatic. He listens as much as he performs, a look of hideous, powerful rapture on his face. Big arched eyebrows that never stop traveling, like a Jew's—wandering-Jew eyebrows. When he plays he beats down piano and seat and wears them away. He is in motion every moment—what could be more obscene? There he is with his great head, fat stomach, and little round piston legs, and long yellow-sectioned strong big fingers, at rest about the size of bananas. Of course you know how he sounds—you've heard him on records—but still you need to see him. He's going all the time, like skating around the skating rink or rowing a boat. It makes everybody crowd around, here in this shadowless steel-trussed hall with the rose-like posters of Nelson Eddy and the testimonial for the mind-reading horse in handwriting magnified five hundred times. Then all quietly he lays his finger on a key with the promise and serenity of a sibyl touching the book.

Powerhouse is so monstrous he sends everybody into oblivion. When any group, any performers, come to town, don't people always come out and hover near, leaning inward about them, to learn what it is? What is it? Listen. Remember how it was with the acrobats. Watch them carefully, hear the least word, especially what they say to one another, in another language—don't let them escape you; it's the only time for hallucination, the last time. They can't stay. They'll be somewhere else this time tomorrow.

Powerhouse has as much as possible done by signals. Everybody, laughing as if to hide a weakness, will sooner or later hand him up a written request. Powerhouse reads each one, studying with a secret face: that is the face which looks like a mask—anybody's; there is a moment when he makes a decision. Then a light slides under his eyelids, and he says, "92!" or some combination of figures—never a name. Before a number the band is all frantic, misbehaving, pushing, like children in a schoolroom, and he is the teacher getting silence. His hands over the keys, he says sternly, "You-all ready? You-all ready to do some serious walking?"—waits—then, STAMP. Quiet. STAMP, for the second time. This is absolute. Then a set of rhythmic kicks against the floor to communicate the tempo. Then, O Lord! say the distended eyes from beyond the boundary of the trumpets, Hello and good-bye, and they are all down the first note like a waterfall.

This note marks the end of any known discipline. Powerhouse seems to abandon them all—he himself seems lost—down in the song, yelling up like somebody in a whirlpool—not guiding them—hailing them only. But he knows, really. He cries out, but he must know exactly. "Mercy! . . . What I say! . . . Yeah!" And then drifting, listening—"Where that skin beater?"—wanting drums, and starting up and pouring it out in the greatest delight and brutality. On the sweet pieces such a leer for everybody! He looks down so benevolently upon all our faces and whispers the lyrics to us. And if you could hear him at this moment on "Marie, the Dawn is Breaking"! He's going up the keyboard with a few fingers in some very derogatory triplet-routine, he gets higher and higher, and then he looks over the end of the piano, as if over a cliff. But not in a show-off way—the song makes him do it.

He loves the way they all play, too—all those next to him. The far section of the band is all studious, wearing glasses, every one—they don't count. Only those playing around Powerhouse are the real ones. He has a bass fiddler from Vicksburg, black as pitch, named Valentine, who plays with his eyes shut and talking to himself, very young: Powerhouse has to keep encouraging him. "Go on, go on, give it up, bring it on out there!" When you heard him like that on records, did you know he was really pleading?

He calls Valentine out to take a solo.

"What you going to play?" Powerhouse looks out kindly from behind the piano; he opens his mouth and shows his tongue, listening.

Valentine looks down, drawing against his instrument, and says without a lip movement, " 'Honeysuckle Rose.' "

He has a clarinet player named Little Brother, and loves to listen to anything he does. He'll smile and say, "Beautiful!" Little Brother takes a step forward when he plays and stands at the very front, with the whites of his eyes like fishes swimming. Once when he played a low note, Powerhouse muttered in dirty praise, "He went clear downstairs to get that one!"

After a long time, he holds up the number of fingers to tell the band how many choruses still to go—usually five. He keeps his directions down to signals.

It's a bad night outside. It's a white dance, and nobody dances, except a few straggling jitterbugs and two elderly couples. Everybody just stands around the band and watches Powerhouse. Sometimes they steal glances at one another, as if to say, Of course, you know how it is with *them*—Negroes—band leaders—they would play the same way, giving all they've got, for an audience of one. . . . When somebody, no matter who, gives everything, it makes people feel ashamed for him.

Late at night they play the one waltz they will ever consent to play—by request, "Pagan Love Song." Powerhouse's head rolls and sinks like a weight between his waving shoulders. He groans, and his fingers drag into the keys heavily, holding on to the notes, retrieving. It is a sad song.

"You know what happened to me?" says Powerhouse.

Valentine hums a response, dreaming at the bass.

"I got a telegram my wife is dead," says Powerhouse, with wandering fingers.

"Uh-huh?"

His mouth gathers and forms a barbarous O while his fingers walk up straight, unwillingly, three octaves.

"Gypsy? Why how come her to die, didn't you just phone her up in the night last night long distance?"

"Telegram say—here the words: Your wife is dead." He puts 4/4 over the 3/4.

"Not but four words?" This is the drummer, an unpopular boy named Scoot, a disbelieving maniac.

Powerhouse is shaking his vast cheeks. "What the hell was she trying to do? What was she up to?"

"What name has it got signed, if you got a telegram?" Scoot is spitting away with those wire brushes.

Little Brother, the clarinet player, who cannot now speak, glares and tilts back.

"Uranus Knockwood is the name signed." Powerhouse lifts his eyes open. "Ever heard of him?" A bubble shoots out on his lip like a plate on a counter.

Valentine is beating slowly on with his palm and scratching the strings with his long blue nails. He is fond of a waltz, Powerhouse interrupts him.

"I don't know him. Don't know who he is." Valentine shakes his head with the closed eyes.

"Say it agin."

"Uranus Knockwood."

"That ain't Lenox Avenue."

"It ain't Broadway."

"Ain't ever seen it wrote out in any print, even for horse racing."

"Hell, that's on a star, boy, ain't it?" Crash of the cymbals.

"What the hell was she up to?" Powerhouse shudders. "Tell me, tell me, tell me." He makes triplets, and begins a new chorus. He holds three fingers up.

"You say you got a telegram." This is Valentine, patient and sleepy, beginning again.

Powerhouse is elaborate. "Yas, the time I go out, go way downstairs along a long cor-ri-dor to where they puts us; coming back along the cor-ri-dor; steps out and hands me a telegram: Your wife is dead."

"Gypsy?" The drummer like a spider over his drums.

"Aaaaaaaaa!" shouts Powerhouse, flinging out both powerful arms for three whole beats to flex his muscles, then kneading a dough of bass notes. His eyes glitter. He plays the piano like a drum sometimes—why not?

"Gypsy? Such a dancer?"

"Why you don't hear it straight from your agent? Why it ain't come from headquarters? What you been doing, getting telegrams in the *corridor*, signed nobody?"

They all laugh. End of that chorus.

"What time is it?" Powerhouse calls. "What the hell place is this? Where is my watch and chain?"

"I hang it on you," whimpers Valentine. "It still there."

There it rides on Powerhouse's great stomach, down where he can never see it.

"Sure did hear some clock striking twelve while ago. Must be *midnight*."

"It going to be intermission," Powerhouse declares, lifting up his finger with the signet ring.

He draws the chorus to an end. He pulls a big Northern hotel towel out of the deep pocket in his vast, special-cut tux pants and pushes his forehead into it.

"If she went and killed herself!" he says with a hidden face. "If she got up and jumped out that window!" He gets to his feet, turning vaguely, wearing the towel on his head.

"Ha, ha!"

"Sheik, sheik!"

"She wouldn't do that." Little Brother sets down his clarinet like a precious vase, and speaks. He still looks like an East Indian queen, implacable, divine, and full of snakes. "You ain't going to expect people doing what they says over long distance."

"Come on!" roars Powerhouse. He is already at the back door, he has pulled it wide open, and with a wild, gathered-up face is smelling the terrible night.

Powerhouse, Valentine, Scoot and Little Brother step outside into the drenching rain.

"Well, they emptying buckets," says Powerhouse in a mollified voice. On the street he holds his hands out and turns up the blanched palms like sieves.

A hundred dark, ragged, silent, delighted Negroes have come around from under the eaves of the hall, and follow wherever they go.

"Watch out Little Brother don't shrink," says Powerhouse. "You just the right size now, clarinet don't suck you in. You got a dry throat, Little Brother, you in the desert?" He reaches into the pocket and pulls out a paper of mints. "Now hold 'em in your mouth—don't chew 'em. I don't carry around nothing without limit."

"Go in that joint and have beer," says Scoot, who walks ahead.

"Beer? Beer? You know what beer is? What do they say is beer? What's beer? Where I been?"

"Down yonder where it say World Café—that do?" They are in Negrotown now.

Valentine patters over and holds open a screen door warped like a sea shell, bitter in the wet, and they walk in, stained darker with the rain and leaving footprints. Inside, sheltered dry smells stand like screens around a table covered with a red-checkered cloth, in the center of which flies hang onto an obelisk-shaped ketchup bottle. The midnight walls are checkered again with admonishing "Not Responsible" signs and black-figured, smoky calendars. It is a waiting, silent, limp room. There is a burned-out-looking nickelodeon and right beside it a long-necked wall instrument labeled "Business Phone, Don't Keep Talking." Circled phone numbers are written up everywhere. There is a worn-out peacock feather hanging by a thread to an old, thin, pink, exposed light bulb, where it slowly turns around and around, whoever breathes.

A waitress watches.

"Come here, living statue, and get all this big order of beer we fixing to give."

"Never seen you before anywhere." The waitress moves and comes forward and slowly shows little gold leaves and tendrils over her teeth. She shoves up her shoulders and breasts. "How I going to know who you might be? Robbers? Coming in out of the black of night right at midnight, setting down so big at my table?"

"Boogers," says Powerhouse, his eyes opening lazily as in a cave.

The girl screams delicately with pleasure. O Lord, she likes talk and scares.

"Where you going to find enough beer to put out on this here table?"

She runs to the kitchen with bent elbows and sliding steps.

"Here's a million nickels," says Powerhouse, pulling his hand out of his pocket and sprinkling coins out, all but the last one, which he makes vanish like a magician.

Valentine and Scoot take the money over to the nickelodeon, which looks as battered as a slot machine, and read all the names of the records out loud.

"Whose 'Tuxedo Junction'?" asks Powerhouse.

"You know whose."

"Nickelodeon, I request you please to play 'Empty Red Blues' and let Bessie Smith sing."

Silence: they hold it like a measure.

"Bring me all those nickels on back here," says Powerhouse. "Look at that! What you tell me the name of this place?"

"White dance, week night, raining, Alligator, Mississippi, long ways from home."

"Uh-huh."

"Sent for You Yesterday and Here You Come Today" plays.

The waitress, setting the tray of beer down on a back table, comes up taut and apprehensive as a hen. "Says in the kitchen, back there putting their eyes to little hole peeping out, that you is Mr. Powerhouse. . . . They knows from a picture they seen."

"They seeing right tonight, that is him," says Little Brother.

"You him?"

"That is him in the flesh," says Scoot.

"Does you wish to touch him?" asks Valentine. "Because he don't bite."

"You passing through?"

"Now you got everything right."

She waits like a drop, hands languishing together in front.

"Little-Bit, ain't you going to bring the beer?"

She brings it, and goes behind the cash register and smiles, turning different ways. The little fillet of gold in her mouth is gleaming.

"The Mississippi River's here," she says once.

Now all the watching Negroes press in gently and bright-eyed through the door, as many as can get in. One is a little boy in a straw sombrero which has been coated with aluminum paint all over.

Powerhouse, Valentine, Scoot and Little Brother drink beer, and their eyelids come together like curtains. The wall and the rain and the humble beautiful waitress waiting on them and the other Negroes watching enclose them.

"Listen!" whispers Powerhouse, looking into the ketchup bottle and slowly spreading his performer's hands over the damp, wrinkling cloth with the red squares. "Listen how it is. My wife gets missing me. Gypsy. She goes to the window. She looks out and sees you know what. Street. Sign saying Hotel. People walking. Somebody looks up. Old man. She looks down, out the window. Well? . . . *Ssssst! Plooey!* What she do? Jump out and bust her brains all over the world."

He opens his eyes.

"That's it," agrees Valentine. "You gets a telegram."

"Sure she misses you," Little Brother adds.

"No, it's night time." How softly he tells them! "Sure. It's the night time. She say, What do I hear? Footsteps walking up the hall?

That him? Footsteps go on off. It's not me. I'm in Alligator, Mississippi, she's crazy. Shaking all over. Listens till her ears and all grow out like old music-box horns but still she can't hear a thing. She says, All right! I'll jump out the window then. Got on her nightgown. I know that nightgown, and her thinking there. Says, Ho hum, all right, and jumps out the window. Is she mad at me! Is she crazy! She don't leave *nothing* behind her!"

"Ya! Ha!"

"Brains and insides everywhere, Lord, Lord."

All the watching Negroes stir in their delight, and to their higher delight he says affectionately, "Listen! Rats in here."

"That must be the way, boss."

"Only, naw, Powerhouse, that ain't true. That sound too *bad*."

"Does? I even know who finds her," cries Powerhouse. "That no-good pussyfooted crooning creeper, that creeper that follow around after me, coming up like weeds behind me, following around after me everything I do and messing around on the trail I leave. Bets my numbers, sings my songs, gets close to my agent like a Betsy-bug; when I going out he just coming in. I got him now! I got my eye on him."

"Know who he is?"

"Why, it's that old Uranus Knockwood!"

"Ya! Ha!"

"Yeah, and he is coming now, he going to find Gypsy. There he is, coming around that corner, and Gypsy kadoodling down, oh-oh, watch out! *Ssssst! Plooey!* See, there she is in her little old nightgown, and her insides and brains all scattered round."

A sigh fills the room.

"Hush about her brains. Hush about her insides."

"Ya! Ha! You talking about her brains and insides—old Uranus Knockwood," says Powerhouse, "look down and say Jesus! He say, Look here what I'm walking round in!"

They all burst into halloos of laughter. Powerhouse's face looks like a big hot iron stove.

"Why, he picks her up and carries her off!" he says.

"Ya! Ha!"

"Carries her *back* around the corner. . . ."

"Oh, Powerhouse!"

"You know him."

"Uranus Knockwood!"

"Yeahhh!"

"He take our wives when we gone!"

"He come in when we goes out!"

"Uh-huh!"

"He go out when we comes in!"

"Yeahhh!"

"He standing behind the door!"

"Old Uranus Knockwood."

"You know him."

"Middle-size man."

"Wears a hat."

"That's him."

Everybody in the room moans with pleasure. The little boy in the fine silver hat opens a paper and divides out a jelly roll among his followers.

And out of the breathless ring somebody moves forward like a slave, leading a great logy Negro with bursting eyes, and says, "This here is Sugar-Stick Thompson, that dove down to the bottom of July Creek and pulled up all those drownded white people fall out of a boat. Last summer, pulled up fourteen."

"Hello," says Powerhouse, turning and looking around at them all with his great daring face until they nearly suffocate.

Sugar-Stick, their instrument, cannot speak; he can only look back at the others.

"Can't even swim. Done it by holding his breath," says the fellow with the hero.

Powerhouse looks at him seekingly.

"I his half brother," the fellow puts in.

They step back.

"Gypsy say," Powerhouse rumbles gently again, looking at *them*, " 'What is the use? I'm gonna jump out so far—so far. . . .' *Sssssst*—!"

"Don't, boss, don't do it agin," says Little Brother.

"It's awful," says the waitress. "I hates that Mr. Knockwoods. All that the truth?"

"Want to see the telegram I got from him?" Powerhouse's hand goes to the vast pocket.

"Now wait, now wait, boss." They all watch him.

"It must be the real truth," says the waitress, sucking in her lower lip, her luminous eyes turning sadly, seeking the windows.

"No, babe, it ain't the truth." His eyebrows fly up, and he begins to whisper to her out of his vast oven mouth. His hand stays in his pocket. "Truth is something worse, I ain't said what, yet. It's something hasn't come to me, but I ain't saying it won't. And when it does, then want me to tell you?" He sniffs all at once, his eyes come open and turn up, almost too far. He is dreamily smiling.

"Don't, boss, don't, Powerhouse!"

"Oh!" the waitress screams.

"Go on git out of here!" bellows Powerhouse, taking his hand out of his pocket and clapping after her red dress.

The ring of watchers breaks and falls away.

"*Look* at that! Intermission is up," says Powerhouse.

He folds money under a glass, and after they go out, Valentine leans back in and drops a nickel in the nickelodeon behind them, and it lights up and begins to play "The Goona Goo." The feather dangles still.

"Take a telegram!" Powerhouse shouts suddenly up into the rain over the street. "Take a answer. Now what was that name?"

They get a little tired.

"Uranus Knockwood."

"You ought to know."

"Yas? Spell it to me."

They spell it all the ways it could be spelled. It puts them in a wonderful humor.

"Here's the answer. I got it right here. 'What in the hell you talking about? Don't make any difference: I gotcha.' Name signed: Powerhouse."

"That going to reach him, Powerhouse?" Valentine speaks in a maternal voice.

"Yas, yas."

All hushing, following him up the dark street at a distance, like old rained-on black ghosts, the Negroes are afraid they will die laughing.

Powerhouse throws back his vast head into the steaming rain, and a look of hopeful desire seems to blow somehow like a vapor from his own dilated nostrils over his face and bring a mist to his eyes.

"Reach him and come out the other side."

"That's it, Powerhouse, that's it. You got him now."

Powerhouse lets out a long sigh.

"But ain't you going back there to call up Gypsy long distance, the way you did last night in that other place? I seen a telephone. . . . Just to see if she there at home?"

There is a measure of silence. That is one crazy drummer that's going to get his neck broken some day.

"No," growls Powerhouse. "No! How many thousand times tonight I got to say No?"

He holds up his arm in the rain.

"You sure-enough unroll your voice some night, it about reach up yonder to her," says Little Brother, dismayed.

They go on up the street, shaking the rain off and on them like birds.

Back in the dance hall, they play "San" (99). The jitterbugs start up like windmills stationed over the floor, and in their orbits—one circle, another, a long stretch and a zigzag—dance the elderly couples with old smoothness, undisturbed and stately.

When Powerhouse first came back from intermission, no doubt full of beer, they said, he got the band tuned up again in his own way. He didn't strike the piano keys for pitch—he simply opened his mouth and gave falsetto howls—in A, D and so on—they tuned by him. Then he took hold of the piano, as if he saw it for the first time in his life, and tested it for strength, hit it down in the bass, played an octave with his elbow, lifted the top, looked inside, and leaned against it with all his might. He sat down and played it for a few minutes with outrageous force and got it under his power—a bass deep and coarse as a sea net—then produced something glimmering and fragile, and smiled. And who could ever remember any of the things he says? They are just inspired remarks that roll out of his mouth like smoke.

They've requested "Somebody Loves Me," and he's already done twelve or fourteen choruses, piling them up nobody knows how, and it will be a wonder if he ever gets through. Now and then he calls and shouts, " 'Somebody loves me! Somebody loves me, I wonder who!' " His mouth gets to be nothing but a volcano. "I wonder who!"

"Maybe . . ." He uses all his right hand on a trill.

"Maybe . . ." He pulls back his spread fingers, and looks out upon the place where he is. A vast, impersonal and yet furious grimace transfigures his wet face.

" . . . Maybe it's you!"

LONESOME BOY, SILVER TRUMPET

Arna Bontemps
1902-1973

One of the outstanding black writers of twentieth century America, Arna Bontemps received many accolades for both his poetry and fiction. He held a National Endowment for the Humanities Grant the year he died, was a Guggenheim Fellowship recipient, and won numerous other awards and honors. "Lonesome Boy, Silver Trumpet" (1955), a tale of a young trumpeter who plays for a "devil's ball," is evocative of an old, warm, folksy, and romantic South.

When Bubber first learned to play the trumpet, his old grandpa winked his eye and laughed.

"You better mind how you blow that horn, sonny boy. You better mind."

"I like to blow loud, I like to blow fast, and I like to blow high," Bubber answered. "Listen to this, Grandpa." And he went on blowing with his eyes closed.

When Bubber was a little bigger, he began carrying his trumpet around with him wherever he went, so his old grandpa scratched his whiskers, took the corncob pipe out of his mouth, and laughed again.

"You better mind *where* you blow that horn, boy," he warned. "I used to blow one myself, and I know."

Bubber smiled. "Where did you ever blow music, Grandpa?"

"Down in New Orleans and all up and down the river. I blowed trumpet most everywhere in my young days, and I tell you, you better mind where you go blowing."

"I like to blow my trumpet in the school band when it marches, I like to blow it on the landing when the riverboats come in sight, and I like to blow it among the trees in the swamp," he said, still smiling. But when he looked at his grandpa again, he saw a worried look on the old man's face, and he asked, "What's the matter, Grandpa, ain't that all right?"

Grandpa shook his head. "I wouldn't do it if I was you."

That sounded funny to Bubber, but he was not in the habit of disputing his grandfather. Instead he said, "I don't believe I ever heard you blow the trumpet, Grandpa. Don't you want to try blowing on mine now?"

Again the old man shook his head. "My blowing days are long gone," he said. "I still got the lip, but I ain't got the teeth. It takes good teeth to blow high notes on a horn, and these I got ain't much good. They're store teeth."

That made Bubber feel sorry for his grandfather, so he whispered softly, "I'll mind where I blow my horn, Grandpa."

He didn't really mean it though. He just said it to make his grandpa feel good. And the very next day he was half a mile out in the country blowing his horn in a cornfield. Two or three evenings later he was blowing it on a shady lane when the sun went down and not paying much attention where he went.

When he came home, his grandpa met him. "I heard you blowing your horn a long ways away," he said. "The air was still. I could hear it easy."

"How did it sound, Grandpa?"

"Oh, it sounded right pretty." He paused a moment, knocking the ashes out of his pipe, before adding, "Sounded like you mighta been lost."

That made Bubber ashamed of himself, because he knew he had not kept his word and that he was not minding where he blowed his trumpet. "I know what you mean, Grandpa," he answered. "But I can't do like you say. When I'm blowing my horn, I don't always look where I'm going."

Grandpa walked to the window and looked out. While he was standing there, he hitched his overalls up a little higher. He took a red handkerchief from his pocket and wiped his forehead. "Sounded to me like you might have been past Barbin's Landing."

"I was lost," Bubber admitted.

"You can end up in some funny places when you're just blowing a horn and not paying attention. I know," Grandpa insisted. "I know."

"Well, what do you want me to do, Grandpa?"

The old man struck a kitchen match on the seat of his pants and lit a kerosene lamp because the room was black dark by now. While the match was still burning, he lit his pipe. Then he sat down and stretched out his feet. Bubber was on a stool on the other side of the room, his trumpet under his arm. "When you go to school and play your horn in the band, that's all right," the old man said. "When you come home, you ought to put it in the case and leave it there. It ain't good to go trapesing around with a horn in your hand. You might get into devilment."

"But I feel lonesome without my trumpet, Grandpa," Bubber pleaded. "I don't like to go around without it anytime. I feel lost."

Grandpa sighed. "Well, there you are—lost with it and lost without it. I don't know what's going to become of you, sonny boy."

"You don't understand, Grandpa. You don't understand."

The old man smoked his pipe quietly for a few minutes and then went off to bed, but Bubber did not move. Later on, however, when he heard his grandpa snoring in the next room, he went outdoors, down the path, and around the smokehouse, and sat on a log. The night was still. He couldn't hear anything louder than a cricket. Soon he began wondering how his trumpet would sound on such a still night, back there behind the old smokehouse, so he put the mouthpiece to his lips very lightly and blew a few silvery notes. Immediately Bubber felt better. Now he knew for sure that Grandpa didn't understand how it was with a boy and a horn—a lonesome boy with a silver trumpet. Bubber lifted his horn toward the stars and let the music pour out.

Presently a big orange moon rose, and everything Bubber could see changed suddenly. The moon was so big it made the smokehouse and the trees and the fences seem small. Bubber blew his trumpet loud, he blew it fast, and he blew it high, and in just a few minutes he forgot all about Grandpa sleeping in the house.

He was afraid to talk to Grandpa after that. He was afraid Grandpa might scold him or warn him or try in some other way to persuade him to leave his trumpet in its case. Bubber was growing fast now. He knew what he liked, and he did not think he needed any advice from Grandpa.

Still he loved his grandfather very much, and he had no intention of saying anything that would hurt him. Instead he decided to leave home. He did not tell Grandpa what he was going to do. He just waited till the old man went to sleep in his bed one night. Then he quietly blew out the lamp, put his trumpet under his arm, and started walking down the road from Marksville to Barbin's Landing.

No boat was there, but Bubber did not mind. He knew one would come by before morning, and he knew that he wouldn't be lonesome so long as he had his trumpet with him. He found a place on the little dock where he could lean back against a post and swing his feet over the edge while playing, and the time passed swiftly. And when he finally went aboard a riverboat, just before morning, he found a place on the deck that suited him just as well and went right on blowing his horn.

Nobody asked him to pay any fare. The riverboat men did not seem to expect it of a boy who blew a trumpet the way Bubber did. And in New Orleans the cooks in the kitchens where he ate and the people who kept the rooming houses where he slept did not seem to expect him to pay either. In fact, people seemed to think that a boy who played a trumpet where the patrons of a restaurant could hear him or for the guests of a rooming house should receive money for it. They began to throw money around Bubber's feet as he played his horn.

202

At first he was surprised. Later he decided it only showed how wrong Grandpa had been about horn blowing. So he picked up all the money they threw, bought himself fancy new clothes, and began looking for new places to play. He ran into boys who played guitars or bullfiddles or drums or other instruments, and he played right along with them. He went out with them to play for picnics or barbecues or boat excursions or dances. He played early in the morning and he played late at night, and he bought new clothes and dressed up so fine he scarcely knew himself in a mirror. He scarcely knew day from night.

It was wonderful to play the trumpet like that, Bubber thought, and to make all that money. People telephoned to the rooming house where he lived and asked for him nearly every day. Some sent notes asking if he would play his trumpet at their parties. Occasionally one would send an automobile to bring him to the place, and this was the best of all. Bubber liked riding through the pretty part of the city to the ballrooms in which well-dressed people waited to dance to his music. He enjoyed even more the times when he was taken to big white-columned houses in the country, houses surrounded by old trees with moss on them.

But he went to so many places to play his trumpet, he forgot where he had been and he got into the habit of not paying much attention. That was how it was the day he received a strange call on the telephone. A voice that sounded like a very proper gentleman said, "I would like to speak to the boy from Marksville, the one who plays the trumpet."

"I'm Bubber, sir. I'm the one."

"Well, Bubber, I'm having a very special party tonight—very special," the voice said. "I want you to play for us."

Bubber felt a little drowsy because he had been sleeping when the phone rang, and he still wasn't too wide awake. He yawned as he answered, "Just me, sir? You want me to play by myself?"

"There will be other musicians, Bubber. You'll play in the band. We'll be looking for you?"

"Where do you live, sir?" Bubber asked sleepily.

"Never mind about that, Bubber. I'll send my chauffeur with my car. He'll bring you."

The voice was growing faint by this time, and Bubber was not sure he caught the last words. "Where did you say, sir?" he asked suddenly. "When is it you want me?"

"I'll send my chauffeur," the voice repeated and then faded out completely.

Bubber put the phone down and went back to his bed to sleep some more. He had played his trumpet very late the night before, and now he just couldn't keep his eyes open.

Something was ringing when he woke up again. Was it the telephone? Bubber jumped out of bed and ran to answer, but the phone buzzed when he put it to his ear. There was nobody on the line. Then he knew it must have been the doorbell. A moment later he heard the door open, and footsteps came down the dark hall toward Bubber's room. Before Bubber could turn on the light, the footsteps were just outside his room, and a man's voice said, "I'm the chauffeur. I've brought the car to take you to the dance."

"So soon?" Bubber asked, surprised.

The man laughed. "You must have slept all day. It's night now, and we have a long way to drive."

"I'll put on my clothes," Bubber said.

The street light was shining through the window, so he did not bother to switch on the light in his room. Bubber never liked to open his eyes with a bright light shining, and anyway he knew right where to put his hands on the clothes he needed. As he began slipping into them, the chauffeur turned away. "I'll wait for you on the curb," he said.

"All right," Bubber called. "I'll hurry."

When he finished dressing, Bubber took his trumpet off the shelf, closed the door of his room, and went out to where the tall driver was standing beside a long, shiny automobile. The chauffeur saw him coming and opened the door to the back seat. When Bubber stepped in, he threw a lap robe across his knees and closed it. Then the chauffeur went around to his place in the front seat, stepped on the starter, switched on his headlights, and sped away.

The car was finer than any Bubber had ridden in before; the motor purred so softly and the chauffeur drove it so smoothly, that Bubber soon began to feel sleepy again. One thing puzzled him, however. He had not yet seen the driver's face, and he wondered what the man looked like. But now the chauffeur's cap was down so far over his eyes and his coat collar was turned up so high Bubber could not see his face at all, no matter how far he leaned forward.

After a while he decided it was no use. He would have to wait till he got out of the car to look at the man's face. In the meantime he would sleep. Bubber pulled the lap robe up over his shoulders, stretched out on the wide back seat of the car and went to sleep again.

204

The car came to a stop, but Bubber did not wake up till the chauffeur opened the door and touched his shoulder. When he stepped out of the car, he could see nothing but dark, twisted trees with moss hanging from them. It was a dark and lonely place, and Bubber was so surprised he did not remember to look at the chauffeur's face. Instead, he followed the tall figure up a path covered with leaves to a white-columned house with lights shining in the windows.

Bubber felt a little better when he saw the big house with the bright windows. He had played in such houses before, and he was glad for a chance to play in another. He took his trumpet from under his arm, put the mouthpiece to his lips, and blew a few bright, clear notes as he walked. The chauffeur did not turn around. He led Bubber to a side entrance, opened the door, and pointed the boy to the room where the dancing had already started. Without ever showing his face, the chauffeur closed the door and returned to the car.

Nobody had to tell Bubber what to do now. He found a place next to the big fiddle that made the rhythms, waited a moment for the beat, then came in with his trumpet. With the bass fiddle, the drums, and the other stringed instruments backing him up, Bubber began to bear down on his trumpet. This was just what he liked. He played loud, he played fast, he played high, and it was all he could do to keep from laughing when he thought about Grandpa and remembered how the old man had told him to mind how he played his horn. Grandpa should see him now, Bubber thought.

Bubber looked at the dancers swirling on the ballroom floor under the high swinging chandelier, and he wished that Grandpa could somehow be at the window and see how they glided and spun around to the music of his horn. He wished the old man could get at least one glimpse of the handsome dancers, the beautiful women in bright-colored silks, the slender men in black evening clothes.

As the evening went on, more people came and began dancing. The floor became more and more crowded, and Bubber played louder and louder, faster and faster, and by midnight the gay ballroom seemed to be spinning like a pinwheel. The floor looked like glass under the dancers' feet. The drapes on the windows resembled gold, and Bubber was playing his trumpet so hard and so fast his eyes looked like they were ready to pop out of his head.

But he was not tired. He felt as if he could go on playing like this forever. He did not even need a short rest. When the other musicians called for a break and went outside to catch a breath of fresh air, he kept right on blowing his horn, running up the scale and down, hitting high C's, swelling out on the notes and then letting them fade away. He kept the dancers entertained till the full band came back, and he blew the notes that started them to dancing again.

Bubber gave no thought to the time, and when a breeze began blowing through the tall windows, he paid no attention. He played as loud as ever, and the dancers swirled just as fast. But there was one thing that did bother him a little. The faces of the dancers began to look thin and hollow as the breeze brought streaks of morning mist into the room. What was the matter with them? Were they tired from dancing all night? Bubber wondered.

But the morning breeze blew stronger and stronger. The curtains flapped, and a gray light appeared in the windows. By this time Bubber noticed that the people who were dancing had no faces at all, and though they continued to dance wildly as he played his trumpet, they seemed dim and far away. Were they disappearing?

Soon Bubber could scarcely see them at all. Suddenly he wondered where the party had gone. The musicians too grew dim and finally disappeared. Even the room with the big chandelier and the golden drapes on the windows was fading away like a technicolor dream. Bubber was frightened when he realized that nothing was left, and he was alone. Yes, definitely, he was alone—but *where*? Where was he now?

He never stopped blowing his shiny trumpet. In fact, as the party began to break up in this strange way, he blew harder than ever to help himself feel brave again. He also closed his eyes. That was why he happened to notice how uncomfortable the place where he was sitting had become. It was about as unpleasant as sitting on a log. And it was while his eyes were closed that he first became aware of leaves nearby, leaves rustling and blowing in the cool breeze.

But he could not keep his eyes closed for long with so much happening. Bubber just had to peep eventually, and when he did, he saw only leaves around him. Certainly leaves were nothing to be afraid of, he thought, but it was a little hard to understand how the house and room in which he had been playing for the party all night had been replaced by branches and leaves like this. Bubber opened both his eyes wide, stopped blowing his horn for a moment, and took a good, careful look at his surroundings.

Only then did he discover for sure that he was not in a house at all. There were no dancers, no musicians, nobody at all with him, and what had seemed like a rather uncomfortable chair or log was a large branch. Bubber was sitting in a pecan tree, and now he realized that this was where he had been blowing his trumpet so fast and so loud and so high all night. It was very discouraging.

But where was the chauffeur who had brought him here and what had become of the party and the graceful dancers? Bubber climbed down and began looking around. He could see no trace of the things that had seemed so real last night, so he decided he had better go home. Not home to the rooming house where he slept while in New Orleans, but home to the country where Grandpa lived.

He carried his horn under his arm, but he did not play a note on the bus that took him back to Marksville next day. And when he got off the bus and started walking down the road to Grandpa's house in the country, he still didn't feel much like playing anything on his trumpet.

Grandpa was sleeping in a hammock under a chinaberry tree when he arrived, but he slept with one eye open, so Bubber did not have to wake him up. He just stood there, and Grandpa smiled.

"I looked for you to come home before now," the old man said.

"I should have come home sooner," Bubber answered, shame-faced.

"I expected you to be blowing on your horn when you came."

"That's what I want to talk to you about, Grandpa."

The old man sat up in the hammock and put his feet on the ground. He scratched his head and reached for his hat. "Don't tell me anything startling," he said. "I just woke up, and I don't want to be surprised so soon."

Bubber thought maybe he should not mention what had happened. "All right, Grandpa," he whispered, looking rather sad. He leaned against the chinaberry tree, holding the trumpet under his arm, and waited for Grandpa to speak again.

Suddenly the old man blinked his eyes as if remembering something he had almost forgotten. "Did you mind how you blew on that horn down in New Orleans?" he asked.

"Sometimes I did. Sometimes I *didn't*," Bubber confessed.

Grandpa looked hurt. "I hate to hear that, sonny boy," he said. "Have you been playing your horn at barbecues and boat rides and dances and all such as that?"

"Yes, Grandpa," Bubber said, looking at the ground.

"Keep on like that and you're apt to wind up playing for a devil's ball."

Bubber nodded sadly. "Yes, I know."

Suddenly the old man stood up and put his hand on Bubber's shoulder. "Did a educated gentleman call you on the telephone?"

"He talked so proper I could hardly make out what he was saying."

"Did the chauffeur come in a long shiny car?"

Bubber nodded again. "I ended up in a pecan tree," he told Grandpa.

"I tried to tell you, Bubber, but you wouldn't listen to me."

"I'll listen to you from now on, Grandpa."

Grandpa laughed through his whiskers. "Well, take your trumpet in the house and put it on the shelf while I get you something to eat," he said.

Bubber smiled too. He was hungry, and he had not tasted any of Grandpa's cooking for a long time.

THE KID NOBODY COULD HANDLE

Kurt Vonnegut, Jr.
1922-

Embraced by our current generation of young people as an articulator of their own insecurities and anxieties, Kurt Vonnegut writes about the cruelty and barbarism of the modern world. "The Kid Nobody Could Handle" (1955) is a fine example of his special vision. The story concerns a wayward youth and a caring adult attempting to reach him.

209

It was seven-thirty in the morning. Waddling, clanking, muddy machines were tearing a hill to pieces behind a restaurant, and trucks were hauling the pieces away. Inside the restaurant, dishes rattled on their shelves. Tables quaked, and a very kind fat man with a headful of music looked down at the jiggling yolks of his breakfast eggs. His wife was visiting relatives out of town. He was on his own.

The kind fat man was George M. Helmholtz, a man of forty, head of the music department of Lincoln High School, and director of the band. Life had treated him well. Each year he dreamed the same big dream. He dreamed of leading as fine a band as there was on the face of the earth. And each year the dream came true.

It came true because Helmholtz was sure that a man couldn't have a better dream than his. Faced by this unnerving sureness, Kiwanians, Rotarians, and Lions paid for band uniforms that cost twice as much as their best suits, school administrators let Helmholtz raid the budget for expensive props, and youngsters played their hearts out for him. When youngsters had no talent, Helmholtz made them play on guts alone.

Everything was good about Helmholtz's life save his finances. He was so dazzled by his big dream that he was a child in the marketplace. Ten years before, he had sold the hill behind the restaurant to Bert Quinn, the restaurant owner, for one thousand dollars. It was now apparent, even to Helmholtz, that Helmholtz had been had.

Quinn sat down in the booth with the bandmaster. He was a bachelor, a small, dark, humorless man. He wasn't a well man. He couldn't sleep, he couldn't stop working, he couldn't smile warmly. He had only two moods: one suspicious and self-pitying, the other arrogant and boastful. The first mood applied when he was losing money. The second mood applied when he was making it.

Quinn was in the arrogant and boastful mood when he sat down with Helmholtz. He sucked whistlingly on a toothpick, and talked of vision—his own.

"I wonder how many eyes saw the hill before I did?" said Quinn. "Thousands and thousands, I'll bet—and not one saw what I saw. How many eyes?"

"Mine, at least," said Helmholtz. All the hill had meant to him was a panting climb, free blackberries, taxes, and a place for band picnics.

"You inherit the hill from your old man, and it's nothing but a pain in the neck to you," said Quinn. "So you figure you'll stick me with it."

"I didn't figure to stick you," Helmholtz protested. "The good Lord knows the price was more than fair."

"You say that now," said Quinn gleefully. "Sure, Helmholtz, you say that now. Now you see the shopping district's got to grow. Now you see what I saw."

"Yes," said Helmholtz. "Too late, too late." He looked around for some diversion, and saw a fifteen-year-old boy coming toward him, mopping the aisle between booths.

The boy was small but with tough, stringy muscles standing out on his neck and forearms. Childhood lingered in his features, but when he paused to rest, his fingers went hopefully to the silky beginnings of sideburns and a mustache. He mopped like a robot, jerkily, brainlessly, but took pains not to splash suds over the toes of his black boots.

"So what do I do when I get the hill?" said Quinn. "I tear it down, and it's like somebody pulled down a dam. All of a sudden everybody wants to build a store where the hill was."

"Um," said Helmholtz. He smiled genially at the boy. The boy looked through him without a twitch of recognition.

"We all got something," said Quinn. "You got music; I got vision." And he smiled, for it was perfectly clear to both where the money lay. "Think big!" said Quinn. "Dream big! That's what vision is. Keep your eyes wider open than anybody else's."

"That boy," said Helmholtz, "I've seen him around school, but I never knew his name."

Quinn laughed cheerlessly. "Billy the Kid? The storm trooper? Rudolph Valentino? Flash Gordon?" He called the boy. . . . "Hey, Jim! Come here a minute."

Helmholtz was appalled to see that the boy's eyes were as expressionless as oysters.

"This is my brother-in-law's kid by another marriage—before he married my sister," said Quinn. "His name's Jim Donnini, and he's from the south side of Chicago, and he's very tough."

Jim Donnini's hands tightened on the mop handle.

"How do you do?" said Helmholtz.

"Hi," said Jim emptily.

"He's living with me now," said Quinn. "He's my baby now."

"You want a lift to school, Jim?"

"Yeah, he wants a lift to school," said Quinn. "See what you make of him. He won't talk to me." He turned to Jim. "Go on, kid, wash up and shave."

Robotlike, Jim marched away.

"Where are his parents?"

"His mother's dead. His old man married my sister, walked out on her, and stuck her with him. Then the court didn't like the way she was raising him, and put him in foster homes for a while. Then they decided to get him clear out of Chicago, so they stuck me with him." He shook his head. "Life's a funny thing, Helmholtz."

"Not very funny, sometimes," said Helmholtz. He pushed his eggs away.

"Like some whole new race of people coming up," said Quinn wonderingly. "Nothing like the kids we got around here. Those boots, the black jacket—and he won't talk. He won't run around with the other kids. Won't study. I don't think he can even read and write very good."

"Does he like music at all? Or drawing? Or animals?" said Helmholtz. "Does he collect anything?"

"You know what he likes?" said Quinn. "He likes to polish those boots—get off by himself and polish those boots. And when he's really in heaven is when he can get off by himself, spread comic books all around him on the floor, polish his boots, and watch television." He smiled ruefully. "Yeah, he had a collection too. And I took it away from him and threw it in the river."

"Threw it in the river?" said Helmholtz.

"Yeah," said Quinn. "Eight knives—some with blades as long as your hand."

Helmholtz paled. "Oh." A prickling sensation spread over the back of his neck. "This is a new problem at Lincoln High. I hardly know what to think about it." He swept spilled salt together in a neat little pile, just as he would have liked to sweep together his scattered thoughts. "It's a kind of sickness, isn't it? That's the way to look at it?"

"Sick?" said Quinn. He slapped the table. "You can say that again!" He tapped his chest. "And Doctor Quinn is just the man to give him what's good for what ails him."

"What's that?" said Helmholtz.

"No more talk about the poor little sick boy," said Quinn grimly. "That's all he's heard from the social workers and the juvenile court, and God knows who all. From now on, he's the no-good bum of a man. I'll ride his tail till he straightens up and flies right or winds up in the can for life. One way or the other."

"I see," said Helmholtz.

"Like listening to music?" said Helmholtz to Jim brightly, as they rode to school in Helmholtz's car.

Jim said nothing. He was stroking his mustache and sideburns, which he had not shaved off.

"Ever drum with the fingers or keep time with your feet?" said Helmholtz. He had noticed that Jim's boots were decorated with chains that had no function but to jingle as he walked.

Jim sighed with ennui.

"Or whistle?" said Helmholtz. "If you do any of those things, it's just like picking up the keys to a whole new world—a world as beautiful as any world can be."

Jim gave a soft Bronx cheer.

"There!" said Helmholtz. "You've illustrated the basic principle of the family of brass wind instruments. The glorious voice of every one of them starts with a buzz on the lips."

The seat springs of Helmholtz's old car creaked under Jim, as Jim shifted his weight. Helmholtz took this as a sign of interest, and he turned to smile in comradely fashion. But Jim had shifted his weight in order to get a cigarette from inside his tight leather jacket.

Helmholtz was too upset to comment at once. It was only at the end of the ride, as he turned into the teachers' parking lot, that he thought of something to say.

"Sometimes," said Helmholtz, "I get so lonely and disgusted, I don't see how I can stand it. I feel like doing all kinds of crazy things, just for the heck of it—things that might even be bad for me."

Jim blew a smoke ring expertly.

"And then!" said Helmholtz. He snapped his fingers and honked his horn. "And then, Jim, I remember I've got at least one tiny corner of the universe I can make just the way I want it! I can go to it and gloat over it until I'm brand-new and happy again."

"Aren't you the lucky one?" said Jim. He yawned.

"I am, for a fact," said Helmholtz. "My corner of the universe happens to be the air around my band. I can fill it with music. Mr. Beeler, in zoology, has his butterflies. Mr. Trottman, in physics, has his pendulum and tuning forks. Making sure everybody has a corner like that is about the biggest job we teachers have. I—"

The car door opened and slammed, and Jim was gone. Helmholtz stamped out Jim's cigarette and buried it under the gravel of the parking lot.

Helmholtz's first class of the morning was C Band, where beginners thumped and wheezed and tooted as best they could, and looked down the long, long, long road through B Band to A Band, the Lincoln High School Ten Square Band, the finest band in the world.

Helmholtz stepped onto the podium and raised his baton. "You are better than you think," he said. "A-one, a-two, a-three." Down came the baton.

C Band set out in its quest for beauty—set out like a rusty switch engine, with valves stuck, pipes clogged, unions leaking, bearings dry.

Helmholtz was still smiling at the end of the hour, because he'd heard in his mind the music as it was going to be someday. His throat was raw, for he had been singing with the band for the whole hour. He stepped into the hall for a drink from the fountain.

As he drank, he heard the jingling of chains. He looked up at Jim Donnini. Rivers of students flowed between classrooms, pausing in friendly eddies, flowing on again. Jim was alone. When he paused, it wasn't to greet anyone, but to polish the toes of his boots on his trousers legs. He had the air of a spy in a melodrama, missing nothing, liking nothing, looking forward to the great day when everything would be turned upside down.

"Hello, Jim," said Helmholtz. "Say, I was just thinking about you. We've got a lot of clubs and teams that meet after school. And that's a good way to get to know a lot of people."

Jim measured Helmholtz carefully with his eyes. "Maybe I don't want to know a lot of people," he said. "Ever think of that?" He set his feet down hard to make his chains jingle as he walked away.

When Helmholtz returned to the podium for a rehearsal of B Band, there was a note waiting for him, calling him to a special faculty meeting.

The meeting was about vandalism.

Someone had broken into the school and wrecked the office of Mr. Crane, head of the English Department. The poor man's treasures—books, diplomas, snapshots of England, the beginnings of eleven novels—had been ripped and crumpled, mixed, dumped and trampled, and drenched with ink.

Helmholtz was sickened. He couldn't believe it. He couldn't

bring himself to think about it. It didn't become real to him until late that night, in a dream. In the dream Helmholtz saw a boy with barracuda teeth, with claws like baling hooks. The monster climbed into a window of the high school and dropped to the floor of the band rehearsal room. The monster clawed to shreds the heads of the biggest drum in the state. Helmholtz woke up howling. There was nothing to do but dress and go to the school.

At two in the morning, Helmholtz caressed the drum heads in the band rehearsal room, with the night watchman looking on. He rolled the drum back and forth on its cart, and he turned the light inside on and off, on and off. The drum was unharmed. The night watchman left to make his rounds.

The band's treasure house was safe. With the contentment of a miser counting his money, Helmholtz fondled the rest of the instruments, one by one. And then he began to polish the sousaphones. As he polished, he could hear the great horns roaring, could see them flashing in the sunlight, with the Stars and Stripes and the banner of Lincoln High going before.

"Yump-yump, tiddle-tiddle, yump-yump, tiddle-tiddle!" sang Helmholtz happily. "Yump-yump-yump, ra-a-a-a-a, yump-yump, yump-yump—boom!"

As he paused to choose the next number for his imaginary band to play, he heard a furtive noise in the chemistry laboratory next door. Helmholtz sneaked into the hall, jerked open the laboratory door, and flashed on the lights. Jim Donnini had a bottle of acid in either hand. He was spashing acid over the periodic table of the elements, over the blackboards covered with formulas, over the bust of Lavoisier. The scene was the most repulsive thing Helmholtz could have looked upon.

Jim smiled with thin bravado.

"Get out," said Helmholtz.

"What're you gonna do?" said Jim.

"Clean up. Save what I can," said Helmholtz dazedly. He picked up a wad of cotton waste and began wiping up the acid.

"You gonna call the cops?" said Jim.

"I—I don't know," said Helmholtz. "No thoughts come. If I'd caught you hurting the bass drum, I think I would have killed you with a single blow. But I wouldn't have had any intelligent thoughts about what you were—what you thought you were doing."

"It's about time this place got set on its ear," said Jim.

"Is it?" said Helmholtz. "That must be so, if one of our students wants to murder it."

"What good is it?" said Jim.

"Not much good, I guess," said Helmholtz. "It's just the best thing human beings ever managed to do." He was helpless, talking to himself. He had a bag of tricks for making boys behave like men—tricks that played on boyish fears and dreams and loves. But here was a boy without fear, without dreams, without love.

"If you smashed up all the schools," said Helmholtz, "we wouldn't have any hope left."

"What hope?" said Jim.

"The hope that everybody will be glad he's alive," said Helmholtz. "Even you."

"That's a laugh," said Jim. "All I ever got out of this dump was a hard time. So what're you gonna do?"

"I have to do something, don't I?" said Helmholtz.

"I don't care what you do," said Jim.

"I know," said Helmholtz. "I know." He marched Jim into his tiny office off the band rehearsal room. He dialed the telephone number of the principal's home. Numbly, he waited for the bell to get the old man from his bed.

Jim dusted his boots with a rag.

Helmholtz suddenly dropped the telephone into its cradle before the principal could answer. "Isn't there anything you care about but ripping, hacking, bending, rending, smashing, bashing?" he cried. "Anything? Anything but those boots?"

"Go on! Call up whoever you're gonna call," said Jim.

Helmholtz opened a locker and took a trumpet from it. He thrust the trumpet into Jim's arms. "There!" he said, puffing with emotion. "There's my treasure. It's the dearest thing I own. I give it to you to smash. I won't move a muscle to stop you. You can have the added pleasure of watching my heart break while you do it."

Jim looked at him oddly. He laid down the trumpet.

"Go on!" said Helmholtz. "If the world has treated you so badly, it deserves to have the trumpet smashed!"

"I—" said Jim. Helmholtz grabbed his belt, put a foot behind him, and dumped him on the floor.

Helmholtz pulled Jim's boots off and threw them into a corner. "There!" said Helmholtz savagely. He jerked the boy to his feet again and thrust the trumpet into his arms once more.

Jim Donnini was barefoot now. He had lost his socks with his boots. The boy looked down. The feet that had once seemed big black clubs were narrow as chicken wings now—bony and blue, and not quite clean.

The boy shivered, then quaked. Each quake seemed to shake something loose inside, until, at last, there was no boy left. No boy at all. Jim's head lolled, as though he waited only for death.

Helmholtz was overwhelmed by remorse. He threw his arms around the boy. "Jim! Jim—listen to me, boy!"

Jim stopped quaking.

"You know what you've got there—the trumpet?" said Helmholtz. "You know what's special about it?"

Jim only sighed.

"It belonged to John Philip Sousa!" said Helmholtz. He rocked and shook Jim gently, trying to bring him back to life. "I'll trade it to you, Jim—for your boots. It's yours, Jim! John Philip Sousa's trumpet is yours! It's worth hundreds of dollars, Jim—thousands!"

Jim laid his head on Helmholtz's breast.

"It's better than boots, Jim," said Helmholtz. "You can learn to play it. You're somebody, Jim. You're the boy with John Philip Sousa's trumpet!"

Helmholtz released Jim slowly, sure the boy would topple. Jim didn't fall. He stood alone. The trumpet was still in his arms.

"I'll take you home, Jim," said Helmholtz. "Be a good boy and I won't say a word about tonight. Polish your trumpet, and learn to be a good boy."

"Can I have my boots?" said Jim dully.

"No," said Helmholtz. "I don't think they're good for you."

He drove Jim home. He opened the car windows and the air seemed to refresh the boy. He let him out at Quinn's restaurant. The soft pats of Jim's bare feet on the sidewalk echoed down the empty street. He climbed through a window, and into his bedroom behind the kitchen. And all was still.

The next morning the waddling clanking, muddy machines were making the vision of Bert Quinn come true. They were smoothing off the place where the hill had been behind the restaurant. They were making it as level as a billiard table.

Helmholtz sat in a booth again. Quinn joined him again. Jim mopped again. Jim kept his eyes down, refusing to notice Helmholtz. And he didn't seem to care when a surf of suds broke over the toes of his small and narrow brown Oxfords.

"Eating out two mornings in a row?" said Quinn. "Something wrong at home?"

"My wife's still out of town," said Helmholtz.

"While the cat's away—" said Quinn. He winked.

"When the cat's away," said Helmholtz, "this mouse gets lonesome."

Quinn leaned forward. "Is that what got you out of bed in the middle of the night, Helmholtz? Loneliness?" He jerked his head at Jim. "Kid! Go get Mr. Helmholtz his horn."

Jim raised his head, and Helmholtz saw that his eyes were oysterlike again. He marched away to get the trumpet.

Quinn now showed that he was excited and angry. "You take away his boots and give him a horn, and I'm not supposed to get curious?" he said. "I'm not supposed to start asking questions? I'm not supposed to find out you caught him taking the school apart? You'd made a lousy crook, Helmholtz. You'd leave your baton, sheet music, and your driver's license at the scene of the crime."

"I don't think about hiding clues," said Helmholtz. "I just do what I do. I was going to tell you."

Quinn's feet danced and his shoes squeaked like mice. "Yes?" he said. "Well, I've got some news for you too."

"What is that?" said Helmholtz uneasily.

"It's all over with Jim and me," said Quinn. "Last night was the payoff. I'm sending him back where he came from."

"To another string of foster homes?" said Helmholtz weakly.

"Whatever the experts figure out to do with a kid like that." Quinn sat back, exhaled noisily, and went limp with relief.

"You can't," said Helmholtz.

"I can," said Quinn.

"That will be the end of him," said Helmholtz. "He can't stand to be thrown away like that one more time."

"He can't feel anything," said Quinn. "I can't help him; I can't hurt him. Nobody can. There isn't a nerve in him."

"A bundle of scar tissue," said Helmholtz.

The bundle of scar tissue returned with the trumpet. Impassively, he laid it on the table in front of Helmholtz.

Helmholtz forced a smile. "It's yours, Jim," he said. "I gave it to you."

"Take it while you got the chance, Helmholtz," said Quinn. "He doesn't want it. All he'll do is swap it for a knife or a pack of cigarettes."

"He doesn't know what it is, yet," said Helmholtz. "It takes a while to find out."

"Is it any good?" said Quinn.

"Any good?" said Helmholtz, not believing his ears. "Any good?" He didn't see how anyone could look at the instrument and not be warmed and dazzled by it. "Any good?" he murmured. "It belonged to John Philip Sousa."

Quinn blinked stupidly. "Who?"

Helmholtz's hands fluttered on the table top like the wings of a dying bird. "Who was John Philip Sousa?" he piped. No more words came. The subject was too big for a tired man to cover. The dying bird expired and lay still.

After a long silence, Helmholtz picked up the trumpet. He kissed the cold mouthpiece and pumped the valves in a dream of a brilliant cadenza. Over the bell of the instrument, Helmholtz saw Jim Donnini's face, seemingly floating in space—all but deaf and blind. Now Helmholtz saw the futility of men and their treasures. He had thought that his greatest treasure, the trumpet, could buy a soul for Jim. The trumpet was worthless.

Deliberately, Helmholtz hammered the trumpet against the table edge. He bent it around a coat tree. He handed the wreck to Quinn.

"Ya busted it," said Quinn, amazed. "Why'dja do that? What's that prove?"

"I—I don't know," said Helmholtz. A terrible blasphemy rumbled deep in him, like the warning of a volcano. And then, irresistibly, out it came. "Life is no damn good," said Helmholtz. His face twisted as he fought back tears and shame.

Helmholtz, the mountain that walked like a man, was falling apart. Jim Donnini's eyes filled with pity and alarm. They came alive. They became human. Helmholtz had got a message through. Quinn looked at Jim, and something like hope flickered for the first time in his bitterly lonely old face.

Two weeks later, a new semester began at Lincoln High.

In the band rehearsal room, the members of C Band were waiting for their leader—were waiting for their destinies as musicians to unfold.

Helmholtz stepped onto the podium, and rattled his baton against his music stand. "The Voices of Spring," he said. "Everybody hear that? The Voices of Spring?"

There were rustling sounds as the musicians put the music on their stands. In the pregnant silence that followed their readiness. Helmholtz glanced at Jim Donnini, who sat on the last seat of the worst trumpet section of the worst band in school.

His trumpet, John Philip Sousa's trumpet, George M. Helmholtz's trumpet, had been repaired.

"Think of it this way," said Helmholtz. "Our aim is to make the world more beautiful than it was when we came into it. It can be done. You can do it."

A small cry of despair came from Jim Donnini. It was meant to be private, but it pierced every ear with its poignancy.

"How?" said Jim.

"Love yourself," said Helmholtz, "and make your instrument sing about it. A-one, a-two, a-three." Down came his baton.